GUTTED

The Code: Time-Tested Secrets for Getting
What You Want from Women—
Without Marrying Them!
(with Nate Penn)

GUTTED

DOWN TO THE STUDS IN MY HOUSE, MY MARRIAGE, MY ENTIRE LIFE

LAWRENCE LaROSE

BLOOMSBURY

Published by Bloomsbury, New York and London
Distributed to the trade by Holtzbrinck Publishers

All papers used by Bloomsbury are natural, recyclable products
made from wood grown in well-managed forests.
The manufacturing processes conform to the environmental
regulations of the country of origin.

Library of Congress Cataloging-in-Publication Data
LaRose, Lawrence.
Gutted : down to the studs in my house, my marriage, my entire life /
Lawrence LaRose.
p. cm.
ISBN 1–58234–392–6 (hardcover)
1. Dwellings—Remodeling—Anecdotes. 2. LaRose, Lawrence—Marriage.
3. LaRose, Lawrence—Humor. 4. LaRose, Lawrence—Homes and
haunts—New York (State)—Sag Harbor. 5. Writers—Homes and
haunts—New York (State)—Sag Harbor. 1. Title.
TH4816.L335 2004
643'.7—dc22
2004000722

First U.S. Edition 2004

1 3 5 7 9 10 8 6 4 2

Typeset by Hewer Text Ltd, Edinburgh
Printed in the United States of America by
R R Donnelley & Sons, Harrisonburg, Virginia

For
Pamela Maraldo
Jeff Steele and Bob McKinnon
Joe and Sue Hine
Norman Stiles and Ellen Dillon.
They put a roof over our heads
when ours was open to the sky.

And especially, Susan.
With you I got into it,
And without you I
would not have made it out.

Before we can adorn our houses with beautiful objects the walls must be stripped, and our lives must be stripped.

Henry David Thoreau, *Walden*

I know not how it was—but with the first glimpse of the building, a sense of insufferable gloom pervaded my spirit.

Edgar Allan Poe, *The Fall of the House of Usher*

Ah, it is difficult to speak of what it was,
that savage forest, dense and difficult,
which even in recall renews my fear . . .
But to retell the good discovered there,
I'll also tell the other things I saw.

Dante Alighieri, *The Divine Comedy*

This Is Not My Beautiful House

I'm looking at a picture of Susan on the front steps of our new home. She's peeking over her shoulder and smiling brightly. A front door carriage light dangles upside down from the siding. Despite the fact that she has a blue bucket and cleaning supplies in her arms, it's clear from her expression that this is a monumental day. Out of frame, I hold a bottle of champagne.

We made the forty-minute drive back from Riverhead, where we just had the house closing, in thirty minutes. With the keys in hand, we are ready to spruce up what now officially—in all its romance and terror—is ours. Tellingly, we are both carrying testaments to our ignorance. Susan grasps a mop that won't be used for ages. This house needs many things, but first on the list is not a good swabbing. But that is typical. Susan enthusiastically charges ahead in most projects thinking it all has to get done at some point, so what if we do the last step first? It'll look that much nicer in the process. Or something like that; I'm still learning how her head works.

For my part, I've bought a crowbar that is far too small. A joke crowbar. Thinking I was getting prepared, I bought a tool that I now see is no match for the job. This house cries for some judicious—ah, hell, even injudicious—demolition, but if I did it all with this dollhouse crowbar it would take us perhaps three decades.

Sound project management suggests we start with a small task, one we can reasonably accomplish, to build our confidence and direct us down the path to larger challenges. I grab the champagne.

"To our new house, our new life," I toast, raising a glass.

"To our new *home*," Susan underlines.

Glasses in hand we walk around the house, reintroducing ourselves to the innumerable charms of this small cape. Innumerable because there are none. Somehow, now that we own it, the house looks even dingier. It is sobering to think that we made the largest purchase of our lives, a decision that will affect us for years, having spent mere hours here. Fortunately, we don't yet know that our future will be defined by hurricanes of dust, fiberglass itches in intimate places, isolation, screaming subcontractors, mind-bending debt, backbreaking work, threats of divorce, and chickens. And that in the next two years, we will ask ourselves, with damnable frequency, "How the hell did this happen?"

Instead, we are drifting away from sobriety, the champagne slowly dulling the reality that is beginning to set in. There is a lot to undo, a lot to demolish, even before we begin to improve the place according to our dreams. To get our feet wet, we remove a few dust-encrusted blinds and tug like terriers at the primeval carpeting. An hour into our labors we have a pile in the dining area that is halfway up to the ceiling. It's clear that we're going to need a Dumpster, fast. The biggest one we can find. We finish the champagne and resolve to start in earnest tomorrow.

Maybe you've read one of those quaint recollections of renovation, typically set in a small town in New Hampshire or Vermont. The tale is plucky and determined, with romantic planning sessions and cheery design discussions followed by a newly minted fondness for getting one's hands dirty and muscles sore.

The tale is punctuated with occasional aw-darn disappointments and unanticipated setbacks, all of it aromatherapied by the restorative presence of freshly cut Douglas fir. Invariably the protagonist in these narratives befriends a local craftsman, named something like Tully or Jenks, who carries his tools in a wooden toolbox, lectures on mortise and tenon construction, and recounts the way things used to be done before all these new-fangled doodads, like nails.

But real building doesn't happen that way. At least not on the east end of Long Island, where some of the country's largest and most lavish estates are constructed at a breathtaking pace. In East Hampton alone, where the median price for a home is $550,000, new houses spring up at the rate of one every day. From humble $400,000 tear-down ranch homes on slab foundations to mansions with more square feet than an airplane hangar, construction moves with a rapidity and swarming work-force that doesn't have time for talk of mortise and tenon, no matter how caring the contractor. Many old homes in need of repair aren't rebuilt. They are knocked down with a bulldozer, and carted away. A new stick home—or worse, modular—is put up in no time. Faster. Cheaper. More profitable.

Susan and I, however, were determined to renovate. Not out of any soft spot for cutesy husband and wife restoration scenarios, but out of sheer financial necessity. As we began looking at homes in our price range—Susan does public relations for nonprofit and philanthropic organizations, and I'm a writer pretending to be, like most of the country, an Internet savant—we soon learned that that range includes a time-share from the Old Lady in the Shoe and fixer-uppers like the small toenail-yellow Cape Cod we eventually bought in Sag Harbor, New York.

Since its construction in 1950, this simple home had been the unwitting and hapless victim of one punishing choice after

another: green asbestos shingles covered over by yellow aluminum siding; airport lounge–inspired wallpaper hidden behind
kiddy-porn grade wood paneling; oak floors smothered by wall-
to-wall shag rug last vacuumed during the Eisenhower adminis-
tration; disheartening layers of linoleum topped by terrifying
ones. Hardly a choice made during its history seemed to improve
the place: not the cinder-block retaining wall bisecting the backyard, not the shower curtains used as closet doors, not the stairs to
the basement resituated directly inside the front door. The place
looked positively forlorn, more in need of Paxil than a coat of
paint.

"It *does* need a little TLC," the realtor said leadingly, barely
disguising her own incredulity.

Susan—who is never speechless—had turned speechless. She
stared at me pie-eyed. Scared almost.

A little TLC? I'm thinking more like CPR.

Moments earlier we were looking at a different yellow house,
one made with wood. Its beautiful clapboards from the 1800s
were painted a light lemon chiffon. The original shutters hung
alertly and clean, gleaming with a fresh coat of paint. The interior
was a warm embrace of period trim detail, original door hardware, tasteful updating, and an airy and well-designed kitchen.
Light streamed in its leaded glass windows, splashing the wide-
plank pumpkin-pine floors. The place hummed with a cared-for
history. Better still, the front porch had broad views of Sag Pond.
The hitch, of course, was the price: more than twice our budget.
And yet the place was inspiring to us; it spoke of what a good
renovation could look like and be worth.

"This place looks fantastic," Susan said, appreciating the
refinished living room. "We should be able to do this."

"We just have to find the right place, and we'll make it like
this," I said in a deluded fit. Despite the price, we walked out

charged up. It was an encouraging "After" shot . . . that is, encouraging *before* we stepped into a real fear-inducing "Before."

Let's go on a virtual tour of our prospective home, this aluminum-clad and barely affordable château. Cautiously approach the residence by walking atop the bicolor yellow and gray checkerboard cement walkway that could be a knockoff of Archie Bunker's. Look around the grounds? Why bother? All the grass is dead. You ascend the front cinder-block stairs and open a creaky metal storm door, careful not to pull the thing off its hinges. Entering the living room you have two choices: You can either make an immediate left onto a generous stretch of grime held together by a carpet substrate, or step forward, where you will likely stab your hand on the handrail decorated with candle-tipped lightbulbs, then pitch yourself headlong down the stairs and tumble into the basement. Welcome to 69½ Union Street.

The living room looks like it has died. Admire the four-wall wood paneling, the pressed-board ceiling tiles, and the vertical blinds that not only block out the light, but effortlessly capture the dust of millennia. As we walk toward the kitchen, be sure to appreciate the sole bathroom in the house, complete with a curled-edge linoleum floor, pale blue toilet, pale blue sink, and— bathroom fixture trifecta—pale blue tub. The sliding plastic shower doors may have been opaque at one point, but they are now slaked with years of soap deposit. Some walls are squishy from moisture that has gotten behind the tile and is trapped, rotting the wood.

Then the jewel in the crown. Do you enjoy a spacious kitchen and eating area where you can cook and entertain friends? Well then, look elsewhere. Here we have 180 square feet that is cut up like a rabbit warren, with a constricted and linoleumed kitchenette (who stole the refrigerator?) and broken chunks of Formica countertop (sporting a cat-puke pattern) that leaves you just enough room to turn around. Tango? Only if you've got insurance. The appliances, though protected from the elements by a surface coat of aerosolized and condensed frying grease, look like they would be maxed out if asked to prepare more than two Lean Cuisines. This utilitarian room is adorned with a pass-through wall to the dining area, an even more penal affair so dingy that it is lightless despite sliding glass doors—which give onto a small, elevated, free-standing deck that sways when too many people are on it. Like two or more.

If you dare, continue to the upper floor. There is a stairwell— again, wood paneled—a shoot so narrow that you'll appreciate how cows feel moments before slaughter. In the lofty recess of the house are two—God I'm getting tired of saying it—wood-paneled rooms, which can (and have) been used as bedrooms. The feeling is both claustrophobic (low ceilings) and open (no doors). The rotting windowsills have been painted dark green to dissuade light from entering. To increase ease of access and cut down on unnecessary wood products, closet doors are actually repurposed shower curtains.

Welcome to Shangri-la. Asking price? $350,000.

Initially I thought that I was being too hard on the house, or by extension too hard on its previous inhabitants; heck, not every house is as well built and maintained as Bob Vila would like. Not everyone's design choices are going to make Martha Stewart melt. But when you have the audacity to ask almost half a million dollars for a dump like that, you are fair game. And in a fair game, that house would be called nothing more and nothing less than a shit heap.

So we bought it. Or, at least, offered to buy it at a lowball price.

The realtor thought that we'd be laughed at. Never mind that the house of blight had been on the market for some time, the climate on the east end of Long Island was so red hot that people were asking stupid prices for real estate, and getting them. Time wasn't necessarily a bad thing, it just meant you had to wait a little longer for a dupe to swim downstream. There are many Hamptons homeowners, we've come to learn, who go hunting in "silly money" season. They routinely put their properties on sale each summer for obscene prices, not because they need or want to move, but if some vacationing sucker is willing to plunk down one million five for a ramshackle saltbox, well, they'll sell you the seats they're sitting in. In effect, we were turning silly money on its head, offering laughably low (though Hamptons chump change is still a small fortune to most of us). Despite the realtor's reservations, and the report that everyone in her office also thought we were nuts, legally she was obligated to tender our offer to the seller.

We let her know on Monday what we were willing to pay, and, honestly, expected to be promptly spanked by the seller. Who knows, maybe we were feeling a little reckless and drunk with hope. We had pursued and lost a different fixer-upper in East Hampton, and the heady buzz from putting our bankbooks on the line was electrifying . . . but beginning to wear off. We needed another hit, another rush from being part of the real estate game. Who cares if we were playing at the penny-ante end of things for them; to *us* it was real money, a real stretch. Clearly rookies with more zeal than discrimination, we were primed to buy something, *anything*, no matter how forlorn it looked. But after our piddling offer, we heard, surprise of surprises: nothing. Not a word for a whole week. Not a rebuke. Not a laugh. Not a guffaw. Then, the unthinkable: a counteroffer!

It was a moment of vertigo: Is he really counteroffering our lowball? Let's buy it! This thought was juxtaposed with the more sensible: Are we really offering more than fifty cents for that shit heap? Let's praise God he didn't hold us to the offer, and run like hell! Mostly, however, we were thrilled. We were shaky with unknown apprehensions. We wanted it. We didn't want it. *What did we want?* We'd only been married a couple of months, had known each other for barely a year, how could we know what was best for us? Exactly the point, we thought in a moment of judicious reflectiveness. Then we decided to buy it.

Rather than look too eager, however, we waited to respond. We countered his counter only after ten days passed. And promptly heard nothing.

Damn it, we waited too long. We were stupid. We will move with alacrity next time. Maybe. Then, miraculously, we had a deal. The agreed upon price was nearly $100,000 less than he was asking. I hung up the phone, told Susan, and we jumped on our apartment's parquet floors. We literally jumped—no doubt angering neighbors below who, from the day we moved in, complained about our noisy perambulating. We jumped. Jumped because we were moving forward. Jumped because we were embarking on a trip to a place we had never visited. Jumped because in our new home there would be no carping killjoys who were primed to complain as soon as we put on our stilettos and cowboy boots and did the Macarena. We would be masters of our own dumpy domain. Free.

We sent in our nonrefundable deposit. It caught me unawares when I learned that nonrefundable in this situation means *non*refundable. No turning back. No second thoughts. No ambivalence without a hefty price tag. Then we started the process of due diligence, securing a mortgage and other unsavory nightmares. The bank, for their part, was like the CIA, asking to look under our paperweights, in our underwear drawers, insisting on insurances and inspections that, in reality, were little more than a side economy of scam artists and charlatans acting under a faux finish of answerability. The inspection required was easily the most ridiculous five hundred dollars we'd ever burned. It was a mortgage necessity, so we hired AmeriSpec, which is an industry biggie, but reading their "exhaustive" report I learned little more than our house was not currently engulfed in flames and it was not falling down thanks to a faulty foundation. At least as far as they could see.

And that is the key, for they can't see any farther than you can. If there were problems *within* the walls—and those are the problems that matter—they can't tell you because they have no authority to look within the walls. In effect, we paid a lot of money for some "inspector" to stroll through our home. There are other, and considerably more expensive, inspectors, who will spend hours at your prospective home, house detectives if you will, unearthing untold horror stories. Trust me: They are worth the added expense. Of course, even Perry Mason on house patrol could not have divined all the problems we would soon encounter.

"Do you feel different?" Susan asked over pasta and clams. We were snuggled in our apartment foyer, which doubled as our dining room, disbelieving that in a few weeks we would be home owners.

"Like older and established, or terrified of the responsibility of fixing that place?" I asked.

"Yes, both."

"Yes," I said, "both."

"But don't you think it will be fun?"

"Fun?" I said, thinking that yes, to actually have the thing cleaned and fixed and then be sipping daiquiris and inviting friends out for the weekend and spending long Saturdays at the beach will be fun, but fixing the place up? I wasn't sure. I was inclined to believe it would be, always having wanted to build or renovate a house but never ever actually having done so. I knew I was one, and suspected she was the other, novice on the job. "I think it'll be a lot of work. But, honestly, I'm thrilled that we're doing it together. That'll be fun."

"Aw, that's so sweet."

"I know, I should shut up."

She flicked an errant peppercorn at me, and then grinned coquettishly.

Had you described this dizzily domestic scene to anyone who knew me only a year earlier, they would have balked in disbelief, maybe even snickered. In 1997, I had gained a bizarre and wholly unexpected notoriety for cowriting *The Code: Time-Tested Secrets for Getting What You Want from Women—Without Marrying Them!* The book's surprising success led to a *People* magazine feature, countless radio interviews, then appearances on *The Today Show* with Katie Couric, *The O'Reilly Factor*, and *Oprah!* The wild ride felt even wilder—and perversely out of whack— when I saw the book featured on a billboard in Times Square. It was a thoroughly surreal turn of events for someone who had spent years of his life toiling in graduate school, sitting in classes with Harold Bloom, and listening to lectures by Jacques Derrida. Suffice it to say, my media-generated "authority" as a seduction Svengali was not only unanticipated but also a genuine blast. In light of the book, indeed because of it, I was hardly considered much of a conventional, old-fashioned romantic. Yet feeling more like a failed romantic, not "the Code guy," is certainly how I was the night I met Susan.

It was a sweltering July Manhattan evening, and I was at easily the worst party I'd ever been to. There were maybe fifteen people in attendance, most of them clumped near the rheumatic air conditioner as it chugged loudly but inefficiently. Still smarting from a doomed and preposterous relationship that had ended a month earlier, I steadied myself with a cold beer and a Jesuit's aloofness, swearing off secular concerns of flirtation, courtship, and long legs that ended in grotesquely expensive shoes sharpened to scrape YOU DON'T GIVE ME ENOUGH across your heart. *Om* was yesterday's mantra; today's was *grrr*. GRRR!

Then I spied a statuesque brunette across the room. She was wearing a light blue floral dress that whispered flattering remarks down her neckline and hugged her flat athletic stomach. A warm walking antithesis of waif, she exuded confidence and spirit. The center of her circle, she occasionally threw her arms aloft for greater laughing power. I thought, *Why aren't I with a woman like that?* This was quickly followed by more questions like, *What do I have to be so angry about?* and *Why am I over here talking to the fridge?*

After I wrangled an introduction, my friend Jonathan torpedoed my chances by saying, "And this is Lawrence. He wrote that best-seller on how not to marry women, *The Code.*"

"No kidding," she said, not registering a word Jonathan had said. How could anyone? For the last fifteen minutes he'd been dancing the Macarena with his pants belted up around his nipple line.

"Nice to meet you, Lars," she said, and then apologized that she was "just leaving."

"No, you're not," I said, surprising myself.

"Because . . ."

"Because your wine glass is empty," I said, fumbling miserably. I convinced her that we could uncork just one bottle, just to try. She agreed, but was unsatisfied. "Undrinkable!" I'd never seen a woman reject wine with such glee. So we tried another. Again, unsatisfactory. "Not fit for a thirsty dog," she announced triumphantly.

I glared at the label. "Let me try that," I said, hoping she'd hand me her glass and cross this most trivial and yet somehow significant of intimacies. With an effortless shrug, she did, handing it to me. "That *is* bad," I said, wincing from the assault. We tried another, and another, without success. Is this woman high maintenance, I wondered, or is she flirting with me?

"One could get a glass of wine where there is real air-conditioning," she prompted.

"One could," I quickly agreed.

We spent the evening at a subterranean and lavishly air-conditioned boîte, *talking*. I had never spoken, or listened, so much in my life. The place was packed, absolutely packed, and yet looking back on it now, I don't remember a thing about that evening except our corner table.

"I play two-man beach, mostly."

"Like Gabrielle Reece?" I asked, surreptitiously peeking at her calves.

"Yes, there are tournaments most weekends. Even in D.C. There were lots of players."

"It's like a parallel universe. *None* of my friends play volleyball. But D.C. . . . what were you thinking?"

"I was working on the Hill," she said, with a hint of embarrassment, as if she felt like she was bragging.

"Doing what?"

"I was working for a senator."

"Which one?"

"From Pennsylvania," she said evasively.

"Who is . . ." I said, leading.

"Arlen Specter."

Cough. "The Republican nut?"

"A-a-a-arlen," she said, mimicking his speech, "is a du-decent man."

I couldn't tell if she was serious, or being polite. "The Anita Hill guy, right?"

"I could tell you stories."

"And guns, too, isn't he goofy for guns?"

"You can't win statewide in Pennsylvania and be against guns. Everyone knows that."

"I didn't know that." And I didn't; it was intimidating. I had absolutely no follow-up. Everyone I had ever dated came from the Manhattan mainstays: publishing, banking, and food. I didn't know from Beltway.

"So what made you move up here?" I asked, harnessing the conversation a little closer to home.

"To work for Cuomo." *Shit, more politics,* I thought. "I ran his communications office in New York City, not that he ever listened to me."

"Which is no doubt why he did so well."

"Exactly," she said, and we laughed.

"Was Andrew around that campaign? He seems so, I don't know if this is a policy wonk's term, but, skeezy."

"Is this on the record?" she joked.

"Totally on background."

"I couldn't tell if he had bad political instincts or if he wanted to sink his father's campaign. Some weird father-son competitive thing going on there."

"Another pinot?"

"Sure, why not, it's early." As in early in the morning: two A.M.

"Tell me about your family," I said. Hold it. Jesus, did I really just say that? Should I really be running downfield so far on the first date? Is this even a date? Her *family?* I mean, shouldn't we have sex first?

"My sister lives out in L.A. A model turned actress."

"Blonde?"

"Be nice."

"Only kidding."

"If you only knew. She was a Fembot. You know, in *Austin Powers?*"

"Uh . . . huh," I said, not sure if she was pulling my leg.

"And the family's best athlete, next to my dad."

"What was your father's sport?"

"Baseball. He turned down the first professional signing bonus to go work with refugees in China."

"Knuckleballer turned knucklehead!" I snorted, with just enough obvious sarcasm not to get on the wrong side of Dad this early. Then I teed off an easy compliment: "You must have gotten your smarts from your mother."

Silence.

Shit, I thought, *her mom's dead.*

"That's complicated," she finally said.

Complicated? What can be complicated? *Not dead, but on life support. In a maximum-security prison. Working covertly with the Colombian guerillas.*

"My mother left when we were young. I was raised by my dad."

"I'm sorry, we don't have to talk about this. And I don't pretend to know what that's like when I say this, but my mother went through something similar. She was six when her father ran off. I don't think she ever recovered from it."

"Well, I got over it," Susan said, and I didn't know whether or not to believe her. "I haven't really had much contact with her for over twenty years. I mean, if you can't count on people, well . . ."

She didn't deliver it with even a hint of warning in my direction, but I heard what she was saying, rolled the thought over in my head. I'd spent years in a state of emotional ambivalence, racing in the front door and sneaking out the back. Now—*why?*—I wanted to be counted on. For *Susan* to count on me.

Landing at her doorstep at four A.M., I was eager to shed my former self, and determined *not* to go upstairs. Fortuitously, I wasn't invited in.

Our first not-really-a-date first date led to more dates, each somehow devoid of the mawkishness you'd expect from people as instantly and obviously smitten as we were. Everything about it felt different, like our dating wasn't prelude to a romance but preparation for a life together. In terms of *Dating for Dummies*, we passed the compatibility test and got extra credit. But having written a so-called dating book, I'll be the first to admit that compatibility tests are about as reliable as a ten-point check from a used-car salesman. Besides, when you're speeding through the early weeks of romance, who can really see what's most defining in a relationship? That kind of knowledge only comes in the rearview mirror.

Three weeks later Susan and I went to a friend's summer share in East Hampton for the weekend. We played volleyball, we played darts, we played tennis. In a crescendo of still more athleticism, we friskily chased each other along the beach, kicking waves. We wound up at a beachside home a few miles down the road in Amagansett. We couldn't get enough of each other. We made love in the den, in the library, in the master bedroom next to the chimney. God only knows whose house it was. When we were there it was still a construction site.

It felt like things were moving exceptionally fast, happily, like we were racing toward some new life that we had long prepared for, some new destination we had long dreamed of, but never quite knew how to get there. The correct circumstances had never quite aligned, the stubborn emotional bureaucracies never gave their requisite okays. Then, suddenly, without any preparation or formal application, we were told that we could go, we could move forward. It was heady and dizzying, and not a little complicated—especially when, just after the wedding, and a perilously short time before the mortgage closing, I was on the street, out of a job.

"You'll have something in no time," Susan said, masking any apprehension she might have had.

"We're closing in days!"

"I did the numbers this afternoon. I can carry us for a while."

It was both heartening and disheartening to hear, reassuring and depressing. I felt "enlightened" enough to believe, intellectually, that whoever earned the bread would support the family. But the reality of it was this: we had barely dried out our swimsuits from the honeymoon and I was being supported by my wife. When she met me, Susan thought I had a stable career at an Internet company. If she was initially worried, she never showed it. I became anxious about my contributions to our fledgling marriage and thought it was a good thing I was the better cook.

"But we gotta dump the house," I offered as a way of budget-trimming sacrifice, hoping to hell she would disagree with me.

"We'll lose the deposit, and we can't afford that."

"Jesus, this sucks."

"You wanna lose the house?"

"I . . ."

"Well, I don't. I don't want to move backwards. Do you want to be stuck in the damn apartment forever? Do you want to rent forever, never own something that creates equity?"

"No," I said, thinking she had said exactly what I was feeling, that we both had been on the starting line of life for some time. We had dated around, traveled, worked, and had fun. But build a life? Truly and fully share our hopes and dreams with someone, or establish an environment to raise a family? No, we had both entered our mid-thirties spending most of our time with the same social pit crews. They were good friends, surely, but when would either of us venture out from the uncommitted comfort of socializing and take a real lap around life? Now. We had darted across the starting line and gotten married, and neither of us was willing to pull back on the throttle. We wanted the house. *Our* house. Reckless, perhaps. But it was recklessness born of certitude, a strong faith in each other in the confidence gained from passing our first big test: getting married. From selecting the guest list, printing invitations, choosing the site, to all number of inconsequential decisions that become unbelievably, maddeningly consequential, planning the wedding was (as almost anyone will tell you) much more difficult than the service itself. From small tasks like choosing stationery to important responsibilities like writing our own vows, it was challenging to define "our" taste before the ceremony that established the "we." What did I learn from the experience? I learned a person can make some very large promises when he's wearing a clean suit.

Ready . . . Set . . . Oh Shit

She's opaque, shrouded by fog. Her hair is a dark Medusan tangle held rigid with layers of dust and fiberglass strands. She breathes heavily and sounds a bit like Darth Vader when she speaks: "Honey, you look like shit."

"And yet I"—*cough*—"feel great!" I say, holding myself against a wall. Or what used to be a wall and is now only a couple of two-by-fours with an orphan tar-coated electrical line hanging uselessly through them. I pull the sweaty safety goggles from my face and get the first clear view of my wife I've had all morning.

"You're as beautiful as the day I met you."

"And you're full of shit, too!" I can't read her tone. Was that funny and lighthearted? Or faint and exasperated? Maybe I should take my earplugs out.

We've been tearing apart our house. People call it renovating, but it feels more like terminating. What do you call it when you kill a house, with malice and forethought? When you unapologetically rip the flipping life out of it? Casacide? Domicilicide? Perhaps the more appropriate question is what do you call it when a house kills you? We've been pulling out the integument, pulling apart an ugly, if neatly upright, paneled wall. It is now a dusty tide up to our knees.

"I wonder if that was a supporting wall."

"Jesus, how many times?" I say, exasperated. "See those two-by-eights in the living room ceiling? They run north-south, same as this wall. This *decorative, nonsupporting* wall."

Susan yanks on a loose piece of ceiling Sheetrock with her pry bar. "But *these* two-by-eights run east-west."

"Shit!" She's right. And damn it, this house is a crazy quilt. I never would have guessed that the ceiling joists would change direction from one room to the next. This complicates matters, as we hope to rip the entire back wall out to expand this kitchen area.

I'm beginning to fill with panic. "Is it sagging?"

Susan looks up again, studies it. "Not any more than it was before."

"You sure?"

"No."

"Well, let's leave the rest of that wall in place until we can figure something out." Figure something out. That means ask someone to save us. "I'll finish pulling out the paneling and Sheetrock and then we'll *know* what's what. You wanna start on the floors?"

That's a dumb question, I know, but Susan says, "Sure, it's gotta go sometime."

Susan is the first one out the front door. I race down the stairs behind her. Dark smoke billows out the door after us in huge gusts. Dust masks cover our mouths, making us look like *ER* extras staring at an accident victim as we gape at our house in astonishment.

"Jesus!"

"Yeah, it got thick fast."

"What *is* that?"

"Everything," I say. "Everything that ever made it in that house and never made it back out again." Dust, dead bugs, cat dander, and God knows what else had been let loose when we began ripping out the walls. I started in on the ceilings with a garden rake—pulling down ceiling tiles with the teeth of the rake, then punching through the Sheetrock, and yanking downward— and it was working ferociously well. I had the living room cleared in minutes, but when I couldn't see Susan tearing up the dining room carpeting five feet away, it seemed like a good time to flee.

We're experiencing what every band of vandalizing teens already knows: Destruction is uniquely bonding. Plus, it's fun. There are no judgment calls or needs for consensus. Everything must go. Ripping, hitting, and sawing indiscriminately are a great release and progress is fast and obvious. After the dust settles we trudge back in and attack some more, hauling everything back to the kitchen area and onto the elevated deck. We've positioned a barge-sized Dumpster below the deck, and it is filling rapidly. By lunch it's half full.

Later that day we are formally introduced to our first large problem. She stands about five feet four.

"You gotta read the booklet," says Sybil, the building inspector's secretary.

"The booklet?" we ask, resting our elbows on the faux–wood grain plastic veneer counter.

"On renovating and historic preservation, from the Architectural Review Board."

"Our house isn't really historic," I say. "It's kind of an old and dilapidated . . ."

"You said Union Street didn't you? That's in the Historic District."

"Oh."

"So any changes have to be approved by the Architectural Review Board, and once they are satisfied you go to the ZBA."

"The . . ."

"Zoning Board of Appeals. Of course you've already read through your file."

"Which file?"

"Your house file. The building department keeps a file on every house in the village. Improvements, changes, code violations. It's public records, you just need to present identification and sign the form."

"Hmm. I think we'd like to read the record," I say, reaching for my wallet and handing over my driver's license.

"It'll be a minute."

Moments later—*whump*—our house file is in front of us. From the thickness of it, I immediately surmise that there must have been a triple homicide and an archeological dig on the premises. What else could account for all this paperwork?

Our neighbors, it seems. *They* could account for all of this paperwork.

When we were considering buying the house, it was offered with a complete set of plans for a renovation, plans that had been approved for implementation. Thinking nothing of it, Susan and I assumed it was a throwaway, an added bonus that really wasn't much of a bonus at all. We looked at the plans and dismissed them, thinking it made our house look like a carbon copy of the house next to it. Little did we know why.

The most pervasive argument presented to the Zoning Board of Appeals, we would come to see, is childlike in its simplicity. "They have a pool, so how can you deny me a pool?" "Their lot coverage is 25 percent. How can you object to my addition if the lot coverage will be 25 percent?" The argument is rather fallacious, for no two properties are the same, no set of considerations line up so squarely. But it is also a compelling argument, one of the toughest the zoning board has to tangle with, playing as it does on an elemental version of fairness and the American zeal for self-definition. It is a difficult argument to dismiss, but in the case of our property's previous owner, Len Schwartz, dismissed it was. Repeatedly, for two *years*. He was denied the right to improve his property according to his wishes for what must have felt an agonizing eternity. Rough treatment for a lifelong inhabitant of Sag Harbor, especially when you consider that he himself was a member of the zoning board.

The weight of our home's file did not come from any felonious activity, but neighborly acrimony. From all appearances, our previous owner and his neighbors hated each other. The file was rife with legal briefs, zoning board applications and reapplications, surveys, and, most hilariously, sun and shade studies. Schwartz's neighbor to the east, Veronique Saint-Pierre, insisted that if Schwartz were to build the mammoth house he was proposing (though smaller than hers), it would impair her free enjoyment of her property, cutting off her sunlight and stifling her cherished plants. Admittedly a valid argument; none of us wants to live in the shadow cast by a Trump building. But the plan backfired, for the biggest impediment to Saint-Pierre's sunlight, the study uncovered, was the stockade fence she had erected so that she did not have to look at Schwartz's unsightly property. He won on that count, but was nevertheless stymied by the letter-writing campaign that Saint-Pierre mounted, asking friends, some who didn't even live on the street, to write in and protest Schwartz's planned renovations, arguing that they would be a blight on the architectural integrity of Sag Harbor and a threat to civilized cohabitation itself.

By the time we turn the last page of the file, our jaws are hanging.

"Uh-oh."

"No shit," I say softly, not wanting to incite Sybil into a librarian's censure. "This is a nightmare."

"I think it's time to make some friends," Susan suggests.

"The neighbors?"

"We could grab that cooler in Pam's basement," Susan says, referring to our bed-sit benefactor, who has been nice enough to let us flop at her home while we begin to fix up our fixer-upper.

Up a windy wooded trail, Pam's house is perched atop a hill in East Hampton. With ample space, and a pool, it is a cherished retreat after a day of sweaty labor. We can sleep, shower, cook, swim, and otherwise live like humans. We may be unsettled but we are comfortable. "We'll get a couple of bags of ice, some wine, cheese, and have people over on Friday."

"The place is a mess. We could cause someone's death."

"We'll host it right on the front yard," Susan says. "Whoever wants to walk through the house takes their life into their own hands."

"Genius."

It's a beautiful evening in late May. The sun is flickering through the large oak at the corner of our lot, dappling our dead grass and making our small gathering of new friends and neighbors look professionally lit. There's a knot of people loitering around the blue cooler, the ad hoc kitchen and gathering spot on the front lawn. The stairs have had their handrail ripped off, and the interior of the house is too messy and uncomfortable to stand in, even for a quick glass of wine. From our initial demolition efforts, the house looks like a bomb hit it, but Susan has stationed potted rhododendrons in front "to make it look civilized." Our neighbors Ted and Steve, alarmed by our paper plate and waiter's corkscrew, have supplied a decorative platter and cheese knife.

"Hi Veronique," says Susan, "glad you could make it to our big soirée." I smile at Susan's targeted messaging, for Veronique affects (or possibly *is*, we're not yet sure) French nobility. I can see her rattling around Paris's sixteenth arrondissement, lunching with retired ambassadors and beating back panhandlers with *ficelles*. Age has mildly hunched her, but she's spritely.

"I'd *love* a glass of wine," she says, though no one has yet offered her one. "And *you*," she says, pointing a hooked finger at our startled friend, Gavin, "I like you, you're a sinner! What brand are they?"

"Marlboro Lights," he says, looking close to tears.

"I might have to pinch one from you before I go."

"I might have to pinch you back," he says, recovering.

We're flush with admiration for our neighborhood. This is precisely what we were hoping to find, but had little reason to believe still existed in the Hamptons. Many of our neighbors on Union Street have already come by to welcome us, some have invited us to dinner, and everyone has expressed enthusiasm for the rehabilitation of our edifice. They can't possibly know what we plan to do with the house since we don't yet know ourselves, but clearly anything will be an improvement in their eyes. Countless conversations slope into the inevitable: "Well, if it were my house . . ." Some ideas are novel, some are positively loony, but the ones we listen to most closely are Veronique's. We are eager to divine if there are matters more than solar theft and encroaching shade that will set her off, for we want her to be an ardent supporter of our little fix-me-up. Otherwise, we're looking at two years of hell; she and her team of devoted letter writers could sink us faster than an iceberg.

"Well, I'm just thrilled a nice young couple has taken over Len Schwartz's house," Veronique says to us. "I looked at that house, you know. My realtor said it would cost at least one hundred thousand dollars just to make it *livable*."

"Is that right?" I say, daunted but hoping Susan heard her, too. It's nice that I'm not the only one telling Susan that her visions of getting this house shipshape in three months for thirty thousand dollars are a little, well, optimistic.

"Oh, it was filthy," she continues, as though we didn't see what we had purchased prior to today. "And I'll tell you. Where I grew up, the Negroes lived on the other side of town. It's just the way it was in those days."

"Hmm."

"And many lived in tar paper shacks. Shacks, I tell you, but they took pride in those homes and they were spotless compared to *his* house." Schwartz's entire family of four lived there, but Veronique always refers to it as *his* house. Even when gleefully (if guiltily) recounting how the garish plastic Mickey Mouse swing that hung in *his* front yard went mysteriously missing.

Humorously, I will hear Schwartz's side of the relationship when I meet up with him a few days later. I have questions about the location of the septic tank and the raised layer of cement in the basement. Schwartz is a throwback from Sag Harbor's whaling days; he looks like a cross between Snagglepuss and Queequeg, with a tuft of yellow hair launching above his brow and a peculiar round growth on the end of his tongue. I can't resist asking him about his days living next to Veronique.

"You had quite a colorful neighbor," I say, opening the door.

"Ha!" he laughs, and shakes his head.

"Didn't quite see eye to eye on everything?"

"I bought a bug zapper one day," he says, referring to the awful black cage with a blue luminescent tangle that hung by an angle iron from the backyard cherry tree. "And the very next morning after I put it up she calls me and says, 'Len, that thing kept me awake all night!' "

"Uh-huh."

"And I said, 'Oh my God, Veronique, imagine what's going to happen when I actually turn it on!' "

We both laugh out loud, but I can't decide if this is comic retribution, pathetic neighborly antipathy, or rural class consciousness. Living in Manhattan was easy: Your neighbors ignore you, and you are expected to ignore them. It is becoming apparent that we have a lot to learn, not just about Union Street, but about living in a little town. The charms of knowing your green grocer, your mail delivery representative, and your cesspool cleaner—ah, what simple satisfactions from a bygone era—are balanced by a know-everything neighborly invasiveness, a rampant protectionism, free-floating antagonisms, and occasionally, a surprising (perhaps imported) litigiousness. At least for those who go for such sport. Many more simply fly under the radar enjoying the small-town ambience.

As the lawn party continues, Susan and I give a few brave, curious souls a tour of the premises. We tempt fate and move to the back deck with our friends Kate and Leo. We swirl the last of our white wine in the shallows of our clear plastic and listen to Sag Harbor lore. Kate and Leo have had a house here for years, seem to know the asking price on every home for sale, and have a good handle on most of the population—at least the gossip-worthy ones. Kate knits her brows in contemplation, and wonders aloud, "Doesn't Hannibal live on this street?"

"Who?" Susan asks.

Kate looks to Leo for visual confirmation, "Hannibal. You know, Hannibal Lecter from *Silence of the Lambs*?"

"Hannibal Lecter lives on this street?" Susan jumpily asks. Her movement causes the deck to move and creak disconcertingly. We look to each other like we might be going down.

"The fava bean guy," Leo confirms as the deck settles, "but he's the character, the author is Thomas Harris."

"Have you met him?" I ask, still somewhat dubious that the master of suspense lives on our street, much less in our zip code.

"Oh, no no no no. Never had the occasion, but I've seen him a few times tooling around town in a black Town Car. Once in the hardware store."

"Buying tools to prepare dinner, no doubt."

Leo gives a rimshot *"Ba-dum-bump!"* to my lame joke. Kate

follows with a request for Chianti, and Susan mercifully calls a moratorium on any more Hannibal jokes.

We head back to the cooler for refills, deciding it best to get off the deck before someone really gets killed.

Susan and I spend the remainder of the weekend ripping the living daylights out of the house. Soon the upstairs paneling is gone, as are the ceiling tiles, the decrepit bathroom tiles, the stairwell carpeting (a mistake: carpeting could have protected the stairs while we dragged heavy, cumbersome, denting objects in and out of the house for months to come), and the linoleum. Layers and layers of linoleum. A particular pleasure is tearing apart the light blue bathroom—everything goes *crack*—but what we uncover is frightening. Neither of us is wearing a mask now. They're hot and uncomfortable and though we remind each other all day, nag each other to put the masks back on, neither of us ever does. It's only demo, right?

"What *is* that?" I say. "That's not just old wood."

"Mold?" Susan says.

"Where's my mask?" I ask, suddenly cautious.

"Around your neck."

I hastily cover my mouth and lean over to examine the wall. "So if it's mold why is it black?"

"Because it's *black* mold."

I stand back up and raise my eyebrows at her.

"I read something about this in *Newsweek*," Susan continues. "People with mold all through their houses and they have to leave them behind. Belongings and all. Burn them to the ground."

"No way."

"It's what it said, gives people cancer, brain tumors, mood swings, weird unidentifiable diseases. Learning disorders in children." She's right, I later learn. In fact, the most toxic mold spores, the *Stachybotrys*, have been blamed for everything from irritable bowel syndrome, mood swings, asthma, skin rashes, memory impairment, even death. While mold is naturally occurring, the fear created by some sensational reports has created a boom in the mold remediation business rivaling that of absestos abatement.

"So, what are you saying? We can burn down the house?"

"It'd be a hell of a lot faster."

"Spray it with bleach."

"That's it?"

"It's mold. Bleach'll kill it."

"I dunno, my wife says it makes people go insane. Shouldn't we use something stronger?"

"Than bleach?"

"I guess," I say, though I'll later learn my instincts are wrong: Using straight bleach is less effective than a 10 percent solution of bleach mixed with water. "Anyway, this is the project." I'm giving the walk-through to a guy named Bill Dexter. He's clean-cut, carries no more than five extra pounds, is well spoken and disturbingly matter-of-fact. If central casting sent him over for the part of building contractor, you'd take one look at him say, "He's not believable. Too pretty." He could pass for a high-school tennis coach. Surely, he's nothing like the other four or five contractors we've already met. There's been the elfin guy who wanted to make everything cozy, with lots of little cabinets and hidden closets; the builder with the reputation, who, at the time of our appointment, slowed his truck in front of the house and then kept on driving; and the close-talker whose bad breath and disheveled comportment led me to believe that, if we hired him, our house would stink and fall over.

My personal favorite was the Range Roving charlatan who went by the name—I kid you not—Cary Grant. Sporting a seventy-five-dollar haircut and Gucci loafers, he had a manufactured enthusiasm destined for late-night advertising greatness. "I'm going to listen to you, and then I am going to say what I see happening here," he started, "so that we get a sense of how we are going to work together and I can give you feedback on what you want to accomplish and . . ." It was a loopy rhetoric to be sure, a smoke screen of verbiage that convinced me that ignorance is an asset and I should go into business tomorrow. His building by mind-meld approach was revolutionary to be sure, and when he narrowed his gaze, he did a really fierce *listening to you*.

But if Mr. Grant was right about anything, it is that a relationship with a contractor is a complex one. It is a marriage of sorts, not a short-term fling, and good communication is uppermost. There will be highs and lows, and even in the best of circumstances *things will go wrong*. You want to pick the contractor who will stick by you in the best of times, the worst of times, and when the proverbial caca collides. And yet, ambivalently, Susan and I want to be only half-married to our contractor. It is not an easy relationship to sell someone on. Dexter is not exactly biting.

"We want to do a lot of it ourselves, since we have a tight budget, but we need some help on the larger pieces, like ripping the roof off, and to guide things."

"Guide things?" Dexter asks. He is used to running the job.

"Protect us from ourselves," I offer, as correction. We are eager, smitten with the romance of building our own home, but we are utterly ignorant of how to go about any of it.

"I don't see how it's gonna work," he says.

"We need some help with the dormer, clearly, and when we have other issues we can call you. We're totally flexible, and you can swing by when it's convenient."

"You got a set of plans?"

"We're meeting with a draftsman tomorrow," we say proudly, like we are already ahead of him, "and he says he works fast."

"A draftsman? You're still gonna need those plans stamped by an architect."

"Yeah, I know," I say, not knowing. But how difficult can that be?

"Do what you gotta do, but you don't want me ripping your roof off without a set of plans. Otherwise I'm here scratching my head to make things work. And you don't want to pay for head scratching. That gets expensive."

"Gotcha," I say, appreciating his forthrightness, and thinking that, boy, we'll just get these simple plans drafted by the draftsman and all will be hunky-dory.

God, what saps we were.

It was our planned cost efficiency that drove us to a draftsman. Besides, we knew what we wanted and didn't need a lot of creative input. The addition would be a simple rectangle extending the back of the house. Rather than hire an architectural idea factory inclined to invoice at lawyerlike rates, we figured we could do an end run on the design discussion and get to work pronto.

We found Claudio the same way you find almost anyone in the home improvement racket, from friends who hired him and didn't think the result was too much of an abomination. Not screwing up your neighbor's project somehow confers credibility, reliability, and skill. We asked our neighbor Mark, who had miraculously restored an early nineteenth-century Federal—built by a prominent Sag Harbor family—to its original splendor. Mark had not only navigated the testy and impossible-to-please Architectural Review Board, but had received a special award for historic restoration. He was someone we admired, revered, and we devoured all his helpful advice. Indeed, I emulated his lifestyle of flannel shirts, work boots, and an enviable cache of power tools. He even had a big truck! Of course, we had our differences. Mark's wife was named Gary, and they hosted an annual July Fourth bash for which they helicoptered in big-city-caliber transvestites. But still.

When Mark mentioned Claudio, I was convinced either he could get our plans drawn or he'd look great in a pair of pumps. Yet I also found it odd, when Mark discussed his own house, that Claudio needed to draw architectural renderings of the (pre-construction) exterior—wouldn't a photograph have worked, *really?*—to restore the building to its original state. Ironic, that is, since the overseers and busybodies didn't prevent the architectural bastardizations over the years. Needless to say, Claudio "drafted" Mark's house, what existed in space, and did so ably. Case closed. Next stop was three doors down, our non-Federal, nonhistorically relevant, totally nonremarkable shit heap. Again, it would be expected that we submit existing conditions and proposed changes. Six copies.

When we first meet Claudio, a Brazilian, he has an easy air about him. Maybe it's inexperience. Under his arm is an oversized photo album with pictures of a couple projects he has worked on: some interesting small additions to large homes in Southampton. He also shows us samples of his work, AutoCAD printouts of previous jobs that are cleaner and spiffier than any blueprints I'd seen previously. To me, blueprints ordinarily seem impenetrable, their blue uniformity and crowds of dimension lines demanding a slow and close read. But Claudio's prints are colorful, appealing, and cleanly delineated. We show him around the project and we saddle up for the awkward money talk, bracing ourselves for a discussion that will lay bare how cash strapped we are and how if he'd like to work on this project for a little less money it might be a good way to make his portfolio even fatter. Like we're doing *him* the favor. Indeed, Claudio is studying to be an architect, and taking on jobs like ours will get him closer to his goal faster. In the meantime, he is also working as a groundskeeper.

Finally, when he says that his hourly rate is twenty-five dollars, we are struck dumb. Could we be so lucky? I stifle myself from screaming, "You're hired!" Instead, I let him know that Susan and I are going to talk things over with one other *architect*—don't believe a word of it—and we'll get back to him soon. We quietly pride ourselves on not only finding a solution to a potentially expensive hurdle but also helping the little guy trying to make his mark in the land of opportunity.

The next day, upon visiting the building department, we are reminded that *we* are the little guy. We pop in at ten A.M. to ask a couple general questions of the building inspector, Arnie Smothers. We want to start down the right road. We're a couple of aw-shucks newlyweds and we just want to be respectful and do the right thing. Sure, there is a little gamesmanship in our visit—it is better if he likes us—but mostly we want to do things efficiently and sidestep as many bureaucratic pitfalls as possible. From village lore we deduce that people who have gotten on the wrong side of the building department now fill an entire wing of the local mental institute. Everyone has a story about someone who butted heads with Johnny Law and wound up with an unfinished house and an aneurysm.

"We were hoping to ask a couple procedural questions of the building inspector," Susan says to Sybil. We could just as easily address Mr. Smothers, who sits alone at his desk, but this is procedure.

"Do you have an appointment?" Sybil asks curtly.

"No, but we only . . ."

"Well, Mr. Smothers has an eleven, an eleven-thirty, and then he has to leave at noon. Could you come in tomorrow?"

"Does he have a ten?" Susan presses, leave it to her. "It's ten now."

"I'll have to ask Mr. Smothers." She says this even though "Mr. Smothers" is so close she could reach out and touch him. It's always Mr. Smothers. *You'll have to show that to Mr. Smothers. Mr. Smothers is free now.* The regal Mr. Smothers also writes a column in the local newspaper under the byline "Arnie 'Big Tuna' Smothers," informing readers when to fish for porgy, where to spot a tern, and why the scallop crop is so poor this year.

Arnie is cupping the phone, waving toward us. "Send them in," he says, before ending his conversation. Sybil is none too happy. It is clear that, no matter how much Mr. Smothers drives the boat, Sybil schedules it, and she doesn't like this unscheduled visit.

"Mr. Smothers can see you now," she says, sulking with feigned perkiness.

We explain our general plan, just to feel him out, see if there are any potential pitfalls in the plan from an inspection standpoint. We want to add a rectangle, twenty by twenty-two feet, to the back of the house. On the first floor, the kitchen will extend ten feet, and there will be a ten-foot deck. The floor below—which attaches to the basement, but as the grade gives way will all be above ground—will create two rooms. French doors will give onto a small patio, perhaps slate or red brick. I underline the doors, to confirm that there are clear ways of egress.

"What are those rooms going to be used for?"

"Um," I hesitate, careful of the minefield. "Probably an office and, uh, storage space?"

"Storage space?" He says, leaning back in his chair, looking down his nose at me. *I'm an idiot. Who puts French doors on a storage space?*

"Or a playroom. Maybe . . . another office." I'm floundering.

Susan steps in. "Is there an issue with that space?"

"Well, today they shouldn't be bedrooms per se, but after the first of the year, when the code changes . . ."

"See," Susan taps me, "Mr. Smothers is trying to help us."

"I'm not helping anyone," he says, leaning his chair back, "I'm just thinking aloud."

"Of course," Susan agrees.

"But your lawyer will be able to deal with all of this."

"We're not using a lawyer," I say.

"You're not using a lawyer?" It's delivered quizzically, like he's never heard of such a thing.

Susan clarifies, "We don't have the money for a lawyer."

"Most people *do* hire a lawyer," he underlines with his I'm-not-helping-just-thinking-aloud tone.

"Truthfully," I say, "even if we did have room in the budget, we don't think it's worth . . ."

His chair creaks as he leans it forward, resting all four legs on the floor. Then he speaks slowly. "You're a very brave man."

Am I being paranoid, or was he using brave *as a synonym for* stupid?

We leave thinking we've made some modicum of progress, but also aware that we are walking out the door with more questions than answers. Why do we need someone's approval to put in new windows? What else will be changing in the building code? Where do we *find* the code? How are we going to get all this paperwork—survey, site map, tax map, existing condition plans, proposed alterations, permit application, and letters of recommendation—in time for the next Architectural Review meeting? Rather than get mired in logistics and bureaucracy, we decide to head back to the house and do something.

Walking up Main Street you can get a sense, under today's picturesque veneer, of the village this used to be. In the early

1800s, Sag Harbor was a booming whaling town, a veritable Long Island Las Vegas, teeming with foreigners and locals making high-stakes gambles on whale oil. After long stints at sea, the whalers would return to port hungry and horny and causing all manner of ruckus. The former brothel today houses a florist shop. And like Las Vegas (and unlike today), early Sag Harbor was not parti-cularly religious. Indeed, the earliest known Sag Harbor society was the Infidels, whose purpose was to attack Christianity. Yet Christianity was not the threat that fire was. A series of con-flagrations alternately trimmed or leveled Sag Harbor, fostering a steadfast local spirit and an incredibly populous and enthusiastic volunteer fire department. The town alarm induces a frenzied response and near lethal traffic surge as every able bodied male races to douse something. When the whale oil market deterio-rated, Sag Harbor turned to watch case making (a Bulova fac-tory), torpedo testing (in conjunction with the Bliss torpedo factory in Brooklyn), and rum-running. Today it is a major manufacturer (perhaps guardian) of quaint. Looking at old photographs you realize that, despite the fires, the general look of downtown defined by the American Hotel and Municipal Building is largely unchanged. It's a cute town, if a little heavy on twee, and worlds away from the hazards and hustle of Manhattan. I'm happy in a way I've never felt before. This feels right. I enjoy knowing that I can call the deli owner by his first name, Rich, or wave to the school crossing guard, the one whose Coke-bottle-bottom glasses make you wonder if she can even see the traffic.

"We're lucky, you know," Susan says, "that Boyd fell through." She's right, and it took us a while to know it. We had had our hearts set on a house on Boyd Street in East Hampton, but we lost out.

"East Hampton would have been a disaster." The town has become the victim of too much success. The stores on Main

Street are high-priced boutiques from Manhattan. Ralph Lauren. Anne Klein. Victoria's Secret. Even Tiffany's jewelers. Humvees and Mercedes SUVs overrun the streets like conquering forces, intent on securing a vacation perimeter. People in lines for coffee and Danish are ruder than they are in the city, if you can imagine, subconsciously saying: "I have worked hard for my leisure and, damn it, I will run you over if I have to to get it." Sag Harbor, for its part, is no stranger to the well heeled, but it has been spared the majority of the stupidity. The homes here butt up against one another. The lot sizes are modest. With notable exceptions, and thanks in part to the strictures of the zoning codes, people can't build McMansions, homes that are more egonomic than ergonomic.

We're walking with our heads in the clouds, letting it sink in that we actually own something here, that our future and this picturesque town are intertwined for the foreseeable future and we're happy about that. We turn onto Union Street and almost get run over—by a bicyclist. Not a Lycra-wrapped Lance Armstrong wanna-be, but a middle-aged woman on an upright bike. A tan beret flattened by the velocity tops her head, and wisps of gray hair feather back in the jet stream.

"Jesus."

"She didn't even look back," Susan hisses.

"She looks familiar."

"She should. She's up and down the street all day long."

I turn to get another look. Hunched forward, gripping the handlebars tightly, she seems on a mission. A small brown corrugated box is affixed on the rear rack. Her legs are peddling madly, carrying her onto Main Street and out of sight. "Really?"

"Nonstop." Susan grabs a pair of imaginary handlebars and leans forward. "I can hear the music from *The Wizard of Oz* in my head now when she passes."

"What music?" I ask, remembering only those crazy monkeys.

"You know, the Wicked Witch of the West—*dat-da-dat-da-daa-da, dat-da-dat-da-daa-da*—when she's peddling her bike like that."

"I think that *was* her. Elphaba has moved to Sag Harbor to retire."

"*If* she's retired."

"Good point," I say. "We don't know what's in that box."

"I'll be so happy to get this thing closed up," Susan says. We are standing at the lip of the stairwell to the basement. Since I tore out the handrail in a fit of demolition glee, our living room looks likes it's been cratered. A three-by-eight-foot hole patiently waits for someone inattentive to fall in and break a leg. She's been asking me to do this for a while, but I've been dragging my feet, busying myself with demo. Truth be told, I'm not sure how to proceed. Can I just slap some plywood over the top? Would that support a couch? No, I should use some supports underneath. But how big and how many? Crossways or lengthways? Does it even matter? All these questions are running through my head, but I'm careful to keep pretending a knowing manliness. "We just need the right wood," I declare, and nod with conviction.

"What wood is that?" she presses.

"Plywood—but we need Mark's truck," I say, stalling.

"Let's just strap it on top of our car."

I can't believe what I'm hearing. Though I shouldn't be so surprised; I've heard this type of mad suggestion from Susan before. "Come off it," I protest, "the thing is like four by eight feet."

"So what?" she says. "Let's do it."

Does she mean that?

Yes, she means that. I might have protested, but it's futile.

Susan is a force of nature. "Let's get it done." She says it like a charge.

I'm beat. "I'll get the keys."

Though I've been pretending a degree of expertise in front of my new wife, I'm unmasked on our first trip to Riverhead Building Supply. I rest against the sales counter like a dusty cowpoke leaning into the bar rail ordering a shot of rye. "I need a pound of galvanized screws, two inch; three eight-foot two-by-eights, Douglas fir; and a sheet of three-quarter-inch plywood."

The sales guy is tapping away furiously like an airline reservationist as I talk. Suddenly he stops short and looks at me. "What kind?"

"What kind what?" I ask, flustered.

"Plywood. What kind of plywood?"

I said three-quarter-inch, I know I did. What could he be driving at? I can feel Susan staring at the side of my head.

"The *wood* kind?" I say, half statement, half question.

"What are you using it for?"

"There's a hole in the floor . . ."

"CDX."

Uh.

"Anything else?"

Yeah, my masculinity back. "Nope, that's it."

"The *wood* kind," Susan snorts, as we head out the door.

"Oh, enough!" I snap unconvincingly. The twitch at the corner of my lips gives me away and we laugh all the way to the car. We drive around the lumberyard and find our CDX and two-by-eights. We strap them to the roof of our beat up BMW 325, and Susan jumps in the backseat. The car recently had a stroke and is completely paralyzed on the right side. Something electrical went kerflooey and both doors on the right and the gas tank access are frozen shut. Susan has to either Daisy Duke it through the passenger-side window or jump in the backseat. The wizened old codger who inspects vehicles leaving the yard, protecting against theft, looks at us quizzically. He can't figure out why I'm chauffeuring a woman around and picking up lumber. "These contractors are sure driving fancy cars these days."

"The truck's in the shop."

"Ha! There was a guy in here last week in a Rolls Royce. The backseat was stacked with ten bags of MortarMix."

"Yeah," I say, "he works for me."

Driving slowly, hazards on, we make it back to Sag Harbor with a three-quarter-inch wood sail strapped to our roof. I thought Susan was crazy to suggest it, but now I'm charged that we actually have some material to work with. After weeks of demo, this will inaugurate the construction phase, the beginning of the beginning. We are, with this minor improvement, crossing the line from demolition crew to builders of a dream. Our dream.

After lugging in the materials together, I address myself to the man's work: the power tools. Looking like one of those panicky home improvers who actually reads the safety instructions, I put on a respirator to counter the deadly dust cloud that will be kicked up by my growling two-horsepower Black & Decker circular saw. Hockey puck-sized filters stick out from both cheeks, making me look like I'm in a biohazard zone. While I awkwardly pull safety goggles (not glasses, mind you, *goggles*) over this contraption, the headband catches, snaps, and propels the safety plastic into my left eye. I don't know how to spell the sound I make, but it means *ouch*.

"Oh my God," Susan says, "are you okay?"

"I'm fine." My eye feels like it's on fire. "I just can't see out of my left eye."

"YOU CAN'T SEE?"

"I'm kidding. But damn, it hurts." Tears stream down my cheek, collecting uncomfortably in the respirator mouthpiece.

"How can I help?" Susan asks.

I shake my head vigorously and blink. "It's fine," I repeat. "Okay, now . . . should I cut one long piece or two short pieces?" I say, thinking aloud.

"What's the difference?"

"I don't know." I stare at the floor joists. I look at the plywood. I look at Susan. She looks at the joists. And so begins our renovation, the two of us harmoniously working side by side, staring at a hole in the floor like it is an SAT question.

"I think one piece," Susan says.

"Me too. Grab the end of the tape and we'll measure."

Half blind and moistened, I squint at the inch marks on the measuring tape, which have gone blurry. "Ninety-four and three quarters, I think."

"You think?"

I determinedly forge ahead, cutting a three-foot length of plywood, while Susan holds. Then we secure it to the joists with a couple hundred screws. Job done. One piece of CDX attached, one cornea scratched. At this rate the house should be done by 2007, and Susan will be a widow.

After taking one long afternoon to repair the hole in our living room floor, it is clear that our renovation is moving at a crackling pace. So, too, my career. In the space of one week, two Internet companies with which I had interviewed—one had all but tendered an offer pending "numbers"—impose hiring freezes. The job market is getting very chilly, standoffish. Even bitchy, it seems, as more and more firms are clarifying that their hiring requirements do not include a master's in comparative literature, a sarcastic sense of humor, or a great appreciation for lunch. In truth the tightening of the economy—dot-com going dot-bomb—makes me, makes *us*, start to think creatively. In other words, we're desperate.

The following Monday, I decide to merge my dual needs—employment and renovation know-how—by trying to get a job on a construction crew in the Hamptons. Meanwhile, Susan will continue to work at her job in the city.

I see a promising ad in the local weekly, *Dan's Papers*:

QUALITY CONSTRUCTION OF THE HAMPTONS

SEEKING GOOD CARPENTERS.

CALL FLOYD 555–1212.

"Oh, sure, I've got some experience," I tell Floyd, thinking back to how I almost knocked my eye out. I also think back to grade school and the boxy house I assembled with popsicle sticks and Elmer's glue, and am at a loss for transferable skills. Truth be told, I've never even built a *bird*house, much less a structure that has to support the weight of humans, bathtubs, and a grand piano. Sure, I've done some painting in my day, but I've never seen a house held upright with Benjamin Moore. I mutter to Floyd that I'm comfortable building "stuff" and feel lucky he can't look into my eyes as I tell him this pack of lies.

More important than experience, it seems, Floyd wants to know if I have tools. "Oh yes," I say, thinking I could scrape together a tape measure, maybe a Phillips-head screwdriver, and a nail sink, "I've got tools."

"Your own chop box?" he asks. I'm not sure if the cellular reception has gone spotty or if guillotines have some efficient use in building.

"Yes, I've got tools," I repeat, adding eagerly, "but I'll be buying some more." Like a hammer, I think.

"You'll start on Monday," he says.

The Land of Floyd

My first day, like a seasoned carpenter, I don't show up. Or call. Today is the deadline for applications to the Architectural Review Board of Sag Harbor. Because the town aims to maintain its historical character (steroidal quaint), every window choice and fence height needs approval—sometimes twice. The Architectural Review Board oversees aesthetics (the zoning board, meanwhile, is all about setbacks, lot coverage, and, if you can believe it, space coverage). Sag Harbor enacted a law stating that a house cannot be larger than an imaginary pyramid drawn from five feet within the four borders of the property. This is an aptly named regulation, if you stop to consider that the Great Pyramids of Giza were built as the final resting place of the pharaoh. Susan and I are already feeling buried by the administrative malarkey.

Our house sits a scant eight feet from the eastern lot line, in flagrant violation of the pyramid law. But since our house was built before the law was drawn we are considered "pre-existing nonconforming." This is the Sag Harbor architectural version of original sin.

Today's crisis is thanks to the crack surveying team we hired. In surveys of 1985 and 1990, the lot measured 6,100 square feet. Our surveyor found only 5,500 of them. On a sprawling East Hampton estate this would be negligible, but on our postage stamp of property, 600 square feet is roughly 10 percent of our land. This, of course, affects how any zoning board member will look at our allowable lot coverage. With less land, the percent coverage of our house—and addition—would be higher. If we cross the 25 percent mark we will almost certainly be denied any more "house." "Could I drop the revised survey off at the end of the day to complete the application?" I ask the building department's Sybil at nine A.M.

"Noon, or it'll be next month's meeting," she says, unbending and artificially sweet. I'm beginning to see Sybil to be the unlikely progeny of a snippy grocery checkout girl and Joseph Stalin. A combination of heard-it-all-before and my-way-or-the-Gulag. Next *month?* Susan will go apoplectic. She does go apoplectic. Racing to our surveyor's lair in Hampton Bays, I phone her at work.

"That's ridiculous, completely ridiculous!" she shouts.

"Don't shout, I'm on your side," I plead.

"This application is to replace *windows*, what do we even need a survey for?"

"Because Sybil says so. Maybe she's been reading Kafka."

"Sorry you have to drive all that way."

"Traffic's not too bad," I lie.

"Oh, some Beyernheimer guy called here looking for you."

"At your office? We need a phone at the house."

"We can't afford another bill right now."

"*Fine,*" I say, grinding my teeth. Without cell phone reception, it is like being in the outback. I could go the whole day without talking to someone, and when you are trying to build a house, that's not a good thing. "So, who is he, this Beyernheimer?"

"That roofer Randolph Duke recommended."

"Is he party material?" I ask, using our subcontractor litmus test. Susan and I had decided that once the house is complete we'll have a backyard clambake, inviting family, friends, and all the subcontractors who worked on the house. Hiring has become a question not only of quality, but whether or not we would want to have this person over for dinner. Despite many party-based nos, the party test produces some superb tradesmen.

"I didn't talk to him, he just left a message."

"Okay, I'll call him after."

"Drive safely."

"Will do," I say, though I'm not. Speeding to Hampton Bays and back I narrowly make the noon deadline to turn in the application, when I realize that the surveyor corrected one error but not another. I hope Sybil won't notice.

I return home to discover that Claudio the draftsman has been by . . . to leave a bill after his three weeks of work. It's tacked to a central stud in the kitchen since we have no door to slip it under, or counter to rest it on. I slide the invoice out of a business-sized envelope and promptly have cardiac arrest. The heart-stopping outrage is there in black and white: BALANCE DUE: **$4,450.00**. I scan up the page, convinced that there is a mistake, that the decimal point hip-checked to the right, turning $445 to $4,450. But no, there is no mistake, Claudio is billing us for 178 hours.

I can't believe it. One hundred seventy-eight hours to draft our dinky hut? The Amish can *build* a house faster than that. Claudio must have been working in a black hole to swallow that amount of time. But then I remember Susan telling me about a meeting she had with him at his garage apartment in Southampton. He was clumsy with the computer program, and she found herself commandeering the mouse to make it go faster. He suggested they work on paper. She suggested they *get it done*. Apparently he did, very methodically. Or ineptly. It struck me like a blow to the head: Susan and Lawrence are paying for Claudio to teach himself AutoCAD. Dropping the invoice to the floor, I looked around the gutted interior of our home and weighed my options: I could kill the draftsman or I could get a job.

As soon as I find a strong enough cellular signal (perfidious Sprint) I phone Floyd and ask for a second chance, pimping out my corneal injury from two weeks ago. He says okay, which is probably indicative of the labor shortage on the east end of Long Island—at least for ersatz carpenters who are willing to work for fourteen dollars an hour. (That's six dollars an hour less than my wife pays her receptionist, she thoughtfully points out, and *she* gets health benefits.) Floyd cuffs my ears for not calling, says instead of working on the Southampton house maybe I should work at his place with a couple of the guys. That doesn't sound good. What can that mean? Then he reconsiders and points me toward Southampton, reminding me to contact Billy when I get there. I'm relieved and I don't know why. One last time I confirm, wearily, seven A.M. "Yeah, seven," he says, "at least that's when the guys are supposed to show up."

Supposed to? I'm sensing a leadership style that is decidedly not hands on.

The address that Floyd gave me was on Cooper's Neck Lane in Southampton. The "Necks" were originally farming territory, the Great and Little Plains of Southampton, but today their only bumper crop is outsized vacation homes for the elite. Each is spectacularly maintained and dramatically private. Most have a service entrance.

Like many roads in the estate section of Southampton, Cooper's Neck Lane is a green tunnel of twenty-foot hedges, precision-manicured to completely (or nearly) obstruct any view of the homes or their inhabitants. Reminiscent of Roland Barthes's conception of the erotic—it exists where the garment gapes—

these hedges make one dizzy with desire, they tease you, dare you to steal a glimpse of the pulchritudinous palazzos. The flagrant efforts at privacy advertise a desire not to be concealed but to be peered at enviously.

My cacophonous drive down Cooper's Neck Lane destroys the green serenity. Windows open, radio blaring, my dilapidated 1987 BMW noisily labors forward, emitting a rotational scrape from worn brake pads and the huffing of mistimed pistons. At any moment I expect a loud clank and a cartoon puff of smoke to signal the sedan's demise. I pull into the drive promptly at seven-thirty A.M. and my jaw drops. The pebbled drive is at least three hundred feet long. It bends in front of a gargantuan—and soon to be gargantuaner—house, then makes another three hundred–foot run back on the other side of the property. A line of London Plain sycamores, easily thirty or forty of them, canopy the entryway and generously shade the lawns.

The house framing suggests something huge and expansive, one of those massive places that will generously stroke its owner's ego and impress legions of sundressed and seersuckered guests for many summer weekends to come. The eventual size of the house, not including decks, patios, and pool house, will be eleven thousand square feet, roughly twice the square footage of our entire *lot* in Sag Harbor. Eventually it will be listed for sale at fourteen million dollars. The immensity of it thrills me, as if by some random mix-up I am invited to batting practice with the New York Yankees. I don't belong here, but damn if it won't be fun to live in the mansion's reflected glory until someone finds out.

I park at the end of a long line of muscular trucks. Not the let's-go-to-the-flea-market-and-pick-up-some-cheap-antiques type, but the kinds of trucks that six-foot men have to stand on tiptoe to see over the front quarter panel.

I get out and loiter around for a few minutes, tie my Timber-lands (which, at four years old, still look as new as the day I bought them), and stare with manufactured purpose into my cluttered trunk. But there's nothing here to help my hastily assumed career, just a set of jumper cables, two canisters of used tennis balls, and a tattered copy of Philip Roth's *My Life as a Man*. After just the right amount of futzing, I nod with satisfaction, slam the trunk, and make my way to look for the foreman. My T-shirt and shorts suddenly seem too clean.

I approach a couple workers and ask for Billy. They point me to a young guy who looks like he could be valedictorian at the community college.

"Are you Billy?"

"Yeah?"

"I'm Lawrence. Floyd said . . ."

"Weren't you supposed to be here yesterday?" he asks quiz-zically. Like *he* might be in the wrong.

I was expecting a Billy of slightly different issue, someone gristled and unshaven, obviously seasoned by mishaps, and more roundly proportioned. But in a spiffy white muscle T, Billy is young, clean-cut, and physically fit. He's got short blond hair, an insufficient chin, and a thin blond mustache that could be titled "The Valen-tino, Smudged." His youth is exaggerated by an air of blinking noncomprehension and, as I observe on the stroll to the tool truck, occasional toe walking. But I count my blessings; I could have encountered a real prick, gruffly swearing that he doesn't need the head office sending another goddamn greenhorn.

"What's your experience?" he asks.

I suppress an urge to say, *I'm great with Quark and PowerPoint*, and try to confabulate something that I won't be held account-able for later. He looks through me, like a television psychic, and I wonder if he can see I have zero experience.

"General."

He stares at me. Hard.

"Comfortable framing, general carpentry, Sheetrock, etc." I'm staccato, inarticulate, verbless. In a word, perfect. I seem to be flying under Billy's radar. Or maybe he just places me a notch, a very small notch, above broom boy. We head back to what the blueprints term the breakfast area. A man is having a light breakfast—a Camel Light. The thousands of previous cigarettes color his fingers, his teeth, and crease his skin more deeply. The years have made him lean and sinewy. He looks like a ponytailed, tattooed, irradiated Jimmy Buffett long after the jukebox has run out of steam in Margaritaville. Billy says, "You can work with Joe back here."

Joe says, "How's it goin'?"

"Awright," I say.

Billy leaves, his job done.

Joe talks through the cigarette that never leaves his lips. "What we gotta do . . . (drag) . . . is we gotta . . . (puff) . . . put some footers under these temporary walls (drag . . . pause . . . puff) . . . down there." He points when he says "down there" to emphasize the unpleasantness of the task. If ever a job was invented for the new guy, this was it.

Beneath the flooring, the crawl space is roughly three feet high. Ten hours of heavy rain over the weekend have flooded it with about six inches of water, a yellowish tide that carries old coffee cups, cigarette butts, sawdust, sandwich remnants, and everything else the workers threw to the floor. It would be possible to pump out this dreadful flood, but, as luck would have it, the bilge pump is broken. And it is dark; only a three-by-five-foot section has been cut out of the plywood flooring to access the crawl space. I calculate how long it would take to retreat, my puny sedan spitting gravel the whole way down the drive. That, and how long afterward my flight would be recounted and laughed at.

The breakfast room is probably eighteen by twenty feet, with a twelve-foot ceiling. A steel I beam is being added to support the increased load from the second and third floors above it. To sink the I beam, the ceiling joists will have to be cut. (Though I don't know it yet, I'll have to do this exact routine—on a much smaller scale—when I rip off the back wall of my kitchen.) Once the beam is slid into place the joists are ticoed to the I beam, which is to be sandwiched with lumber through-bolted top and bottom, every twelve inches on center. Ticos are those U-shaped metal joist hangers that hold one board firmly perpendicular to another. Of course, to make those cuts in the beam and raise the I beam, something else will have to support the floor above us: the temporary walls. Those walls are built within the room, but the support must go to the foundation, to the cement slab beneath us, otherwise the floors we are standing on will buckle and force the room out of alignment. That is what necessitates us going into the watery hell.

But—a gift from God—Joe says he's going in the hole. We lower cinder blocks into the water and rest two-by-ten-inch boards on top of them. This creates a miniature, if precarious, dock to work on. A foot-long fluorescent bulb dangles over the opening to give some meager light. I mention the potentially lethal consequences, should the light get bumped into the water. Joe shrugs it off and I see myself reading him his last rites. He bends a nail over the cord as if to appease me. Then he hunches under the floor joists and sets to work. It is Zolaesque in its cramped, fetid demands, a *Germinal* of the Hamptons. While Joe's in the hole, I'll be in charge of cutting the two-by-four-inch boards that will serve as the footers.

A note about safety equipment: No one uses any. None. At

home, with goggles, respirator, and gloves, I look ready for a moonwalk. Here, none of that has a place. Too cumbersome, too hot. Too pussy. In fact, some safety mechanisms are removed or overridden to make the many repetitive motions quicker and less burdensome. The blade guard on the circular saw, for example, can slow down cutting, or even interfere with straight lines, since the resistance on the spring-loaded guard presses against the board unequally. Joe's saw guard is propped open with a small piece of scrap plywood, so the circular blade is exposed and ready to cut as soon as the trigger is pressed.

Joe hunches in the hole and pops up with a measurement to cut, "Forty-seven and five eighths, heavy," or asks me to trim one that doesn't quite fit, "Take a blade off that," which I do, sawing off only the width of the saw blade's kerf. The first board—partially brown from the blade's burn marks—took me a good fifteen seconds, I was so determined not to screw it up. But ten swipes later I'm getting the hang of working here and becoming comfortable with the saw. I cut another stud and put the saw down, forgetting the blade guard is jammed open. Its teeth dig into the plywood flooring, and the saw tears around my feet like a scorpion. Joe's head pops out of the hole like a prairie dog's.

"Gotta watch that," he says, as I repress a shout. At this rate, my ignorance will betray me before noon.

Another guy shows up at about eight-thirty. He's probably five feet six and roundheaded like Pig Pen from the *Peanuts* comic strip, grown-up and in the construction trade. Torn jeans. Ripped T-shirt. Sawdust covers his baseball cap like frosting. There is a cast on his left hand and forearm, mottled gray and brown from work and sweat. He looks moderately unstable.

"How ya doin'?" I ask in mock familiarity.

"I'm Dale," he says.

Joe calls for another board. I cut it and surreptitiously toss some sawdust on my clean cap. Dale is placing headers above a couple of the door frames in the room where we are working, and the way in which Joe speaks to Dale dismissively makes me think Dale did these headers once before, wrong. In platform framing—colloquially referred to as stick construction—two-by-fours or two-by-sixes spaced at sixteen-inch intervals transfer the weight from the floors above them and create the walls that separate one room from another. When an opening like a door or a window exists, that same load has to be transferred, but there aren't boards within the opening to do so. Hence headers, which are more rigid and move the load laterally to additional studs and jacks.

Needless to say, two two-by-twelves cut at three-foot lengths are a significant and unwieldy amount of weight for a healthy man, much less one short dude with a broken wrist. I watch Dale struggle. He holds the header between one hand and the crook of his wounded arm. He also must carry his Paslode nail gun, which, in a way, you could blame for this madness. Introduced in 1986, the Paslode framing nail gun revolutionized building—speeding construction, reducing carpenter fatigue and (it seems) turning every home into a lightning rod, thanks to the tenfold increase of nails. Pull the trigger—*cha-thunk*—a ten-penny nail is bulleted flush into hard wood. It's a split second affair that doesn't require one hand to steady the nail and another to swing the hammer.

To get the header in place, Dale has to climb a six-foot stepladder. He drops the nail gun on the fourth step up the ladder, leaving him aloft, adrift, and frustrated. I seize the opportunity to make a quick friend.

About that time, Bob roars in. "Who's the new guy?" he says, less interested in the new guy than with making clear that he's the veteran. Bob, from appearances, was confronted years ago with a decision: Be a lounge singer à la Dean Martin or Tom Jones or go into construction. He chose building. In place of a tuxedo, he wears a lavish tool belt, eschewing the more rudimentary tawny leather variety for black ballistic nylon with more pockets, pouches, and hooks than I can count. His hair is combed, his shirt is tucked in, and his black work boots are not only relatively clean, but tied. Bob's inquisitiveness is not gregariousness, I'll later learn, but from his quasi-managerial role (as an informer, reporting on other's work habits) when Floyd is not around.

Working in the adjacent room is a loudmouthed guy named Ritchie. He is a Trinidadian bisexual. Deafeningly bisexual. Married, two kids, an unrepentant job site thief—"They take hours off me paycheck, I take some bundles a shingles, square!"— Ritchie is boisterous, and his noise level is in inverse proportion to how much work he gets done. "Watch me!" he announces, in a mock tutorial flair, suggesting that his few momentary efforts are not simply accomplishments, but artistic. "Watch me!" More often, Ritchie is a master at getting others to do his work for him. Though he has no position of authority, he does not let that constrain him.

"Wheh's yah tool behlt?" he sneers at me, anxious. Unbeknownst to me, but very beknownst to everyone else, an entourage of "big heads" has arrived on site. The architect, builder, and project manager move in a tight pack from room to room. Everyone, even stationary and loquacious Ritchie, is suddenly hammering with abandon.

"Yah tool behlt, wheh's yah tool belt?" he whispers loudly.

Bam, bam, bam. "I need to buy a new one tomorrow," I say, lamely, mumbling that my "old one" is *mumble mumble*, and so tomorrow *mumble mumble mumble*.

"Come," he commands. "We will have to find you something." We stomp around the ground floor until Ritchie finds a tool belt under the main staircase leading to the second floor.

I hold the unexpectedly heavy belt in my right hand. The rain over the weekend soaked the belt, and everything in it. An old carpenter's hammer has a patina of rust. The nails are corroded. The chalk line is caked, gummy. The initials "N.S." are scratched into the side of a utility razor, which releases a stream of water.

"Put it on, or you don't look like a worker."

I do. The contraption hangs uncomfortably around my waist like a pair of wet cutoffs. It gives me an instant authenticity. My domain is not lumber remnants and sawdust! I'm not here just to jack up the billable hours! I'm a carpenter.

"Good," Ritchie affirms, "now look busy." I leave Joe stranded in the hole while carrying unrequested lumber from one side of the house to the other. The "big heads" keep moving around like observant sharks. I feel like a teenager working at Burger King with an assistant manager who recites corporate If You Got Time to Lean, You Got Time to Clean axioms. This crew is expert at leaning.

After a half hour of frenetic faux work, the supervisory mob is gone, and we are back to normal. I am peering into the crawl space and cutting two-by-fours. Joe is smoking and calling out measurements. Dale is teetering atop a ladder under the weight of a door header, and Ritchie is mouthing off. "Whaht are you doin' in that pit, Joe? You couldn't get me down there. That's nigga work!" In stark contrast to the tolerance with which everyone treats Ritchie—he's harassed, sure, but not for his sexuality or race—he is easily the most bigoted on the crew. "That's nigga work," Ritchie repeats. Joe doesn't say a thing, but his stare evinces a blue-collar stoicism, as if Ritchie is his carping wife, complaining that they never go anywhere anymore.

Amid the din of pounding hammers, screaming circular saws, and punctuations of nail guns, I hear a scream echo off the plywood walls. "ROACH!" It seems like it came from above, but the echoes make it unclear, and all work suddenly ceases. "Roach!" "Rooaach!" "Roach!" It's like I'm caught in a reverse Raid commerical, where the insects have finally won, and we are merely carpenter carrion for the vanquishing bugs.

Through the studs I see a silver commissary truck ambling up the long driveway: the Roach Coach.

Break is a serious business. Everyone stops work immediately, except Dale, who is visibly struggling. He is determined to get one header up before facing the others at break. "Goddamn it," he swears at the board, and swings the Paslode around to whack it into place. The gun roundhouses wildly and he nearly nails my ear to the side of my head. In ninety short minutes it has become clear to me that Dale is someone to avoid, or at least give a wide and constant berth. "Sorry," he says sheepishly. I scowl back, pulling rank on him already.

Numerous people I haven't yet seen are now swarming around the back of the truck, like piglets searching for a teat. There are at least twenty of us. "Work it, work that Roach," chants the driver, a nervously gregarious guy. It's unclear if his humility stems from being the water boy, bringing coffee and eats to the real men doing hard work, or if he's just careful not to appear boastful that he's got the cushy job.

I elbow into the trough and survey the concessions: doughnuts, petrified bagels, polyester lemon cake, soft drinks. I grab my second large cup of coffee for the day, and spy a cherry Danish. I'll look like a wimp with a cherry Danish, I think. I grab a double cheeseburger. It's wrapped in a cellophane sarcophagus that traps the moisture in, and lets none of the pestilence out.

Various groups sit apart on different patches across the lawn. There are the Colombians who, because they speak Spanish, most everyone refers to as the Mexicans. This includes Alex, who was born in Brooklyn. Another group, who are skinheaded and exhibit a beer-pudgy muscularity, are dubbed the Gangbangers, both for their look and their group cacophony as roofers. They have surgically attached sunglasses, never wear shirts, and are turtle-tanned—dark on their backs, light on their fronts. The older guys on the crew, Bob and Joe among them, hang near the backs of trucks and talk about motorcycles and their old ladies.

Sitting in the shade, with my legs in front of me and my back against a tree, I unwrap the burger. I take one bite, give it a muscled swallow, and realize the huge mistake I've made. Looking into its gray despair, I see it appears to be a burger made out of chicken gristle and CO_2, put together with a cheddar-colored adhesive that attaches itself to your esophagus like a supergluc made by NASA. It's best not even to mention the bun.

I stuff the burger into my empty coffee cup, trying to contain it, then lean back onto my elbows to relax. For the first time I realize the day is radiant, crystal clear, seventy degrees with low humidity, and a light breeze. A great day to be at the beach, or on break and not staring at a crawl space flooded with fetid water and cigarette butts while intermittently snorting lines of sawdust.

After break, Joe and I are in the kitchen area again, moving on to the other end of the temporary wall. To get the footers in, we can either continue an elaborate pier system beneath the flooring to the far end or simply rip up another piece of the plywood subflooring. We opt for the latter. "Grab a cat's paw out of the truck," Joe instructs. Great idea, I think, but what the hell is a cat's paw?

I head toward the truck, unsure how the hell I am going to retrieve a tool I have never heard of before. Climbing into the truck, my suspicions are confirmed: Things aren't labeled. Luckily, someone is coming, but I am loathe to ask outright for help. How would that look? The way Joe said it, cat's paw sounds as quotidian as fax machine. A big black guy climbs into the tool truck and we meet. As Chris concerns himself with saw blades, I roughly open one drawer, then another. I open a cabinet. I peer into a carrying case and slam it shut. Then, semi-exasperated, I say, "Hey, Chris, have you seen the cat's paw?" I deliver the line as if to suggest that cat's paws have a habit of moving around like inmates on a prison break. On other trips, I'll vary the inflection as if to suggest that the person I am asking had something to do with its disappearance.

"Yeah, it should be in the first drawer," Chris says, "on the left."

The first drawer on the left is packed with paraphernalia. Pry bars, a stray drill bit, bit sets, countersinks, plum line, combination square, strange pointy tools left over from the Inquisition, orphaned hammers, and, somewhere, a cat's paw.

Thankfully, not a whole lot of tools can actually look like the paw of a cat. There is a small crowbarish apparatus with a rounded end that has a V cut out of it, similar to the claw end of a hammer. I think I'm on the right track, but feeling apprehensive, I hand it to Joe. Will he uncover my stupidity?

"You idiot, that's a shark tooth."

A what?

"Oh, right, you asked for a *cat's* paw?" I race back to the truck and return with a slightly larger tool, which I'm convinced is either a cat's paw or one big-ass shark tooth. Luckily, this time I'm right. He pounds the paw into the plywood, shortly in front of a sunken nail. It bites, and, with a twist, the nail is out. We remove the rest of the nails from the sheet and create new access to the crawl space.

Joe crawls down into the hole. In between cutting studs I realize something is different. It is peculiarly quiet. Not no-hammering quiet, mind you, but no-Ritchie quiet. I look around the adjoining rooms and, sure enough, he has fled the work site, presumably for the day. Like a temperamental housewife after someone sniffed at her housedress, Ritchie stormed off after someone told him to work.

The whole operation seems more loosely organized than Enron.

Next on our task list for the day is some door framing on the second floor. I locate Joe upstairs sitting on a sawhorse, smoking a Camel. Above the first-floor kitchen area is a master bedroom, and a master terrace off to the south. Two guest rooms on either end—with separate bathrooms in between—share the central terrace, which spans a good forty feet. Joe and I take a moment to sun ourselves like pretend home owners. Before us is a panorama of verdant horizons. The terrace floats above the pool, an expansive brick terrace, and a lawn that spills forth to Cooper's Pond. It is a glorious view. Ducks float nonchalantly and snorkel in the shallows for food. On the other side of the pond the grass is even greener, a lush carpet of Kentucky bluegrass. It belongs to one of the most exclusive clubs in the Hamptons, the Southampton Tennis Club. Old money is an understatement. They were probably playing tennis on those lawns right after they snookered the Shinnecock Indians out of their land and turned them into ball boys.

Ladies in regulation whites flit to and fro playfully. On their side of the pond the sun seems cool, the breezes light. On this terrace, the sun is blistering, and the noise is punishing. It feels like I'm watching a ballet while standing in a coal pit. Beyond the tennis courts and courtly clubhouse they can watch the vast expanse of the Atlantic Ocean. A postcard.

My eyes pan to the right, slightly west, and I can't believe what I see. Claudio's house. Our tireless draftsman, who can work— well, *bill*—thirty-two hours a day, lives above the garage on the expansive beachfront estate he caretakes. I look expectantly, convinced that I will see him running around the property like Rommel, barking orders. I wonder what the range is on one of these nail guns. Joe interrupts, "Well, I guess we oughtta . . ."

In short order, we cut out a couple of door openings. Rather than cut plywood to fit around windows and doors, it is faster to wrap an entire house in plywood, then cut out the openings with a Sawzall. Fortuitously, this is exactly what I have to do on my own house next month. It feels more like sculpture than construction, shaving with the rabid toothy blade, for a Sawzall may go fast but it doesn't give a damn about going straight. The long blade is only connected on one end and flaps about like a swordfish. In no time we're done, and on to something else, something more life-threatening.

"*Roach!*"

This time the coach alarms ring in my ears with less urgency, more foreboding. Or maybe that's just the cheeseburger repeating on me. Regardless, I decide I can't possibly face that food again, and make a break for lunch in Southampton. I pull into Schmidt's, which you could call a country grocery, but you'd be wrong. Sure, it has all the trappings of a country grocery, mind you, the polished apples, the milk in glass bottles, the sweet corn stacked like cords of wood, but Schmidt's isn't exactly catering to the country clientele. It is decidedly Hamptonian, the kind of place where patrons drop dimes in the take-a-penny-leave-a-penny tray. I suppose I wouldn't have even noticed a week ago, but today at the sandwich counter I do, standing sweat soaked and sawdusted next to a tall blonde in a bikini top and diaphanous sarong. She cuts in front of me to order tuna fish, and I feel the distance I have traveled since yesterday, the distance between "us" and "them." Or, maybe worse, I have embraced them both but am truly neither.

*   *   *

I'm pulled over on the side of Cedar Street, not too far from the fire department in East Hampton. It's one of the hot spots where I can get a signal on this lousy Sprint cell phone. Pam's house on the hill has one crackly phone line, so if I want to call Susan in the city I have to get in the car and drive near a tower. The communication age has not made it to the east end of Long Island.

"Another Dumpster arrived!" I announce, relaying the only change that occurred to our house while I spent the day working for Floyd.

"Whoo-hoo!" Susan is both thrilled with progress and mocking of this non-news. Dumpsters have been arriving with a frightening regularity, as we pull more and more junk out of our house. Our chant of "The demo never ends" is becoming "The demo never fucking ends." The previous owner of our house, Schwartz, seems to have had a love affair with wood paneling. We are ending that affair.

"That makes number six," I say.

"We're going to go broke from garbage!" And she's right: at five hundred bucks for a thirty yarder we're racking up quite a tab in refuse.

"You know, if we stacked all the Dumpsters together they'd be bigger than the house."

Then Susan says, out of nowhere, "We should've bought Boyd."

"No, we shouldn't have," I say, trying to convince us both. "And there'd be almost as much garbage there."

"You think?"

I think. "No."

We both let out an exhausted laugh.

Susan leaves it, moving on to announce, "In other good news . . ."

"Uh-oh."

"Those apartments I looked at are no good." Every night, Susan is searching after work for a new apartment in the city. Our current lease is up, and we just can't afford it anymore. Susan is paying the lion's share of the bills with her salary. With a tool belt around my waist I can afford to feed myself during the week and pay for a fraction of the supplies. Or, looking at it another way, work building mansions doesn't pay enough to renovate shacks. We need a cheaper apartment in the city to bring our expenses in line, keep progress moving.

"What was wrong with them?" I ask.

"One has no light whatsoever—"

"What do we need light for? We just need a place to flop."

"This is where I live during the week, remember?"

"Right, sorry. But if we just hang onto the apartment for a little longer. The moving costs alone . . ."

"I can't carry that apartment *and* the mortgage *and* the renovation. It's too much. We have to find something cheaper," she says, raising her voice. The stress is amplifying our conversation. We've both been working seven days a week for several months, and the fatigue is eating at us in more ways than just physical, making us overly sensitive and short tempered with each other.

"Then maybe we should pull back our expectations?" I say it like a dare. Our expectations aren't that high. A roof, clean walls, no linoleum.

"Can you come in and look at some apartments? This week is crazy for me."

"When? Between working for Floyd and gutting our place at night?"

"Well, I can't do it all alone."

"*I* can't do it all alone. There's plenty of 'all' for both of us!" I snap. "More 'all' than when we were single."

"You're not happy married?"

"I'm just saying there's more. A lot more. More than I expected. We bit off a lot."

"You want to sell the house?"

"Susan. We're both tired." And that's true. And being separated during the week cuts into the opportunities to comfort and reassure each other. I can't really sell the pep talk without being able to drive it home with a hug, however—and I'm having serious doubts myself. "It'll get better," I say in my best rendition of upbeat.

"When?"

"Soon," I say.

But it won't. It's going to get worse. Much worse.

Real Work, Real Love,
Real Estate

I wake up in a strange bed, alone and in pain. I throw a right toward the alarm clock and feel an ache all the way from my finger joints to the middle of my back. Worse, it's not isolated: I feel the same dull ache on my left side and in my thighs. Is this what it feels like being married?

The alarm brays again at six-thirty. I'm going to be late. Memories of my former job, writing copy at a dot-com disaster, take on a luxurious color: five of us in a cramped, windowless office; the air quality of a high-school locker room after the game; a chief financial officer giving market updates on his bowels—"a real growler"—and carpal tunnel syndrome in uncontested ownership of my right hand. The business model seemed preposterous, but I was wooed by the same blind new-economy enthusiasm that launched an armada of stupid Internet ideas, the same fascination with quasi-celebrity that our CEO thrilled at exploiting in almost every business meeting he recounted in our cramped offices. Finding new employees, securing venture capital, buttressing flagging morale, it was all propped by the same dispiriting pimp's progress.

"We're a part of Edwin Schlossberg, Incorporated."

Blank stare.

"He designs interactive spaces. You could say the Internet is one big interactive space."

". . ."

"And he's married to Caroline Kennedy."

"Technology, eh? How much money were you looking for?"

But while that job felt fake—a scam—the pain in my arms is feeling very real. With exertion I roll over without coordination and stretch one foot to the floor, thinking a hot shower will go a long way to loosening up the soreness from—I'm embarrassed to admit—two measly days labor.

But I'm still aching as I leave for work. With such soreness, it is easier to appreciate the simple things. The cool wind flies through the open windows, the sun sparkles off the waves, traffic is light, and, most important, it is not yet work. I slow down another five miles per hour. I arrive late, but Floyd, who's ostensibly running this job, never shows up before ten. Pulling into the drive, the tires crunch on the gravel, and I feel oddly happy to be back.

Joe's there, and he's already smoking. He offers one to me. After the requisite how's-it-goin's and it's-gonna-be-a-hot-ones, Joe steps on his cigarette butt and says, "Well, I guess . . . ," not bothering to finish the line. We're going back at it. Upstairs. Up to finish the lath. I walk through the wide rough opening for French doors giving onto the second-floor patio and appreciate the early morning view some lucky home owner will have one day. The sun twinkles on the pond. A delicate morning fog still hugs the shady bank and pond grasses. Dew makes the carpet of tennis grass shine. I imagine Claudio, that damnable draftsman of mine, sleeping in, comfortable in his carriage house bed, and I unload a strip of tens into the Paslode and nail loudly into the door jack. *Thunk, thunk.*

Looking upward along the roofline I see yesterday's unfinished business. "I'll cut, you nail," Joe says, securing himself shaded work under the roof.

"Okay, but first I want to fix that," I say, pointing up. A piece of lath—the five-quarter-by-three-inch boards that ladder horizontally up the roof onto which the cedar shingles will be nailed—sticks northward from the roofline like a giant hangnail. I climb up and try to rip it out, but my hammer is no match for six eight-penny nails. Nails out of a Paslode gun have the added benefit of glue, and these guys are stuck good. I try a three-foot crowbar, which makes me look like I'm attacking an anthill with a bazooka. Tilting away from the house for two-handed leverage, I'm suddenly aware that success will mean failure. The board will pop free, and I will catapult to the ground thirty feet below. Is this when I admit I'm in over my head, or do I wait to explain to the ER nurse that my insurance lapsed because I was confident I'd have a new office job by now?

"Shave it down with the power planer," Joe calmly suggests.

Why not? Back up on the roof, I'm hanging on for dear life with my toes and knees. It's barely eight and I'm drenched in sweat. I never should have accepted the cigarette. Trying to be one of the guys, I guess. It's one of those brands you've never heard of, like Matador. My head is spinning. That's when I turn the power planer on. A wild gyroscope of razor blades, it feels like an angry rodent in my hands, pitching me left and almost off the house. Then I plane. And plane some more. I crawl back down cautiously and look back up at my handiwork.

Joe looks, too. "Better pull it out."

Not an auspicious start, but despite my blunders with the lath, Joe isn't perturbed. More than that, he's downright talkative, telling me about his former firewood business. "That's how I got that," he says, pointing to a scar on his face. Amid his wrinkles from sun and a couple thousand cartons of cigarettes, it kind of blends in with the rest of his facial topography, but it's there,

slicing from his left eye up to his hairline. "Chainsaw fuckin'
kicked back and nailed me right there."

"Jesus" is all I can find to say.

"Made it to Southampton hospital and they were pullin' bits of
skull out of my hair."

"Jesus."

"But I don't do that anymore. Firewood got too cheap about a
year ago; it ain't worth the time."

"Or the headaches, I imagine."

The lingering questions I had about Dale are effectively put to
rest when he arrives some time after ten o'clock, swerving and
swearing, and surprisingly cleaned up. Before, his hair was greasy
and flattened against his scalp; today it is as thin and light as a
Silkience commercial. With mirrored aviator sunglasses and a
day's growth of beard, Dale looks like a brutally inebriated John
Mellencamp. He's walking around ranting, trying to engage
people, though he invariably gets treated like he's contracted
the Ebola virus. He says he intends to work, but no one's biting.
Why is he even allowed to walk around the site, I wonder. He
approaches Joe for some sort of oblique confirmation or recognition, and Joe just walks away. A wind catches Dale's hair, parting
it, and I see for the first time a big healed gash on the side of his
head. The scar is easily four or five inches long. As much as Dale's
drunken, plaintive commentary says things are bad *recently*, the
scar suggests they've always been this way.

"Just can't catch a break. Fuckin' cops, you know. Pulled me
over speeding last night and impounded my car. How the hell am
I supposed to get to work? It's like I'm marked or something. Just
when I think that things are working, it gets all fucked up." I nod
slowly, and let him trail off.

Then Dale heads back downstairs. His timing couldn't be

worse. A black Mercedes is crawling up the long drive. By the time it turns in front of the house, Dale is off the front landing and in the morning sun. "Fuck, man, let's get to work," he says to no one in particular, swerving. "Where the hell's my belt?"

Out of the Mercedes steps a silver-haired guy in a blue suit: the developer's father. Tarzano père. He has come to check on its progress. Bob and Billy lasso Dale and call him a cab, but the damage has been done.

The remainder of the morning, Joe and I work on door openings and lath. I make a couple of stupid measuring mistakes, but not being a visible threat, a Dale, is a real feather in my cap. I have to borrow Joe's speed square again to mark a two-by-four and he says, "Keep it. I've got three of 'em." If this were a made for TV movie, that would have been the Hallmark moment, strings up, lambent and golden light, the transference of symbolic speed square from mentor to pupil. But this isn't Hallmark TV; it's Hamptons construction. "Thanks," I say, trying to catch a look of recognition. He turns to light up another cigarette.

Shortly after lunch, the "look busy" shouts ring around the house. Floyd is moving up the driveway, and all of us who didn't look busy suddenly make sure we do. Joe and I set to work reframing a window opening in one of the second-floor bedrooms. It is a massive opening, probably eight feet wide by three and a half feet high. The owner wants it moved an inch and a half to the left.

I squint with disbelief. Joe catches it, and repeats the instructions we've been given. The owner wants *the exact same size window*, just an inch and a half to the left. I could envision the importance of this change if the wall were, say, nine feet wide and the discrepancy were glaring, but the change within this fifteen-foot wall is preposterous. And it is a *change*, Joe stresses, not an error on the part of the initial framing. The owner simply changed his mind. I roll my eyes and plug in the Sawzall.

"Well, he ain't yelling," Joe says. "That's a good sign."

"Floyd?" I ask.

"Uh-huh."

Floyd's short, maybe five foot five, and taut, like an over-inflated Barney Rubble. Standing with Bob and a couple other guys I haven't met, however, it is clear that Floyd is the one in charge. He bounces on his toes and gesticulates more. His forearms fly out, making his points more forcefully, his pronouncements more grandiose, his small frame more commanding. I should probably go introduce myself, but I avoid him. Why call attention to myself? And why risk being pulled off this job and sent to help on the repairs Floyd wants done on his own house? He mentioned the possibility in my phone "interview," and I don't have any desire to drive further west than I already have to. Moreover, I envision fixing a mailbox post or building a swing set at chez Floyd. Despite the backbreaking work, I actually feel fortunate working on this massive and elegant house.

Word travels fast. Less than half an hour after Floyd leaves, everyone knows that there are going to be a lot of change orders. Not orders that mean a picture window one and a half inches to the left, but big, architectural changes. The library, on the south end of the house, is now moving to the north end. The kitchen is making the opposite migration.

Or so we think. The architect is getting pressured to hurry his ass, but so far nothing significant has been issued. The rumor is that the owner wants to put in a stop-work order until the architect gets his drawing done. Everyone cackles at this suggestion. If the owner puts in a stop-work order, he effectively screws himself. He'll never get this crew back on his job anytime soon.

The building boom is still moving at such a pace that all the good carpenters are already snatched up for the summer. A stop-work order would mean the professionals would be working elsewhere tomorrow, and another crew couldn't be assembled for weeks. For me, I'd be out of a job. Everyone snorts at the preposterousness of his changes, amounting to $250,000. I can't quite believe my ears. My entire house cost that much, and that's what this yahoo wants to spend on changes! Everyone walks around with an if-this-guy-knew-what-was-good-for-him swagger, demonstrating that we hold the cards.

With that, the afternoon ambles along slowly. Once our work is completed, I tell Bill that I'm ready to pack up. "Leaving early? You can't leave early."

"Have you got something for me to do?"

"Cut me a piece of fascia, fourteen three and a half."

Okay, great, I think, is that in the produce section? I scramble down to the room where all the trim is stored, a huge pantry of preprimed finger-jointed pine, sixteen-foot-long sections. There must be ten different varieties in as many stacks. Which the hell am I looking for? Jason, the pot-crazed broom boy, shuffles by in a haze.

"Where's the fascia?" I say, as if to suggest it's hidden somewhere. I'm grabbing a piece of one-by-four casing.

"That's casing. The fascia is on that side."

I can't believe I'm relying on the clean-up junkie for help. I'm tempted to thank him in French.

Meanwhile, Joe is leaving early; he just had the intelligence not to tell anyone about it. "Whatcha doing?" he says, wrapping the cord of his circular saw.

"Cutting fascia for Bill," I say, holding it up so that he'll look at it and save my ass if Jason has steered me astray.

"Yeah?"

"He wants it fourteen three and a half," I add for no reason.

"That long point or short point?"

I'm mute. Long point. Short point. *What the hell's the difference?*

"Better check," he says.

I do, and it's long point, which of course is trickier. I lay the board underneath the chop and see that it is set for something completely other than what I am doing. I need to make a weather cut, a thirty-degree bevel so the board both dispatches water more efficiently and hides any gap that may appear when the wood naturally shrinks and swells. I'm staring at the saw as if it's a reactor and any blunder by me could release radioactivity. The blade on a compound miter box can move in six directions and I know only one of them: straight. This is not good. Why couldn't I have just left early? Why did I have to ask Bill if he needed anything? I'm convinced I'll be found out any second. Bill has now been waiting atop a ladder for this board for what feels like half an hour. I know I'm sunk. Which way can I run?

By an act of God, Joe, having forgotten his cigarette lighter upstairs, walks past and agrees to help me. Generously, not once does he mutter "fuckin' idiot."

The train pulls into the Bridgehampton station and releases a tide of beach-bound summer Hamptonites. A full fifty percent of them exit the train while talking on their cell phones. They wear madras shorts and Gucci loafers without socks, summer dresses and strappy sandals. Others are in pin-striped suits, ties pulled askew and shirttails flying, looking like this is their first breath of fresh air since commencement day for their Stanford MBAs. The practical ones carry L.L. Bean canvas bags brimming with the essentials: board shorts, beach towels, flip-flops, sunscreen, and rum. Others carry manuscripts and stock analyses and string bikinis in bags made by Fendi and Louis Vuitton. The buzz of activity is more reminiscent of the Grand Hotel at rush hour than a corn-country train station.

I stick out like a sore thumb among this crowd, filthy and sweaty in my construction attire as I wait for Susan. I bear no resemblance to the man she married. Down the platform I can see her slicing through the crowd. She's wearing a sleek olive-colored Tahari pantsuit and a black fitted top. I hurry to greet her.

She gives me the once over twice, not sure if the sweaty mess in front of her is really me. "My blue-collar husband," she clucks.

"Very funny." I open my arms mockingly wide. "Want a hug?"

"A kiss would be just fine."

I grab her bags and we head back to the car. She Daisy Dukes it through the paralyzed front window, miraculously not tearing her suit.

"I've got some ideas about the living room," she says, as soon as we pull out of the parking lot.

"You don't say?" I spy a copy of *Home* magazine peeking out of her briefcase.

"Yes. I'm thinking rather than white, it should be more of a cream, then we can—"

"That's still white."

"It's a softer white."

"But I thought you wanted our *bedroom* white," I say, already having a difficult time keeping track of all the design conversations we've had.

"Exactly. That's why I want the living room softer, warmer."

"Warmer? All this white I'm going to feel like we're living in a snowstorm!"

"We can't have every room red!"

"I only suggested that for the half bath . . . kind of carnival-esque. You know, you walk in thinking, 'Just another bathroom,' then *ka-pow!*"

"That's just what I want to be thinking in a bathroom."

I crack up. "Okay, so maybe that wasn't a great idea. And I don't love white—"

"But . . ."

"Let me finish? I'm just throwing this out there, but maybe we should Sheetrock the rooms before we paint them. Get a feel for the space?"

"That reminds me . . ."

I punch the gas, thinking if we get to the house faster we'll start talking about the work in front of us, rather than the work way ahead of us.

"This," she says, holding up a tattered napkin with a thicket of black lines, "is my idea for the kitchen layout." Susan makes these drawings at every opportunity, scribbling on bar napkins, place mats, matchbooks. Later, the downstairs bath will be jotted on my work pant leg by Susan with a Sharpie. "Whaddya think?"

The wind keeps catching the edges of the napkin as I speed down the road at Mach 3. "I don't see a thing. Looks like you sneezed India ink." That comment merits a glare, and an annoyed holding of the napkin flat against *Home* magazine. "Rather than putting the island like an L like Claudio suggested . . ."

"That idiot."

"Why not make it straight like this?"

"More like a galley kitchen."

"Kinda. A big airy galley. And it brings the old house and the addition together. We can walk back here, cook away, prepare stuff, guests can sit on barstools on this side, or whatever. We can eat breakfast there, work on the computer." Between the bleeding ink and the wind shear, I can barely make out the napkin rendition, but it seems like a perfect solution to our problem. We thought we'd have one cramped end and one open end of the kitchen, and this basically eliminates ends.

"Genius. I know why I married you."

"Thank you," she says.

"It's not gonna be white, is it?"

Susan has a look on her face like someone just stole her puppy. Then she says feebly, "Well, the cabinets . . ."

"No!" I'm talking firmly to a substance abuser now.

Susan's parents, Ray and Monica, are the first intrepid souls to visit our "new" house. First, no doubt, because they have an easy avenue of escape. They'll ferry over from Connecticut, and if we don't surreptitiously puncture their tires and force them into servitude, they can ferry right back unscathed. As either of them will tell you—vigorously—they should not be considered "handy," not by even the most liberal of standards. But that is selling them short, as I quickly learn upon their arrival, for they certainly know their way around a home improvement project. Indeed, they bring the tool that is quickly becoming the most essential: alcohol.

Susan and I are working outside and greet them at the curb when they drive up, toting an entire case of wine in the backseat. They roll down the window and peer out, impressively blank faced, offering neither legitimate shock nor false enthusiasm.

"Are you guys hungry?" Ray says.

"Don't you want to see the house?" Susan says, more a statement than a question.

"Oh, I see it."

"It gets a lot of sun," Monica offers keenly.

"Yeah," I say, "it does, and I can't figure out why that half of the lawn is all moss under the Japanese maple."

Susan manages to pry them out of the car and we haul the wine into the living room. Something about it looks preposterous, premature, sitting there on the rough surface of ripped-up carpet and glued-down remnants. We give the entire tour, specifying how that wall will be gone, how that hole in the wall will metamorphose into a dining area. They look daunted. I feel daunted, too, but put on a brave face rather than betray any loss of confidence, any compunction about giving their fair daughter one of the biggest headaches of her life. Is it my imagination, or are they moving out the door like they've just felt a tremor? Susan calls after them, "So how do you like it?"

Ray peeks his head back in the front door. "Come on, let's go eat!"

After a round of ice teas, club sandwiches, and family news, Ray clears his throat, and then tentatively asks, "So what's the next step?"

"Dessert?" I suggest.

"No, I meant . . ."

"I know. The next step is the same as the last step," I say. "We have a lot more ripping out to do. A few last windows, the siding that is still on there."

"More ripping?"

"And we have to talk to the engineer at some point to make sure it'll stay standing the way we want to rebuild." At this point the entire back end of our house is open, like the tail end of a bus ripped off.

"Do you know what color you're going to do the living room?" Monica asks, proffering the first decorating question. I stop in my tracks; did she just ask about paint? It can't be genetic: Monica is Susan's stepmother.

Susan clears the table in front of her, preparing to spell it out on a napkin. "I want to do it in whites."

"I thought you said cream?" I jibe.

"Really, whites?" Monica asks. She has impeccable taste and I'm hoping she'll save me, steer Susan toward a color—sea mist, uber ecru, worn saddle, anything—but she doesn't. "That sounds really nice for a beach house, crisp." A stake through my heart.

"Tell her about your kitchen idea," I suggest, thinking this design chat can be guided to something positive, something I like. By this point, Ray is seriously tuned out, eyeing passing patrons for someone to talk to, rescue him.

"Oh. I had another thought on that . . . ," Susan says.

Check!

Later, after lunch, and after showing off Sag Harbor's high tide of antiques shops, we walk home and pack Ray and Monica in their car for the return trip home. The carcass of 69½ Union Street looms in silent judgment of the whole afternoon. I can see Ray searching for words, wanting to say something to his eldest after she has shown him around her new home, but nothing is coming. Similarly, it is clear that Susan very much wants to hear what he thinks after this momentous change in her life, the biggest decision since she threw herself into marriage.

"So, Dad," she says finally, "what do you think?"

"Well," he says in an unassailable fit of honesty, "the town's nice."

Black Haus Monday

Monday morning. The general mood is hungover and uneasy. Everyone is walking around doing the Look Busy. There is no work to do since the tool truck hasn't yet arrived. Twenty guys are busy nailing already sunken nails, measuring lengths of board that won't be cut, and picking up wood scraps and tossing them in the Dumpster.

I stored my belt in the tool truck over the weekend, and without it I feel naked and exposed, a sensation aggravated when a trio of black SUVs suddenly pulls up. The big heads.

"Where's yah belt?" Ritchie snaps at me.

"On the damn truck," I say, feeling like quarry.

"Look busy."

I *am* looking busy, I think, though mostly we're all just busy hiding, keeping one wing of the house between us and the bald, steely-eyed architect with the hair lip. The scrap lumber has been cleaned up, so we move around hunched like *The Gleaners*, extricating miniscule bits of lumber from desiccated shrubbery, unearthing stray nails, and collecting gum wrappers.

Pete Taranzo, the developer and the man Floyd answers to, jumps out of a black Ford Expedition. A hands-free headset dangles from his ear, and he parades conspicuously around the site, never addressing or acknowledging any of us. He's slick, barrel-chested, and wearing dark glasses. He looks like one of those guys who goes to the gym and only works on his upper body; he probably loves to play golf and, because of his top-heavy physique, looks dumb doing it.

He perches on a sawhorse in the backyard and stares into the rising sun. Talking, talking, talking. Talking too softly to be overheard, and believe me, I'm trying. I've climbed to the second floor of the house and peer from behind a wall. Hair Lip the architect meets up with him and they walk around the house. I follow stealthily on the upper floor to overhear. All the body language suggests there are even bigger change orders than we had contemplated.

I head back downstairs and bump into Ritchie. This once I am happy to see him because he has something for me to do. "Cut this boahd for me." To sheath the interior of the elevator enclosure we need to build a platform over the shaft on which to work. Soon, Ritchie and I are both wedged in the tight shaft, measuring.

"Don't get soh close!" Ritchie says.

"I'm . . ."

"You perverts'll do anything to geht yah hands on me."

"I am so hot for you, Ritchie," I joke, and he smiles like a lizard, the tip of his tongue poking out beneath a chipped incisor. I did not sign on for this.

Chris walks by just in time. I figure I can ask him about this Tarzano guy, rather than get date raped by a Trinidadian in an unfinished elevator shaft.

"He's part of the old boys club," Chris says. Should I believe that? Chris is a military man and a nineteen-year construction veteran, but a conspiracy theorist?

"Yeah right," I say, thinking, *Go pull someone else's leg.* Tarzano looks to me like an over-pomaded pizza tosser. But part of a construction syndicate?

Chris shrugs his shoulders. "Ask him," he says, nodding in Ritchie's direction. "You know who he is, right?"

"Yah, buncha crooks."

Chris says that Tarzano is part of a network of about ten contractors who handle the mansion-sized projects. They all confer, bid a project the same. One guy bids low because it's his turn. Price-fixing to milk all the city swells who come out to the Hamptons with better things to do than count their pennies. I'm dubious. "No one's caught on?"

"Who'd wanna tell?" Chris goes on to say that Tarzano is worth billions. "Not millions, *billions*."

By now I find myself swearing just to fit in. "No fuckin' way," I say. Chris shrugs.

Tarzano and Hair Lip continue walking around, talking con-spiratorially, then get in their cars and leave without saying a word. Rumors start that we aren't even supposed to be on the job this morning, but no one can confirm this until the builder's offices open at nine. At least that's what I'm told; the chain of command gets more confounding and government-like by the minute. I'm beginning to wonder what I am doing here. And if my irregular path to home improvement hasn't been a waste of time. Worse, with the feeling that this job could end. I'm anxious that my career in carpentry could end. That I'll be failing, again. I certainly haven't gained enough knowledge to sell myself to another contractor. How many Floyds can there really be out there to take on a pretender like me?

Everyone else is pretty sure that they can find a new job, if need be, in no time. It's proud talk. "No fuckin' problem." Only Chris has the circumspection to point out that most of the good jobs have crewed with the people they need for the summer, and any jobs left will be on smaller jobs, lower paying than Floyd.

"You can pay lower than Floyd?" I ask.

"Well, no."

We're all waiting for Floyd. We are a pack of Estragons and Vladimirs pulling at our work boots, hammering on about nothing, waiting for Godot. Instead, we get Floyd. He arrives at the crack of ten. He's redfaced exiting the truck. "Those fuckin' fucks!"

We got kicked off the job. All of us.

Now, twenty miles west, we are staring at the tanned, bikini-clad posterior of Sherri, a blond twenty-two-year-old who's cooler-diving for beers at an oceanside bar called Summers. David Lee Roth detonates out of the cracked mammoth deck speakers, nearly pushing back the surf.

"Beats work," I half-shout, tipping my head conspiratorially toward Sherri's ass, which moons in our direction. (How depleted can the ice be at noon on a Monday, for crissakes?)

"Yeah," says Bob unenthusiastically, "for a *day*."

Despite his lounge-circuit crooner good looks, Bob, like me—like all of us on this sunny, majestic Monday—suddenly looks like shit. Maybe it's the sawdust and sweat. More than likely it is the financial uncertainty into which we've just been cast.

The fifteen of us—work boots, torn shirts, and dirty cut-offs—hold the perimeter of the bar. Young new arrivals in board shorts and floss bikinis catch each other's eyes over sunglasses, lips pursed. Are we the only ones popping off to the parking lot, pulling cheaper store-bought beers out of Ritchie's trunk?

Chris looks at me quizzically. "What are you doing *here?*"

"I'll pitch in," I say uncomfortably, thinking he is talking about the beer. I reach into my pocket for spare singles. "How much . . . ?"

"Forget it. It's not that."

Now I'm really confused. "Then what?"

"I thought you were," Chris says, grabbing a Coors from the cooler, "a spy."

A who? "A spy," I say unconvincingly, knowing they trapped Robert Hanssen just this way.

"Yeah, there's always one. Usually it's the clean-up guy. Bottle opener?"

"Thanks."

"But you wouldn't be here if you were, would you?"

Counterespionage Chris is paranoid, sure, but also observant enough to see that I'm not just one of the crew. He is one of those construction guys that make women melt: Denzel Washington–good looks with a worker's broad shoulders and strong hands. My wife will never be allowed near him.

I confabulate some story about having worked in a paper mill recently, having been out of the construction racket for a few years, to cover for my unscarred and comparatively feminine hands. I'm not sure he's buying one word of it.

"Anyways," he continues, "I think it was Tarzano with his binoculars from across the pond."

"At the tennis club?"

"Exactly. Too much screwing around."

We head back up to the bar. Floyd is swearing, teetering, insisting that he'll have another job in two days, and ordering more shots for everyone. Of course, that doesn't mean he's buying. Sickly sweet alcoholic accelerants line the bar. I wink woozily at the three o'clock sun and . . . *"Bottoms fuckin' up!"* . . . knock back a shot of Black Haus. If this is being one of the guys, I want my desk job back.

Instead I'm recruited for an impromptu game of volleyball. Foreman Billy has been strutting around with his chest out preened for a little Monday afternoon infidelity, and he figures a display of athletic prowess will have the beach nubiles on him like he was R. Kelly driving a Bentley.

"Why not?" I say woozily.

Six of us in work clothes stumble around like the Munsters on a beach vacation, straight backed, stiff legged, and sending balls at preposterous angles. On occasion I am able to hit one squarely as I had been taught, months previously, by Susan and her coterie of volleyball aficionados.

"Come on, California, hit the damn ball!"

I overhand it just to shut him up. Billy scrambles, trips, nose-dives, and comes up with a mustache full of sand. He's pissed.

"Fourteen serving three," I say. I send the ball over again, this time in a gentle arc. Chris and Jason are too far left, but for Billy, it's totally getable. More than getable, it hits him square on the chest, yanking his attention back from two passing bikinis, and falls to the sand. Game over.

Beers are empty, so everyone wants to quit. I figure it's a good moment for some face time with my esteemed employer, Floyd, before heading out.

"Those lyin' fucks," he continues on his rant to everyone theatrically. "I'll never work for those fucks again, not if they *beg* me!" Yeah, *that's* likely. He growls and spits unproductively on the deck boards.

"I'll make three calls and have five jobs!" he shouts. Katrina and the Waves keep buoyantly "Walking on Sunshine" as the Mexicans do beer funnels. Floyd's chest beating is a limp attempt at wagon circling, hoping his crew won't desert him by sundown.

"You have my phone number, Floyd?"

"Two days, Lawrence. Just give me two days!"

Dreams and Their
Relation to the Subcontractor

With no Floyd to go to, I spend the next day ripping off the aluminum siding from Union Street and have no problem making it to the Architectural Review Board meeting at five P.M. Our house is last under discussion, but I arrive in time to observe the process, scope out any minefields. Cletus Ripley heads the board, calling new business with a nasal whine. His sloped shoulders give him a turtlelike appearance when he lifts his neck up from his files. He is flanked by a crisply dressed realtor, a young design specialist, and two older members, a light-skinned black woman who is attentive and commonsensical in her approach and a short gray-haired guy—the historical register of the board—who is fighting to stay awake.

Several townspeople present their plans in succession. Each discussion metastasizes from a small issue, like the placement of one upstairs window, into heated colloquy debating the placement of *all* the windows in the house. Then a quasi-philosophical deliberation on the purpose of windows qua windows. The fractious argument then boomerangs back onto the applicant's plans and a groupthink ensues. "Let us redesign your home," they seem to say. Walking out with an approval, any approval, is a victory. Go in asking for a new window, come out with a tool shed: You're a winner! The man submitting his plans now is trying to keep calm, as his application for a pool is being turned down. I fear his head is going to explode. "You approved building the pool *house*," he says through gritted teeth, "but now you are not approving the pool?"

Finally, I am called upon to present our plans.

"Yeah, yes," I start nervously. "I'm Lawrence LaRose. My wife, Susan, and I own 69½ Union Street. And we seek to destroy the historic nature of our house."

Even the gray-haired guy is awake now.

"The historic nature of this house being yellow aluminum siding, asbestos shingle, and rotting single-pane windows."

"What do you propose to do?" Ripley questions humorlessly.

"We would like to re-side the house with cedar shingles, put a small dormer on the second floor to accommodate a bathroom, and replace all the windows with new ones."

"What kind?"

"Weathershield."

"Mmm."

"They're six over sixes, true divided light. All wood. The dimensions are all there on the plans."

"This looks nice," says the chestnut-haired woman.

Then, for safety's sake, I turn obsequious: "But I'd like your advice," I say. "When we do phase two, should this rear roofline follow the original, or should I move it down below the window, *here?*"

"Why would you do that?" Ripley asks.

"Just wondering if it would look like one big block, from the side, if I carried the original roofline all the way back."

"Oh, I see what you mean," says chestnut.

"Huh?" asks sleepy.

"They both look good to me," says Ripley.

"Yes, they're both nice."

"So," Ripley closes, "whichever you want, if it's within the pyramid, of course."

It is. But *whatever I want?* That's unheard of. It would be nice to say playing the ignorant rube was a savvy strategy, but there was no playing. I *am* the ignorant rube and a lucky one. Or maybe it was the end of the meeting and time for them to go to bed.

I'm thrilled and can't wait to get outside to call Susan with the good news. I skip all the way home. Well, I didn't *skip*, but damn it I felt like skipping. And the next morning, on my way to pick up our building permit, I'm still walking on air, even looking forward to seeing Sybil.

"Which application?" she asks, as if I hadn't been in there forty-five times already.

"69½ Union Street. LaRose."

"That's on for the next meeting."

"But it already—it was on *last* night's meeting. And no one had any objections. That's why I'm here to pick up the building permit."

"Last night it was only on as a discussion item."

"What the . . . what is a discussion item?"

"When you have an item you want to present to the board for discussion."

What! My brain freezes, just freezes.

"This is unclear to me," I say slowly, resisting the compelling urge to reach for the scissors on Sybil's desk. "I had the paperwork in. I was on the schedule. They all liked my plans."

"That's good."

"No it isn't. I need to get started."

"Look, you are second on the next meeting, it sounds like it should be no problem."

"When's the next meeting?"

"In one month."

I want to murder her. I want to launch into a tirade, shove her *discussion item* right down her throat. My thoughts boil. *Don't you know that we need a place to live? I haven't got a month! Maybe you enjoy this obstructionist game, assuming the upper hand, pushing around the big city muckety-mucks, but let me tell you something, missy,* they *can afford to wait out your gamesmanship in well-appointed splendor. Me, I can't afford that. I'm surviving on the generosity of friends. Where do you get off, you needle-nose, bifocaled obstreperous harridan!*

That's what I want to say. But I don't. Instead, I look her dead in the eye and say, "Thank you."

When I pick up Susan at the train station, I tell her about the morning's disaster—which I characterize as a hiccup—how Sybil had entered us as a "discussion item" rather than as a full-fledged candidate for approval. "Didn't you tell her . . ." she starts, racing past disappointment and blossoming into anger.

I cut her off: "Tell her what? *What?* That we wanted to be on the itinerary, not a discussion item? I didn't know there was such a damn thing as a *discussion* item!"

"Well . . ."

"Exactly," I snap.

I stare down the road and relay in a monotone all the great feedback we received from the board. It's not making either of us feel any better. Susan planned to take off—*is* taking off—the remainder of the week from her office to help with the house, kick things into gear. Instead, we are stalled, forced to sit on our hands, and Susan is in a position to get less work done in either place, the city or the country. To make matters worse, we scheduled Dexter to start on the dormer roof tomorrow, and if he doesn't start tomorrow there's no telling when we'll get him back.

"This isn't a hiccup; this is a disaster," Susan exhales.

"You're telling *me.* You should try dealing with those people. It's crazy making."

"What are we going to do about Dexter?"

"I mean infuriating. We're *improving* the house, the neighborhood, and they prevent us . . ."

"Lawrence, that's not helping. What do you want to do about Dexter?"

I roll it over in my head. We could wait another month for the next meeting, get the approval that is almost certain, reschedule Dexter (if we can), *then* get the work done, and be roughly two months behind schedule. Another two months, that is. Meanwhile, Susan has taken time off to be out here and we are dying to make some visible progress.

"Who's gonna know?" I say softly. "It's on the back side of the house."

Susan smiles conspiratorially. "That's what I was thinking. But would anyone say anything?"

"What, like town spies?"

"Well . . ."

It's a long shot, but there *have* been more than enough incidents of municipal McCarthyism, neighbors informing on neighbors for picayune matters.

"It's on Veronique's side," I reason out loud. "We've shown her the plans. She likes them. They're smaller than Schwartz's approved plans. I think we're fine."

"I agree."

But our criminal resolve melts only a few hours later, over dinner. "We can't do it," I say.

Susan exhales. "No, probably not. They catch us and it won't be a month. We'll be held up for a year." I get up to make the difficult call to Dexter, tell him that tomorrow is a no-go. Returning to the table I see Susan hunched over an unfolded napkin scribbling, and I begin to appreciate just what this newest delay is going to mean. More redesigns.

*   *   *

I fear our month-long delay will mean losing Dexter for longer, but he shows up the day after we finally receive our permit. That's the kind of reliability that makes you suspicious of a carpenter. Doesn't he have any other jobs?

Nevertheless, the day Dexter starts I have to run errands in the morning, so Susan mans the project. When I return at eleven A.M., Dexter already has the roof off and is starting to frame. (We are lifting the roofline to accommodate a bathroom and closet space in the rear bedroom.) He's moving with lightning speed.

"Can you believe this progress?" Susan enthuses. She gives me a hug like we just set sail aboard the *Queen Mary*. "Isn't this great?"

I open my mouth to respond, but it's not my voice that comes out. It's Dexter, from upstairs. "We've got a problem, people," he announces.

Susan and I scramble up the staircase. "What kind of problem?" Susan asks.

"These plans are worthless," he says. He doesn't sound mad or amused, just firm and authoritative.

"What's wrong with them?" I ask, genuinely perplexed, since they seemed perfectly clear to me, and not one person at the Architecture Review Board had any issue with them.

"Well, for one, there aren't any dimension lines."

"And that's bad?"

"That's very bad," he says, explaining that he might as well have a Polaroid to work with, as both give a sense of the building but neither specifies how to build it, how tall or long things should be without doing calculations to figure it out on the fly.

"And so?" Susan says.

"Well, then I have to pull the numbers myself—which isn't a big deal but it takes more time."

"I see."

"The bigger issue . . ."

"Uh oh."

"Is that the bathroom doesn't fit. You cannot get a toilet, a sink, and a shower in this room. Certainly not as drawn in these plans. They won't fit."

That fucking Claudio. How many times can I hate that guy?

"They *have* to fit," Susan says, "we already own them. We can find a way to make them fit, can't we?"

I grind my teeth with exasperation, not knowing how to fix things, but knowing that we are entering into, *on the very first day*, undesirable head-scratching territory.

Dexter looks at the two-by-fours he has cut and laid on the floor to mark out the room to be built. "Well," he says, "the easy part is to move the south wall out, here. But the other issue is this shower."

"Too big?" I ask.

"Not exactly. You've got it on the outside wall, where the dormer slants its lowest point, just over six feet."

"What about the claw-foot tub?" Susan asks, referring to a cast-iron number we had bought at a yard sale for a song.

Dexter raises his eyebrows and says, "It's going to be a problem," in a tone that communicates that it's not a problem, it's an impossibility.

Susan, however, is loathe to sacrifice her yard sale find. "Why can't it fit? It's not that big."

"Well, with the claw-foot tub in that spot," Dexter says, drawing it out with his finger, "the shower head would have to spray *up* to hit your head. And you are going to be hunched over because the tub is an additional six inches off the ground. Basically your head will be hitting drywall."

Susan starts fiddling with the boards on the floor to find a workable solution. I just sigh.

"Any architect should have seen that," Dexter says, grinning.

"Very funny."

"What if we move it to this wall?" Susan suggests, pointing to the imaginary inside wall where the dormer is at its highest point.

I look at the floor where she's pointing, to the ceiling above it, and back to the worthless plans. Dexter is skeptical. "I don't think that's going to be a whole lot better, if you're going to use the claw-foot."

"But we love that tub," Susan says.

"It's a nice tub," I say, "but not if we have to break our necks to use it."

"It's your call," Dexter says, "but why not make a nice-sized shower stall on that wall, skip the claw-foot."

We think it over for maybe a second and realize that it's the only decision that makes sense. It doesn't make giving up the tub any easier, but necessity demands it, and, as they say, necessity is the mother of red-headed stepchildren.

Susan and I return downstairs. The bottom tread cracks as I land on it heavily. Neither of us laugh. We stand mute and slump shouldered, sharing a glance, but knowing there's nothing to say. I'm not even sure our disappointment concerns the tub primarily. It's more about the knowledge that we aren't in control. We thought and planned as best we could. We spent good money to realize our individual hopes for the house, and in the first hours of its renovation we're realizing we're wrong. As a result, we have to decide on the fly, concede our dreams, and live with the consequences for years. It makes me wonder if we are renovating the house or if the house is renovating us, breaking down our cheap assumptions that we can plan the future, and replacing those assumptions with resilience during change, adversity, and compromise.

Coincidentally, miraculously, the plumber we are hiring to reroute the plumbing arrives twenty minutes later.

"Hiya," Goodnough says, climbing the stairs.

"Morning, Barry, your timing couldn't be better," I say.

"Good, thought I was a little late. One of the new guys drove a truck into a telephone pole this morning." Susan and I love this guy. He talks a mile a minute, enthuses about building, and recounts how he and his wife renovated a house while living in it with two young kids. Not only does he share helpful advice, but his very presence is encouraging: If he survived renovation, so can we. More encouraging still, he's able to smile about it.

"We're moving this bathroom around and wonder if we can put the shower here," I explain.

He asks after a dead relative. "The claw-foot?"

"No, not enough headroom. A shower stall."

"Ah."

"Does that work for you?" I ask.

"Depends, what's beneath us?"

"The other bathroom," I say.

"The full bath that is becoming a half bath and a closet," Susan clarifies.

"I can run the vent up this wall. That's no problem," Goodnough says, slashing lines through the open air. "But I need more space for the exit line."

I ask, "How much space?" and fear for the answer.

"Well the PVC is bigger than these two-by-four walls," Goodnough says, using the abbreviation for the plastic, polyvinyl chloride, that has made his occupation much easier. PVC is lighter, easier to cut, and more quickly joined together than the old standard cast-iron pipe. (Susan and I pulled out the cast iron because it was old and corroded on the inside, and altogether in the wrong place once we started rearranging the floor plan.) The downside of PVC, however, is its increased demands on fire evacuees. Just a few ounces of burning PVC will release enough hydrogen chloride gas to kill someone in minutes, and it's pretty bad for computer chips as well. And for that reason—death, not the computer chips—most commercial building codes don't allow for PVC in high-rises. People just can't run fast enough.

"Are we stuck?" Susan asks, wondering if our head-scratched plans are going up in smoke, too.

"Let's go look at the downstairs bath." All four of us travel down the stairs in a herd. I'm not sure if this counts as head-scratching time or group-thinking time, but I am conscious of the fact that Dexter's helpers are getting nothing done without him upstairs.

"How far is this closet going back?" Goodnough asks.

Susan is in charge of dimensions. "Two feet."

"Can you make that wall two-by-six?" Goodnough asks, looking at Dexter.

"I can make it two-by-anything, whatever you want," Dexter says.

"As narrow as holds the pipe, right?" I ask Susan.

"As long as we can fit hangers in here, two-by-six is fine," Susan says, concluding the case.

What we didn't discuss, because our budget has made our decision for us, is that PVC makes noise. Unlike cast-iron piping, which is silent, PVC transmits sounds surprisingly well. Someone elsewhere in a house can tell when a shower is being taken or when a toilet is being flushed if they are within earshot of the exit line. Rich people use cast iron. Less rich people, who are still concerned about the acoustic impact of departing detritus, put up a double layer of Sheetrock on a piped wall to deaden the noise. Me and Susan? We're going to throw the pipe in the back of a closet and play the music loud.

"So, when do you think you guys can start?" I ask Goodnough.

"We'll be here first thing Monday morning."

"Fantastic."

Now that Dexter has begun, and will most likely be done by the end of the week, we are eager to start the rough plumbing. After framing, plumbers go next since their materials are rigid, and the straighter every shot the better. Electricians, on the other hand, come later, as wiring can be moved around with serpentine variety. The one other big consideration at this early stage is heating and air-conditioning; ducting takes up a lot of space, most often an entire sixteen-inch bay, and in smaller homes this can conflict with the demands made by the plumbing.

Our house was constructed with cast-iron baseboard heating, a superb solution. Unfortunately we are getting rid of it, because we are moving the front door from the left-hand side of the house—where it squanders the most light-filled side of the living room—to the center. Moreover, if we want to add central air we would require two entire heating and cooling systems in this small house. We decide to consolidate them into one system. Of course, shortly after ripping out the cast iron, we learn an alternate solution is not as easy as we had thought.

Our house is a Cape Cod, which effectively has no attic. On a hot day like today, this does not go unnoticed. Above the bedroom ceilings, which we have raised a foot so that we can sleep without feeling like hobbits, there is a triangular space perhaps a foot and a half high. Behind the knee wall that meets the east, downward-sloping side of the ceiling, there is a rhomboid space, again small. Neither of these spaces will accommodate an air handler. Our improved insulation will help, but with no attic the upper floor heats up early and stays warm late into the evening. Air-conditioning is necessary. What to do?

"Sanyo makes a very quiet wall unit," offers Cory from East Mountain Air.

"You mean my bedroom is going to look like a deli, with some big unit and a hose going out the window?"

"That's a window unit. A wall unit . . . here let me show you." He hands me a four-color leaflet with the Sanyo 4600, a rectangular unit that sticks out from a wall only a few inches. "It could go right above that closet. It's pretty unnoticeable."

"It's still gonna make my house look like a deli. A good deli, maybe."

"Sorry, but you just can't fit ducting into this house."

Fuck! Nothing fits in the damn house, I think. *No ducting. No claw-foot tub. No closets. The only thing that seems to fit in this house is frustration—and expense. How can something so small incur bills so large?*

All this talk about delis soon reminds us it's time for lunch.

"What are you getting?" I ask Susan, a short walk to the corner later.

"I'm still reading," she replies, raising her hand. This could be a while. We could eat at the Madison Market every day—and we do—and never get through all the sandwich offerings. Chalkboards line the walls with different selections numbering in the hundreds.

"I'm getting a 105," I say, "what do you—"

"Hang on." The hand comes up again.

"You should get the 7, you always get the veggie."

"I'm reading the specials, okay? Grab us some Cokes and a bag of chips. And water, we need water at the house."

"Fine." I pad off to the refrigerators and grab the Cokes. Some kid is sneaking the penny candy into his front pocket and I throw him the raised eyebrows. He reaches into his other pocket and petulantly slaps a quarter on the counter.

"Let's walk down to the beach for lunch," I suggest. "The house won't fall over if we're gone for five minutes."

"I was thinking the same thing."

We backtrack up Union Street, carrying a 105 and a 7, and stroll down the shady side of Division Street toward the beach. "What's going on there?" I whisper.

"Where?"

"There," I say, lifting the bag of sandwiches to point across a lawn as desiccated as our own. There's a dilapidated house with an old sofa next to the back door, but I'm not pointing at the sofa.

"That's a car behind a tree, Lawrence."

"That's a maroon Delta 88, Susan. Take another step."

She does. "Oh my God."

"Shhh. Not so loud."

"A Delta 88 . . . with both front doors open, and a man sitting inside wearing . . ."

"Nothing but underwear."

"Tightie whities," Susan clarifies, sounding both awed and appalled.

"When in Sag Harbor?" I suggest, raising my shoulders.

"It *is* hot out."

The man is far enough away that he doesn't see us staring at him. I'm not sure he'd care if he did. We walk on and resume speaking at a normal level. "I really like that the car wasn't even on, but he had both hands on the steering wheel."

"He did?" Susan asks.

"Yeah, ten and two, just like they teach you in driving school."

She looks at me, smirking. "You're crazy."

"Crazy enough to marry you."

"Very funny," she says, slapping me on the ass.

In a few more minutes we're at the shore. Amazingly, we discovered this beach only after we had bought the house. For reasons we can't comprehend, the realtor never showed—didn't even mention—the beach to us. I find this all the more startling considering that this beach is the best attribute our house currently has. Sure, it's a bay beach, and a kiddie beach with swings and playground paraphernalia, but *still*. It's a block from our house! Today the bay has a light chop, a steady breeze pushes sailboats along the horizon. In the distance is the Cedar Point lighthouse, which guided ships in and out of Sag Harbor for almost a century. Abandoned since its deactivation in 1934, it is a prime candidate for some home improvement of its own.

We eat our sandwiches and watch seagulls kamikaze into the sea for fish. Susan puts an arm around me. "Did you ever think you'd be here, a year ago?"

"This is pretty good, isn't it?"

"Yes. But really, could you have ever guessed that night at that party?"

"That was a bad party."

"*Hey!*"

"I remember. Late last summer. Lying on the beach in East Hampton. Our toes pointed to the sea, looking at one of those mansions."

"I remember that day."

"Do you remember what you said?"

"What?"

"You said that you didn't want one of those huge houses, that you . . ."

"That I'd be much happier with you and a little shack," she finishes.

I give her a kiss. "Be careful what you wish for."

We finish our sandwiches and get up to leave. Susan takes my hand as we walk back to the project. "I still feel that way, you know."

"Me too, honey," I say. "Me too."

"Really?"

"Really. But what worries me is," I say, before things get to saccharine, "are we gonna end up like that guy in the car?"

"Tightie whities?"

"Yeah."

"For one, we couldn't, even if we wanted to."

"Why's that?"

"All our car doors don't open."

"Very funny."

Susan looks up at the sky. "It's so beautiful; I wish I were out here full time."

I reflect on the last nerve-racking week and the backbreaking work. "Yeah, it's like this every day," I say, half sarcastically.

"I don't see how you can complain about being out here," Susan says, gesturing to the gorgeous view.

"I'm not complaining," I say, but I am complaining. At least I think I am. Maybe I'm not. I don't know what I'm saying. I do know that I have been out here for a few months and despite the blisters, cuts, pulled muscles, hammered thumbs, and a scratched cornea, I've got nothing to show for it. I feel like I just arrived. On the other side of it, the seclusion seems like it's gone on for years. It feels like I'm working at an outpost; I have no social circle save the guy from Riverhead who drops off lumber. "Where do you want it?" he says, and I say, "Over on those kickers," pointing to a few two-by-fours I've thrown on the ground to keep the wood off the moist soil. That's a whole conversation. I've burrowed so far into renovating this house, I'm losing the ability to meet new people. Every day I feel farther and farther from Manhattan, my network of friends, and the web of personal contacts who, in whatever fashion, large or small, helped give my life direction, support, and identity. Sure, hoards of "summer people" (SUMMER PEOPLE, SOME ARE NOT is a favorite bumper sticker among the resentful locals who like to bite the hand that feeds them) come and go like the tides—Susan among them—but that doesn't foster a community. Constant work doesn't bring me into contact with anyone other than the subcontractors I meet on a revolving-door policy and the coffee klatch at Floyd's.

Susan works equally hard, to be sure, but because she is both in the city and in the country I don't think she has any idea what I'm talking about. No doubt it's exacerbated by our ungainly arrangement and the inability to establish any rhythm in our lives together. We should be spending our first year learning how to live together, not amassing paint chips, tile samples, and lighting brochures. It occurs to me that most of our life together has been in a state of urgency, most of it positive, but urgency nonetheless. The whirlwind romance, the speedy engagement, the extreme sport honeymoon in Thailand—racing to see it all, from Bangkok to the Golden Triangle, from Pat Pong to the Phi Phi Islands—the job loss, the pitching economy, the quick and questionably timed leap into home ownership, and the brakeless roller coaster of renovation.

I have a vision of some far-off day when Susan and I calmly recline on a new couch, our feet cradled by an ottoman as soft as a cloud bank. The phone doesn't even think of ringing (perhaps someone has thoughtfully buried it in the backyard). Fantastic music—the Brandenburg Concertos or Etta James—dances on a gentle breeze passing through our dustless living room. The relative humidity is perfect! Cool glasses of champagne or orange juice or Poland Spring—it doesn't even matter what we're drinking, things are so good—are held aloft theatrically and we toast to this fine day . . . and simultaneously ask, "Who the hell are you?"

The Hampton Bays Anaconda

Floyd's promised "two days" stretch into ten, and when he calls to say we're going to be working at his house for a few days, his tone is fake casual. It's clear that his "three calls" have not resulted in "five jobs." "I'm waiting on two big projects," he says. "In the meantime we can finish some stuff around my place."

I think of begging off, feigning that I'm such a hot commodity I'm already working with another crew, but I don't. I still don't know a damn thing, and I'll drive forty minutes to Hampton Bays to keep working. Besides, at home we're in a holding pattern. Goodnough didn't show up on Monday to rough the plumbing, we're waiting on the window delivery to finishing ripping out the old ones, and we're still dancing the building department tarantella.

The next morning, I'm bouncing down a dirt road, slaloming around cars on blocks and gunshot RVs, thinking that this can't be right. I must have taken a wrong turn. In life, that is. In my fledgling career as a Hampton's carpenter I'm right where I am supposed to be: There's Floyd's house now, a brown board-and-batten house that might be called "rustic chalet" by someone insane and deceitful enough to try and sell it. In reality, it is a coffee-colored ode to the unexceptional, an abbreviated ranch home that looks like some constipated cow's labored deliverance. Not that I am casting aspersions, mind you; compared to my house it looks damn livable. Comfy even.

I grab my tool belt, wondering if I'm the first one to arrive, given how quiet it is. As I walk toward the backyard, a neighbor's rooster shrieks as if to announce me. In the backyard are the Mexicans, Ritchie, and some red-haired guy I've never met before. The Look Busy has clearly not been sounded; people are doing next to nothing. Indeed, I look around and it's unclear what needs to be done. The house is built, and there is no visible remodeling project going on at the house. From appearances, the more talented crew members are sitting this one out, either too proud or too well paid to work down market. Perhaps they are waiting Floyd out, waiting for him to get a big contract, rather than coming here and doing his domestic chores.

Billy's not around so there is a leadership vacuum. There's no foreman and Floyd is still in bed—sleeping off his drunk, it is said. Not even Ritchie bothers assuming the reigns. Only the red-haired guy, Rick, busies himself with work. I ask him what's what and he garbles something incomprehensible.

"What's that?" I say.

"I'm not being foreman or whatever, not getting paid for that. So whatever."

"I'm not asking you to run anything," I say, "just what's being done. I mean, what's going on here?" There is a desiccated lawn with a large crater in the middle, a row of sheds that looks like a townhouse development, scrap lumber cast hither and yon, and a trio of goats in a rear pen. Rick stops marking the board he's measuring, and looks up.

"You never been here?"

"No."

He smiles, tucks a pencil behind his ear. "That ditch in front of you is gonna be a fish pond. Maybe some turtles."

"Uh-huh."

"And next to the goats is gonna be the pigpen when I'm finished. Then there's the chickens, and next to the chickens is the monkey hut."

"Monkey hut?"

He shrugs his shoulders like *What the fuck do I know?* and I leave it at that.

Monkey hut. You don't have to look at too many real estate circulars to realize that there are as many definitions of dream home as there are architects with a slick sales style. Chasing that dream has given us split-level ranches, modernist cubes, tepee-inspired spires stuck on colonials in fickle postmodern contortions. In the Hamptons many of the dreams center around money, enjoying or advertising it to your neighbors: gold-leaf foyers, Italian tiled driveways, indoor pools, personal bowling alleys. Some are cozy cabins—abandoned railroad stations moved to the seaside and fitted with bedrooms—some are mansions with twenty bedrooms and nineteen baths . . . in the guest house. The one that has caught the attention of environmental protectionists, the disdain of local farmers, and the ire of the rich who have been outdone, is Ira Rennert's one hundred thousand square foot compound Fair Field. Considered by some to be the world's greatest polluter, Rennert's holding company, Renco, deals in Kentucky coal, Utah magnesium, and Humvees. Notoriously secretive, Rennert and his Fair Field compound have been a source of a lot of speculation, ever since the asleep-at-the-wheel Southampton board approved the plans. In addition, Ira has raised the ire of locals by hiring (almost) no workers from the area. All work on Fair Field is being done by union labor from the city, or by specialized artisans flown in from around the globe.

At the other end of the spectrum, Susan and I dream of a simple starter home, with the look and feel of good craftsmanship that has weathered decades: wide plank pine floors, rescued door hardware, cedar shingles. The centerpiece will be a large kitchen area where we can cook, uncork wine, and mix margaritas. An airy social space acknowledges that everyone always winds up in the kitchen, so why not make it comfortable and accommodating? We plan a guest room and an office/guest room on the lower level so that we can put up friends and relatives all summer long. Well, maybe not all summer long, but frequently, and comfortably.

Floyd's dream is something altogether different. Eschewing the arrogance of Rennert's beachside empire as well as Susan's and my *Home and Gardens* simplified livability, Floyd is aiming for something perpendicular to all of us. He aspires to monkey hut greatness. I learn that this hut, which is being outfitted with a skylight, electricity, plumbing, and a drywell, is actually much more than chimp quarters. Floyd also plans for chinchillas, rabbits, ferrets, a fat-tailed gecko, a rough-scaled python, a bearded dragon, and an anaconda. Yes, anaconda. Phylum *Chordata*, class *Reptilia*, order *Squamata*, family *Bodaie*, and home *Hampton Bays*. Having seen a few short fulminating displays of spit and cussing, I know that Floyd can speak *like* an animal, but *to* the animals? I want to learn more from the master of the monkey hut.

"Does Dr. Doolittle need a permit for all these animals?" I ask Ritchie.

"Whaht you care?" he says.

"I don't really, but it seems like they'd make him get one."

"Floyd? He's naht gonna tell no one. I see you got your belt on."

"Yep."

"Look busy."

I have been trying to look busy, cleaning this and that, but I've gotten bored and am beginning to feel conspicuous. I ask Rick what needs to be done and he says that the pigsty needs to be roofed, pointing to a pile of three-tab shingles next to the chicken coop. This isn't exactly what I had in mind when I first thought of sneaking onto a Hamptons crew. But what the hell do I know about roofing? I figure it's worth a shot.

"Great," I say, "can you set me up?"

He looks at me like I'm stupid. "I said the three-tabs are *right there.*"

"Yeah, but do you want to get me started?"

Rick doesn't understand what I'm saying. *Hello, I'm ignorant, stupid!*

"I've gotta get this door squared, and I've got three things after that," he says, pressed. "Leon can help you." In Spanish, he calls over Leon and tells him to work with me on the roof. Leon seems of equally dubious shingling provenance, based on our first five minutes topside. We scramble around the pigs' quarters, trying to smoothly roll out a layer of tar paper. It's not staying in place too well because—*thunk, thunk, thunk*—I'm hitting it with the wrong side of the slap hammer. No staples are going into the paper, just dents. Leon grabs the slap hammer, *"Perdon?"* and gets the thing into place.

A promising development, but a misleading one. After that we are lost, looking to each other vacantly, unsure about next steps. I turn to book learning, reading the side of the shingle bags for some sort of insight. I tell Leon to set up the pneumatic nailer so I can read and, more significantly, because I don't know how to. It feels totally corporate, not knowing what the hell to do but bossing someone else around. Turns out Leon is as green as I am and we spend thirty minutes trying to connect the nailer to the compressor and the compressor to the generator.

Over by the turtle pond, a new guy is futzing with the electrical outlet. He's not on our esteemed crew, I don't think, but he looks familiar. Holy shit! It's Joe from Gang of Four Electric. The same Joe from Gang of Four Electric that was giving Susan and me a quote to wire our house. Can there really be so few qualified electricians on the east end of Long Island that Floyd and I are using the same guy? No doubt Joe knows how ignorant I am—heck, I told him so—and if he spills the beans to Floyd I'm toast. It's comical that I'm afraid of being unmasked for incompetence while standing on top of a pigsty, but I can't deny that I am. I pull my visor down lower. With the heat rising, the noisily clucking chickens are becoming overpoweringly rank. The fetid odor makes me swoon briefly and I stumble to the edge of the sty roof. Just then Floyd, our punctual boss, walks out his back door, groggy and pajama-bottomed at ten A.M. He's on me like a beat cop.

"Lawrence, what are you doing?"

"Roofing a pigsty," I say, disbelieving the words as they come out of my mouth. Countless years of higher education, I think, and now I'm keeping swine dry.

"Like that?" he asks, making me think that my vast expertise— hell, I read tar paper instructions—is at odds with judicious Floyd's building practice. "When's the last time you roofed?"

"A few years ago," I lie.

"A few years ago?" he roars. "What the hell are you doing up there?"

"I wanted to do it," I say. Which is true; like a junior associate with real drive I jumped in to learn something I know nothing about.

"Wanted to do it?" he booms again, revealing his trademark mimetic rhetorical style. Floyd has seven habits of a highly effective contractor, and they're all screaming. At this point I'm stranded aloft, conspicuous as a hog on ice.

"So why you doing it like that?" he persists.

"It's the way . . ."

"That's no way," he screams, and continues in his tutorial style, yelling. "You gotta snap a line, twelve inches. All 'round. Sides first. Start your first course. Don't reverse 'em like that. Got it?"

"Got it."

I have no idea what he just said.

"Just fucking stupid," Floyd mutters. His soliloquy of swearing continues on idle as he surveys the yard for someone else to shout at in his mystifying shorthand of cursing and construction patois. Mid-fit I see that Joe has recognized me. A smile spreads across his face. I put my forefinger to my lips as discreetly as possible.

"Are you fuckin' laughing?" Floyd roars at me.

"Allergies," I say, "was about to sneeze."

"Just fucking *get it done!*"

Leon dismounts the roof, Floyd having declared, "That's not a fucking job for two fuckin' guys," and I am aloft. Alone. Badly informed. I can feel the sweat running down my front, my back, my legs. It is absolutely sweltering. Carrying a load of three-tab asphalt shingles up an aluminum ladder in one-hundred-degree weather, I am just now learning, is not fun. It's not even in the same zip code as fun. The strain literally dizzies me, and I'm losing my balance well off the ground. I flip the shingles off my shoulder and clutch the ladder tightly until my head clears. For the first time I have doubts that I can do this, physically do this. There's always the fear that my idiocy will undo me, but my fitness? And I'm not an unfit person. *I've run marathons goddamn it*, I think to myself, *and this is overwhelming me.*

It doesn't help that Jason is smoking us out. At the instruction of Floyd, who wants to avoid paying for any Dumpsters, Jason is burning all the scrap lumber around the yard. Since there are seven of us producing scraps, cutting lumber for the pigsty, the monkey hut, and a tree fort for the kids (they're going to be able to drive by the time it's ready), there is no end of fuel for Jason's fire. Most of the wood we are using is pressure-treated, and the sickly sweet smell catches in the back of your throat. I'm beginning to feel like beef jerky. I climb up the ladder with another bunch of shingles, my head pounding, wondering if I'm hallucinating.

"Lawrence, you've goht a tight ass!"

I don't even have to look. "Fuck off, Ritchie."

"I mean, a really nice ass!" he says louder, so more people can hear. I make it up the ladder, drop the shingles, and shake my head at Ritchie, laughing. Where do you file a sexual harassment complaint out here, I wonder? "I was climbing atop the pigsty, when this guy, this Trinidadian hussy, comes over from the monkey hut . . ."

After I finish the roofing, Rick calls me over. He's my new friend. He calls me "buddy." Then he tells me a wall needs to be built between two stalls inside the pigsty. For a guy who doesn't want to be foreman, he has no problem giving me the crappy jobs. It stinks, and it's cramped, but it is mercifully shaded inside. At the end of the day, I look back at the sty with a modicum of accomplishment, which makes the whole experience all the more hilarious. I genuinely feel satisfied that I got the job done, and I have a feeling I never had working for an Internet company. It is not Versailles, but I built something that is going to last. And those are going to be the driest pigs on Long Island. Driving home it dawns on me, don't pigs like to be in the mud?

I call Susan and fill her in on all the day's accomplishments. She laughs, but there is an unmistakable undertone of *And how is this helping to get our house built, exactly?* She says that the apartment search is a fiasco. Two more dumps today, one with a higher rent than we are currently paying. A softening economy is not softening the real estate market. This could effectively spoil our chances of trimming costs and using those savings on our renovation.

"Maybe we should just live out there full-time, give up on this idea of keeping a place in the city." Susan says it, but I can hear the reluctance in her voice.

"That'd be great," I joke. "I work out here and can't even pay the phone bill."

"There's got to be something better than what you are doing," she says. "If the city market is so bad, maybe you could find a solid job in the country—something other than underpaid construction jobs, that is."

It irks me that she thinks I haven't considered the options out here. It also irks me that we have this conversation, or one like it, almost every week. The solutions to our immediate problems— which include my job situation, our declining economic situation, and the fatigue we both feel from working seven days a week— seem like one huge game of three-card monte. One week we feel the answer is in the city, with all its promise, as well as social and cultural opportunity. But then we remember its vices, the high prices, the hassles involved in getting to recreation and sports, the subservience to landlords, the pollution. So the next week we decide we have to put all our energy into the country. Then we go to Riverhead Building Supply and nurse our dirty little secret, creating more credit card debt. Perhaps we vacillate in this discussion because continuing to keep the conversation open permits us not to talk about the real issue: We didn't sit down early, and at every step of the way, and talk clearly about money.

After speaking with Susan I suddenly realize how tired I am and decide not to go back to work on our house. Instead I call our neighbor Mark to see if he wants to grab a burger and a beer later. He wants Mexican, but we're on. I feel odd after one margarita. Not tipsy, but woozy. Intelligence suggests there is one prudent course of action in these situations, and I follow it. The second margarita doesn't make me feel any better than the first. I leave half of it, and apologize for having to call it an early night. I'm whooped and can't get into bed fast enough.

A sweaty, haunted night of twisting later, I sit up in bed with the worst hangover of my life. My eyes feel painfully big in their sockets, and it's like my head is stuffed with concrete. It feels like food-poisoning and altitude sickness combined, though I suppose that's impossible at sea level. I force myself up—I need the day's pay—and grab a coffee from Bagel Buoy, thinking I'll walk over to the docks for some fresh air. This isn't working. I need to curl up somewhere like an old cat and expire. I get back in my car and go off in search of a suitable spot. Then I Linda Blair it all the way down Bay Street, my head an overinflated balloon, vomit screaming out of me iridescent green.

That's when I know it wasn't the margaritas. It was the CCA-treated wood. Jason's bonfire poisoned me, us. The lumber was introduced in the sixties to great acclaim, replacing the even more environmentally unfriendly creosote-treated lumber. Containing the majority of the forty million pounds of arsenic used in this country every year, CCA touches all of us, especially children, in applications like decks, playgrounds, docks, and buildings at the ground line. Indeed, some homes in Florida, where insects and moisture are a massive threat, are built entirely of CCA-treated wood. The wonder wood has been proven toxic, carcinogenic, and teratogenic (able to cause birth defects and fetal malformation). Burning scrap CCA releases arsine gas. There is enough arsenic and hexavalent chromium (*paging Erin Brockovich*) to cause dry mouth, severe nausea, vomiting, internal bleeding, kidney-related problems, and more, says the EPA's "Hazard Summary for Arsenic and Its Compounds." Like many people, I assume that if something is bad for a laboratory animal it is bad for me. Not entirely accurate. Humans are *more* sensitive to arsenic than lab animals—by a factor of three hundred. Which explains why lab animals, when they're not in the lab, are building their homes in the ground rather than with supplies from Home Depot. It's safer.

My First Gun

"I'm gonna kill him," I say, theatrically.

"He should be fired!" Susan fumes.

"We're going to kill him, then we're going to fire him," I say, strangling the steering wheel.

"No questions asked."

"Exactly."

Speeding down Hampton Road with fire in our eyes, I hit the left onto Union Street hard.

"Unforgivable!" I mutter.

"I don't care if he does show up," Susan says, "he's still gone. Agreed?"

"Agreed. You wanna do it, or me?" We're furious and felonious but in our hearts neither of us really thinks the damn plumber is going to be there as promised. Again, we'll be frustrated for the opportunity to fire him, call him names. There is a peculiar force in renovation that pushes otherwise law-abiding citizens over the edge. Not simply crossing the line of propriety to the point of shouting and treating people harshly, but fantasizing their demise. It's an emotion I haven't even felt at the DMV: I want someone dead. Susan does too. Is it the loss of time, and by extension money? Is it anger in the face of broken appointments, the implied disrespect? Goodnough was such a nice guy, but a flake. Asshole! More than anything, it's the feeling of powerlessness, a feeling made worse by our own culpability: We invited him to the dance, and now he's got us by the balls. We dubbed the real charlatans—Good-nough and Gang of Four Electric predominantly—Terrible Williamsons, after the original Terrible Williamsons, a band of roving Scottish gypsies, miscreants and flimflam artists that traveled in the home repair racket, giving a farmer's barn a two-thousand-dollar paint job that lasted until the first rainfall, or scaring widows about their leaking gas furnaces, near-collapsing roofs, or almost imploding cellar walls, turning small repair fees into years-long payoffs. While scare tactics and bait-and-switch made the Williamsons terrible, they certainly weren't alone. Senate hearings in 1968 were aimed to direct the Federal Trade Commission to investigate swindling in the home improvement industry, which to this day rates as the second highest (after car repair) source of consumer complaint. Local contractors across the country had a host of scams, posing as city inspectors (threatening to condemn unless certain improvements were made), installing bathroom fixtures attached to no running water or exit pipe, overcharging tenfold, and failing to perform services paid for. In truth, most of our subcontractors so far (save the draftsman) are skilled professionals—at least we think they are. Only Dexter has spent any real time here.

I speed up. Ready to fire someone. We turn the corner. "Holy shit!" I shout.

Susan doesn't believe it either. "Oh . . . my . . . gawd."

Not one, but *two* white trucks emblazoned with black lettering: GOODNOUGH PLUMBING, RESIDENTIAL AND COMMERCIAL.

"I don't believe it!" she thrills.

"They'll never know how close they came," I say, elated, relieved, and marginally irritated that we can't fire them. Strike that: I'm not even *thinking* of firing these plumbers.

"Hey," a portly young plumber says, poking his head out of the upstairs bathroom. I repress the urge to hug him. It's been written that abused children often seek love doubly from the parent who is abusing them, convinced they can keep the mistreatment at bay. "Get you anything?" I ask.

"Nope."

"Did you have any questions on the layout?"

"Nope."

"Okay, just holler if you need us. Oh, and we've got lemonade."

Susan and I go back to what we do best: tearing things apart. Today we are finishing the asbestos shingles that we discovered under the yellow aluminum siding. Ripping off the aluminum siding made a racket, pulling and snapping the interlocking strips like an area rug being cleaned, but it was quick and painless, save for the few lacerations. Asbestos shingles are a different matter. They are not in long strips. They are not interlocking. They are nailed in individually and they must be taken off individually. Plus, they're dangerous. At least we think they are. But we've been ripping off a lot and living in denial. When we first called the realtor to say that we had found asbestos shingles, and did she have any advice on their disposal, she said that it is okay to throw them in an ordinary landfill. Really? Yes, she said, she had asked around. That was the good news.

In the weeks after conferring with the realtor, we continued ripping and reading, and discovered the bad news—bad not only because it is bad/dangerous, but bad/contradictory. The literature is totally contradictory. Read three different articles on asbestos shingles and you will have four different answers. When we saw a home improvement show with outfitted professionals wearing disposable garb and placing shingles in large plastic bags, we pretty much decided to start drawing up a will. It didn't help to learn that asbestos is implicated in five thousand U.S. deaths a year, or that it has been used in everything from popcorn ceilings to toothpaste.

Asbestos is all around us, in tiles, linoleum, vinyl flooring, sheathing on electrical cables, Sheetrock, brake pads, and clutches.

The truth of the matter is that there are three types of asbestos: chrysotile (white), amosite (brown), and crocidolite (blue), with chrysotile being used in the vast majority of housing applications. The distinction to heed, however, is between friable and non-friable asbestos. The former you can crush into a powdery state with the force of your hand. Imagine the asbestos insulation that was formerly used around piping—that's friable. It can be crushed and the dangerous fibers can be released, acting as dangerously as a slow-moving Ebola. When the strands are released and become airborne, if you are not wearing a face mask—or an insufficient one (respirators are the best)—and inhale the material, the strands lodge in your lungs. They cannot be broken down. Unlike all that dust and pollen your lungs "digest" without harm, asbestos strands travel around your lungs, find a comfortable bronchial duct or alveolus to call home, and sit there. Like any unwanted guest that won't leave, this is irritating, and the surrounding lung material starts giving angry glances and rude comments to the unwelcome strands. It can take fifteen to twenty years to develop, but this unhappy relationship can develop into the only word more hateful than asbestos: *cancer.*

Nonfriable asbestos, where the strands are locked in a cement or cementlike substrate, poses less of a health threat. Thankfully asbestos shingles are nonfriable. They only release those dangerous strands when they are sawn, drilled, or abraded. We're not sawing or drilling the shingles to get them off, but using pry bars to crack and loosen the shingles from below is doing some serious abrading.

The best technique to remove asbestos shingles, we learn after we've been pulling from the bottom to top for days, is to remove them from the top down. Start high on the house, reveal the nails on the first course, and move down the overlapping rows. This minimizes the amount of breakage and potential strand liberation. It is also good to wet down the work area with water to keep any stray bits under wraps.

So, in the end, how dangerous *are* asbestos shingles? Well, as you'll learn if you do some more reading on the subject, that depends on which state you live in. There are wildly different requirements for treatment imposed by different states. And even more interesting, in our politically correct times, asbestos shingles are no longer called asbestos shingles. They are called fiber-cement shingles. Thus eradicating the danger with adjectives.

We are resituating two ladders, his and hers, as we move around the back of the house to pull down the final shingles up high. Susan clunks her ladder against the side of the house and steps back.

"Can I ask you a question?" she says.

"Uh."

"What did we buy?"

"A shit heap."

"No, really. Like what the hell did we buy? What's left?"

It's a good question. We've been at this for four months, and there is less house than when we started. We've ripped out every window. Every door. Torn up every floor. Pulled down all the ceilings, every sheet of paneling and Sheetrock, all the insulation, plumbing, and electrical. We've removed the siding—and though we don't know it yet, will remove it *again*. We'll also pull down the leaky gutters, the rotting exterior trim, demolish a flimsy rear deck, pull out the toilets, the bathtub, all the kitchen cabinets, and—how could we not?—the kitchen sink. I'll have to saw a large hole in the cinder-block wall in the rear of the basement to connect to the addition—not even the foundation will go unmolested or unmodified.

"Honey," I say, putting my arm around her waist, grandly surveying our domain, one with so many holes in it you'd think it was a tree fort, "we bought an address. A goddamn address."

Best Damn Haircut

The weekend mornings at Pam's house, the hilltop hideaway, are glorious, but brief. A hastily eaten bowl of cereal, a rapid inhalation of fresh air and birdsong, and we're on the road back to Sag Harbor to work.

Now that we've spent four months in "our" town, we've come to realize it is a deceptively peculiar place. The charms, of course, are undeniable: We are a short walk to town and a bay beach, our lot has a fistful of old-growth trees that shade us from the torrents of sun, and there is a dive bar within walking distance that has a nice survivalist's flair. The dartboard is inches from the front door, and patrons making hasty and inattentive entrances get spiked right in the temple with a dart.

The town's quirks, however, are incontestable. In addition to Disorganized Norman, who walks up and down the street no fewer than twenty times daily, there is the Wicked Witch of the West (aka Witchie Poo), Norman's biking counterpart. Beatrice, an elderly and myopic crone, denies that her cats are sick—"Oh, they're fine"—despite their bloody and suppurating eye infections. They sit curbside like a couple of feline androids in need of spare parts, simultaneously instilling one with sympathy and fear. The building inspector invariably arrives groggy and smelling of the sea. And then there is Stan the War Activist/Gardener who drives his fatigue-green Econoline van around with political exhortations—STOP BOMBING VIEQUES, NO WAR IN IRAQ—hand-drawn on the sides in multicolored chalk. The local Republican majority look at him not so much with contempt but slack-jawed befuddlement. In any case, his sincerity (he was arrested and incarcerated in Vieques) and renegade patriotism are inspiring.

These people, and many more, continue to define the town, honor it with real small-town personality, despite the increasing onslaught of city dwellers. Indeed, it is this small-town feel that ensures the arrival of more city slickers, who glibly sign a million dollar mortgage and then trill about living in Sag Harbor, the "un-Hampton."

The feel of Sag Harbor is also preserved in some of its old storefronts, businesses that would be priced out of town in the tonier hamlets of Southampton or East Hampton: The Variety is a genuine five-and-dime (except in pricing); the independent movie theater, with its stuccoed exterior and neon lettering, could be the backdrop for a James Dean movie; the local grocer makes news when he upgrades his meat counter. And the checkout lines everywhere move agonizingly slow because people talk, trading updates on children, asking after elderly relatives, and offering condolences for the hospitalized basset hound.

For me, the storefront that most typifies Sag Harbor is Marty's Barbershop. Marty still works there, or at least I think he does. A lackadaisical crowd of potted plants loiters on the front windowsill, making it tough to see in, but they aren't the only ones keeping business away. Marty is only open three days a week. After repeat attempts, I catch him on a Thursday. The sign in the window says Open, but I still feel like an intruder. My entrance disturbs the silence of the place. Marty sits in the last chair, his nose in an outstretched newspaper. I close the door sharply. No response. I clear my throat. Still nothing.

"Are you open?" I ask.

"Yes," he says without getting up. Calmly he brings the wings of his paper together, folds them in half, and looks me over. "You have long hair."

"Yes, I do," I agree, having let it grow to well over my ears and collar.

"Do you want it short?"

"I would like it short*er*," I confirm uncertainly.

"I don't do that."

His response catches me by surprise. Never in my many comings and goings have I ever seen someone flattening the cushions in Marty's chairs, and here he is turning away the visibly hirsute. His unique aptitude for staying in business while performing no business whatsoever impresses me marvelously. I entertain visions of Marty as a Sag Harbor consigliere, ministering to and being handsomely supported by some east end mafia. Haircuts? No. But you can pay him for his back alley advice. (Alas, I will soon learn that I am wrong, when I begin to notice an entire population of crew-cut lovers in town. Marty's boys.)

"Could you recommend someone?" I ask impotently, thinking surely he must know someone among his barbering brethren who leans toward the trendy, who is willing to reduce hair lengths from long to less long. Marty tells me of a place down the street and to the left, though he can't quite remember the name. I traipse off in search of this, umm . . . salon, and can find only a marina and—good God—a Pilates studio. Clearly, the place of which Marty spoke either never existed or had long since caved to the locals' entrenched predilection for flattops.

Irked and still lavishly tressed, I ask passersby if they know of any such place. None do, but one has a suggestion that points me in another direction. And that is how I come to put my head in the hands of Homicide Harriet.

*   *   *

Harriet is a French-trained hair professional, hailing from one of the finest salons in Paris. Or so I am told. On her way to make her mark on New York City she detoured to care for a sick grandmother, a woman sick enough to need care, but not so sick that she, well, would cease to need care. Harriet no longer lives with her, but visits frequently now that she has settled in to Sag Harbor. Interestingly, her grandmother got markedly better after Harriet signed a lease.

"I also managed to rack up some hospital bills," Harriet says, giving me a wet comb over. "Do you part it here?"

"Yes," I say, mulling her odd revelation. I have to ask. Sure it's personal, but how personal can it be if she just confessed it? "Hospital bills?" I prompt.

"Yeah."

"How so?"

"I stabbed my boyfriend." I watch as she pulls my hair between the teeth of her black comb and cuts the ends off with a long exquisite snip.

"That must have been some accident," I say.

"Oh no," she corrects, "I meant to kill him." I tilt my head up slightly and get caught catching her eye in the mirror. I avoid any sudden movements.

It seems Harriet's boyfriend, *ex-boyfriend*, she underlines— betrayed her in a most despicable way. Moreover, Harriet confides that the original decision to stay in Sag Harbor was not because of her ill grandmother, but really for her (ex) boyfriend. She had passed on good jobs in the city to stay with him. The act of betrayal, seducing and squiring her best friend in her bathroom during her thirtieth birthday party, was too much and Harriet speared him in the thigh with a serrated steak knife. He was rushed to the hospital. The ex, out of remorse—and, perhaps, blood loss—said that he would not press charges if Harriet would cover his stay, as he lacked medical insurance. The story tests credulity, but I fear to ask for clarifications lest the whole saga turn into *Tosca*. Besides, I need to pace myself. As the stray hairs are swept from my aproned front side, and the hand mirror circled around my back, it is clear I will see Harriet again.

"You look good," Susan says as I walk up to our house.

"Thank you." And she is right. I just had the best haircut of my life.

Advice for Singles

We're fed up. Spent. Tired to the bone and it's not even noon. We dangle our feet out the rough opening for the front door and talk about what to attack next. A makeshift parade of rubber-neckers drive by and gawk at the house like it's a ten-car pileup. This one, in the silver Lexus LS, has come to a full stop. He's saying something to the woman in the passenger seat. He looks back at the house, then at us, then at the house again, and shakes his head.

"Screw it," Susan says, "let's go pick up some high hats."

"Yeah, that'd be a blast."

"Come on! We're both pooped and we're not getting anything done sitting here."

She's right—and I *am* pooped—but recessed lighting? We won't need that for at least . . . well . . . too much time for any viable optimism. Susan, however, likes to buy things ahead of time so they act as silent encouragement to hurry up and use them. I see only more clutter to move around whilst delaying any progress. And clutter seems to have enveloped us, started to define our lives. Our clothes and random belongings clutter Pam's house, where we are beginning to feel we are overstaying our welcome. In Sag Harbor, tornadoes of debris—architectural plans, window brochures, how-to books, lumber receipts—collect in the corners. Random tools are scattered in every room. Even the house itself has taken on a disorganized identity: The old windows have been torn out, some new ones wait to have countless nail holes filled before being installed; the concrete front steps (half demolished) now lead to a closed wall, the new front door opening drops off to the ground; the shingles and aluminum siding are gone from the front and sides but still mar the rear; old gutters dangle uselessly and need to be removed; all the old insulation has been removed and the house gets quickly hot and inhospitable in the late July sun.

"Okay," I say, at last relenting, "what the hell."

"Seriously?"

"Yeah, seriously."

"Woo-hoo, progress!" Susan shouts, jumping to her feet.

I glance up at her suspiciously. "I thought you said you were pooped?"

"Not for shopping! Let's go."

Typically this decision is not arrived at so easily. Once I get set up and working I want to make the most out of one day. Susan, on the other hand, has no trouble picking up and setting down tasks. This troubles me. Worse, she likes to race so far ahead on projects that it verges on fantasy. She already has fistfuls of paint chip samples, for instance, and there is not so much as one Sheetrocked wall in the house. I'm process bound, and convinced that a methodical step-by-step approach will create fewer mistakes and save more money. As a corollary argument, I suggest we live with our house for five minutes, to get a feel for it, the habitable space, before we race forward and decide on all our decorative decisions. Before you see the finished room, how can you tell what color it should be? As it turns out, you can't—Susan just has a lot less reluctance to paint and repaint. How did she get this way?

This is what I am thinking, anyway, after Susan has persuaded me into the car, and we are driving around looking for peril. Lo and behold we find it: Home Depot.

Interestingly, no one ever writes about this do-it-yourself danger; instead they concentrate on hazards like saw blades and asbestos. Trust me, the real danger is shopping. Home Depot is a precarious endeavor in the extreme. If you are single, the place may swallow you whole. With luck you will get out alive, but you can bank on being scathed, overwhelmed, and abraded. If you are not single, Home Depot will show you in four thousand cavernous aisles just how unalterably Other your significant other really is.

The widespread silence on this issue is a national disaster. You won't see university studies linking Lowe's to depression, Home Depot to divorce. You won't see home shows exhorting you to holster your charge card. Even the literature on renovation is conspicuously mute about the mental, emotional, and marital hazards of superstores. Indeed almost every book on building or home renovation instead relies on citing Henry David Thoreau, as if that is going to guide you when you're overwhelmed with rows upon rows of flooring samples. *Walden* is reverently referred to as an example of Yankee ingenuity and sober purpose. Everyone loves how Thoreau went alone into the woods to "live deliberately." His materials list is fawned over as a testament to efficiency, to stalwart building. Well, let me tell you something: Thoreau was a pussy. If he had any strength of character whatsoever, if he *really* strove to communicate something valuable about living, real *living*, not some bachelor's rustic getaway weekend, he would have gotten his lazy New England ass married and gone to Home Depot, the land of infinite decision.

"D'you like the squared-off tank, or this nice one with the softer contours?" Susan asks, sellingly.

"I think the squarish. It looks more classical."

"Really?"

"Yeah," I say, with about 50 percent conviction.

"Hmm."

"But were you thinking the round bowl, or elongated?"

She doesn't hesitate. "Round, definitely."

"Seriously? I think I like the elongated."

"You're not just saying that, are you?"

"Whaddaya mean?"

"You're not just saying you like the elongated 'cause I like the round? I mean you said you like the squareish one when I like the softer contours."

"So you're asking . . . ," I start, feeling like a bobble head.

"If that's what you really like or if you're just saying the opposite of what I like?"

"Why the hell would I do that? It's what I like, but it doesn't really matter. The round looks fine, the soft contours *great*. I'm sure they'll both work just as well."

"Exactly."

"Super, let's throw two in the cart."

"But you don't think it looks too stubby, the round one?"

"Let's not undecide. We had progress. Genuine toilet progress."

"I'm just thinking with the other fixtures, in the space we have . . ."

"The round one will leave more room," I explain, "but the elongated one is better for the male 'machinery.'"

"But what's two inches?"

"I beg your pardon?"

"The *toilet* bowl, the difference is probably two inches."

"So you want the elongated one?"

"Well, maybe for the guest bath?"

"The *guest* bath? If we get the comfortable big ride it should be upstairs."

"Let's get one of each and decide which goes where later."

"Done. Now let's haul ass, we need some lighting."

Every trip like this—to Home Depot, to Lowe's, Riverhead Building Supply, or Southampton Brick and Tile—confronts me with the same unassailable truth: I married a woman I don't know. When we met we shared similar political opinions, a passion for travel and outdoor sports, enthusiasms about recent CDs and Hollywood releases, as well as convictions about what constitutes a good life. But, goddamn, if you want to know somebody, *really* know somebody, go to Home Depot and pick out a sink. A toilet. A front door. That's how you find out how someone's mind works. And indeed, how your own mind works. Confronted with an avalanche of options, a limitless list of decisions—since when does the color of grout matter to me?—Home Depot is a metaphysics of material goods, a dialectics of domesticity, a land of self-discovery. And that never comes cheaply.

We get our toilets, then debate our way through the lighting department, exercising a purer reason than even Immanuel Kant could appreciate. As Susan is plucking the last four-inch halo high hats from the shelf, I feel an unmistakable rustling. A primal urge.

"I'm gonna go check out the *mumble* department*mumble*."

"The what?"

"Yeah, I'll meet you up front," I say quickly.

"Lawrence."

I feel guilty, like saying some friends and I are going to a strip club on Friday. Harmless, to be sure, but who falls into any *good* there? "The tool department. I'm going to the tool department, okay?"

"What do we need?" she asks, responsibly.

"Nothing maybe. Just looking."

I enter the cordoned *haut*-security tool area and in five minutes

I am holding in my hand just what I came for. A gun. A Paslode Impulse Framing Nailer. What can I say? I was going to be impulsive. To my benefit, Home Depot has a liberal return policy that allows cagey contractors who need a nailer for only a short period of time to buy one and swiftly return it for a full refund within the ninety-day return window. The guns are then professionally refurbished and sold at a discount to people like me who are eager for real firepower but a little phased by the $450 price tag for a new one.

"What's that?" Susan asks, suspiciously eyeing the bright orange carrying case in my hand.

"A hundred bucks off, not bad huh?"

"What is it?"

"A nail gun, we're gonna need it," I say, which is true. Now that all the old decrepit windows have been taken out of our house, we will have to reframe some rough openings to accommodate the new larger windows. What I don't say is that I am also eager to look a little more professional on Floyd's crew. Just last week while toiling on Floyd's backyard zoo, a short Italian guy named Ray asked to borrow my circular saw so he could cut some paneling for the monkey hut. I held out my plastic Black & Decker and he looked at me like I was handing him a dead squirrel. "That's a home owner's saw," he cracked, mocking its amateur-grade amperage. Truly, with such little power it huffs and it puffs and cuts along a chalk line like a drunk driver at a roadside test. Ray doesn't demand a lot of the tool—cutting plywood—but for the rest of the day I was known as Black & Decker.

"Can we go now?" Susan prods, trying to avert any more danger.

"Just a sec." I scan the big names, the professional-grade saws in front of me. Makita (solid), DeWALT (Black & Decker with juice), Hitachi (the TV manufacturer?), Milwaukee (tough despite its name), Ryobi (a cheap pretender), and Porter-Cable (the choice of almost everyone I've been working with).

"Don't we have a saw?" asks Susan.

I take a deep breath. Being questioned like this, by my wife and conscience in tandem, demands a diplomatic response, a selling response, one that I believe myself.

"We need a *stronger* saw."

"Oh," she says, and starts pushing the cart. That was remarkably easy, I think to myself. Then she turns back around.

"Why?"

Why? What kind of question is that? Women.

"The other one's been jamming up," I say. This is a flagrant exaggeration, but true in an I-can-see-the-future-and-there-are-screaming-overtaxed-Black-&-Deckers sense. Besides, where does she get off trying to deny a man his tools? I hold up for her inspection a Porter-Cable 347k, a cast-magnesium beauty that combines light weight (though twice the poundage of my home-owner's saw) and raw power. It will cut tirelessly and along a straight line—at least in the hands of someone who can control it.

"Are you going to be happy all weekend, then?"

"I'm always happy." This too is a lie. I've been getting grumpy, frustrated with the slow progress of the home and a career that risks mimicking Floyd's cranky job-site line of work. "I'll be happy all *week*," I say.

"Then buy whatever goddamn saw you want."

And then, gloriously, triumphantly—*no homicides*—we make it to check out. Our decision-making bruised us, but our decisions bind us, and with packages stuffed into the sedan, we leave elated as looters. Our joy lasts all the way back to the house, where, as we stack our purchases in the basement, we discover something that previously escaped our notice. Goodnough's crew has completed only half the rough plumbing. The bathroom lines shoot into the basement, but aren't connected to the exit line.

Morning comes with a jolt. I wake up at six-forty-five startled, scared that I'll be late for work at seven. It's a thirty-minute drive and I haven't even showered. Shit, why didn't I set two alarms? Then something strikes me. Susan's hand on my chest. Phew, it's Saturday. We snuggle for fifteen minutes before it dawns on me: The house is not building itself; *let's get a move on.* What do you mean what's for breakfast, we have a lot of work to do. I try to extricate us from the borrowed comforts of the hilltop retreat, determined to get us on the road and in Sag Harbor so that we can get something done before noon.

We clamor around the kitchen, cobbling together a pitiable repast of muesli and grapefruit juice. I need coffee, lots of coffee. We tumble into the car. It's too early in the morning for gymnastics, so Susan climbs into the backseat rather than jump through the passenger-side window. It's sad that this feels normal, my wife alternately sitting in the backseat and crawling through windows.

"Let's go to Riverhead," Susan says, referring not to the town, but the lumberyard, Riverhead Building Supply.

"No way." I see delay, the loss of the morning, no work done, and down the road, being blamed that progress isn't fast enough.

"We need stuff," Susan says.

"What stuff? We just went shopping yesterday."

"Window trim," she suggests.

"Would you like me to tell you what has to be done before we do window trim?"

"Well, for one, *putting the windows in.*"

"Exactly. But before we can do *that* we have to finish reframing the walls, tar paper the exterior, put window plastic around the opening, flashing along the bottom . . .''

"How do you know this?"

"Dexter told me."

"Do we have tar paper?"

"No."

"We could get that."

Damn it, she's right.

"Okay, but we're outta there in ten minutes."

Of course we're not. We lose an entire hour, and by the time we get on Hampton Road back toward East Hampton, I'm speeding unnecessarily, cutting maybe fifteen seconds off our travel time and stupidly worrying: Is that a cop up ahead? No, that's not a cop up ahead. Is that a cop up ahead? I think that's a cop—no, it's not.

"*Shit,*" I say, punching the brake.

"What?"

"Cop."

We pull up to our house on Union Street and drag the tar paper out of the trunk. The front of the house is now one big plastic sheet, covering the openings from the excised windows. After we moved the door from the right side of the house to the center—more light!—the wall we cut out to accomplish it now rests like an overextended drawbridge from the landing to the ground.

The first order of business is moving all of the plumbing supplies that crowd near the door. It is impossible to get into the basement, where I store some supplies and hide my home-owner-grade tools. Until we return the stairs to their original position—we pulled out the stairwell and boarded it up—we have to run around the house and enter the basement from the rear. That's not nearly the problem that all this clutter is. The basement is full with toilet bowls and tanks, the kitchen stove, the dishwasher, and all the cast-iron heating we pulled out from upstairs. Additionally, I ripped out the electricity, so we can't see a damn thing.

"These toilet tanks are really helpful right now," I snap, as I wave the flashlight around our ankles. The yellow beam glances off the useless porcelain.

"We're going to *need* them," Susan says, omitting the emphatic *duh* on the end.

"Yeah, but first we have to fix the bathroom subfloor, Sheetrock the walls, spackle, tile, grout . . ."

Susan rolls her eyes. This is maybe the ten thousandth time she's had to hear this litany from me.

"We could lose an hour looking . . ." I start.

"It's right here," Susan says, moving aside a stray piece of insulation.

The Sawzall—borrowed from a friend—is the third man on our Saturday crew. The hardest worker. The tireless, underappreciated, molar-rattling Sawzall. We grab a couple extension cords and move upstairs to the south side of the living room, the side that gets drenched with sun from noon to sundown, the side where we want to be lavish and put in a four-by-eight-foot window. The center panel will be fixed, with twenty-four small glass panels, and there will be two double-hung windows on the ends. Maybe that sounds a little too cute, but it's good enough for the Historical Preservation and Architectural Review Board, and we're damning the torpedoes.

To prepare for the new window, we will need to reframe the entire twelve-foot wall, or almost. We will need a new, stronger header with two jacks on each end because of the expanse and weight. Jacks are the two-by-fours that are cut to a length beneath the header, to support that weight, and two studs that run from sill plate to top plate to help keep the floor above us where it belongs. Up.

The header itself is a weighty affair. Two eight-and-a-half-foot lengths of two-by-twelve-inch Douglas fir with an equally sized piece of half-inch plywood in between. The plywood adds rigidity (probably more strength than either two-by-twelve) and makes life easier down the road. Since lumber measurements are nominal, two-by-four actually measures one and a half inches by three and a half inches. When two one-and-a-half-inch boards are nailed together and put in place as a header, they do not rest flush with the three and a half inches of the stud. The half-inch piece of plywood makes up for this gap. Many contractors will skip this step, saving the pennies and leaving a small pocket above your window. Is this a big deal? Not really. It may influence how neatly you attach the window trim, since the drywall can move in that space, but the house isn't going to fall down. In any event, I am still at a point in the process where I am scared to do anything other than the best way for fear the house will implode or I'll be laughed at by Dexter for cutting corners and I'm still jazzed to make the best damn renovation I possibly can—though my perfectionist tendencies are starting to wear on Susan. "Let's just get it done," she urges as I cut a two-by-four one more time, fitting framing material as closely as I would fit finish material. It's not going by the book, I'll later learn, but I think it is.

The morning and afternoon wear steadily on. I can feel my fingers and forearms being deadened, my arms falling increasingly asleep. The constant rattling vibration of the Sawzall carries right through my thick gloves and makes my hands numb. In tight spots, where the wood pinched too tightly, the blade catches, and the entire tool continues in a herky-jerky fashion toward and away from the stud I am cutting. The sawdust has me covered. It is nothing like the happy-scented sawdust of fresh fir; this has an annoying overtone of must and mildew. The boards are tough as concrete, having been dried out over time.

Finally I have all the studs cut free, and I zip effortlessly, rewardingly down the sheathing. It's free. "Stand back," I say, more for drama than effect—Susan is well behind me, standing over the sawhorses looking at tile samples. With a few kicks and a judicious push the entire wall loosens and starts to tilt to the outdoors. One more kick and the top falls from the house, slowly at first, like a sawed tree, then faster, landing powerfully with a thunderous crunch and siroccos of dust. It lands on a ghetto of shrubs, a thorny thicket of vegetation left over from the previous owners' landscaping malfeasance.

"Wow," Susan says. And it *is* wow. The whole wall is gone and the room feels infinitely better. It is exciting, but a little depressing, that we spent so much money for something that, like a pair of designer jeans, is only made more beautiful in its obliteration. The less of the house we retain, the better it looks.

But that open-air beauty fades as we race to get the wall reframed and sheathed. Susan clears the sawhorses of her tile samples and drags a few two-by-fours in from the front yard. "Why don't I cut and you nail?" she suggests.

I look over. She's serious. The saw, *my* saw, my new professional-grade saw is in her hand and she looks poised to cut something.

Clearly, she's lost it. She's never even held a nail gun before, and now she's Handy Andy? "Um." I start thinking. She's usurping my power-tool domain, the male domain, and there's nothing I can do about it. I knew she was a feminist going in and now I'm cooked.

"Would you rather cut and I'll nail?" she asks, sensing my hesitation.

"No, that's fine." This could work, I'm ready to believe, it really could. But if it doesn't I'm the schmuck. I'm the guy who let his wife cut her thumb off. Worse, I'll be the ass that almost forced her into it. I call out the first board, "Ninety-one and three eighths."

Susan is hunched over the two-by-four, extending the Stanley tape measure. "Which are the eighths, the little marks, or the really little marks?"

"The little ones."

"This one?" she says, pointing to the spot with a dull pencil. *Oh, holy Hannah.*

"No, that's three *quarters.* This is three eighths, here. See? There are eight of them in an inch."

She looks up from the tape, eyeballing me. "You don't have to get sarcastic."

"I'm just trying to save time."

"Lecturing isn't saving time."

"No, you're right, it isn't," I say, trying to calm things down—and put an end to this hell. She finds her mark and cuts methodically, so slowly that a small plume of smoke emanates from the blade-scorched lumber.

It's something to behold. She looks exactly like I did so many long months ago, my first day working for Floyd. Of course, I don't tell her that.

"Thanks. We need six more of the same, and four more at seventy-nine and seven eighths." As soon as she cuts, I nail the studs into position with my new Paslode. I risk turning the house into a lightning rod, enthusiastically rifling every exposed face of the stud repeatedly. We hoist the header into place and nail it off. Then we cut the sheathing, the three-quarter-inch plywood, which matches up with the patchwork of original siding still on the house. Now, at last, we are ready to tar paper the exterior.

The tar paper is another of Dexter's counterintuitive suggestions. Many people love Tyvek, which is made out of Kevlar and thus is tough, lightweight, and clean to work with. Hung on the exterior of a house it looks like the world's largest FedEx envelope. Doubtless it is strong, but as Dexter points out, strength is not what you are after here. Waterproofing is. Since we will be installing cedar shingles to the exterior of the house, there will be roughly three thousand nail holes through the sheathing, which means three thousand small opportunities for water to gain access to the home. A good home is one that breathes, but not one that inhales a lot of moisture that will remain trapped. Moisture will cause the deadly black mold, and we will soon run around like lunatics.

Here, Dexter argues, the protective capabilities of the old-fangled tar paper have a slight edge. Since the tar paper has a melty tar component—obviously—heat will soften it and cause it to self-seal around each of those nails, doing a better job of impeding moisture. When you nail through Tyvek, on the other hand, the hole size remains constant. A big risk? Probably not huge, but why take it at all?

As the sun is setting, we finish slap hammering the final length of tar paper onto the house that exists so far. To avoid as much unnecessary water entry as possible, we will wait until the windows arrive to cut out the openings. As we leave for the day, heading back to Pam's house, our project looks like an oversized and very square hearse on the bottom, a hurricane victim on the top.

Monster Garage

After interminable days of smoke-curing and shouts, we are going to move from Floyd's reptarium and rabbitat. With the monkey hut erected and anaconda accommodations up to reptilian code, we can start on the new job Floyd has secured in Remsenburg, which is even further west. Mercifully this travel is a reverse commute—most everyone in the "trade parade" travels from west to east, from middle island communities to the Hamptons. I will be driving a dizzying forty-five minutes west, but that wouldn't even merit a complaint in the trade parade.

We meet up at Floyd's at seven to ready the tool trucks. Besides me, there's Bob the lounge singer, Rick the redhead, Ray the Italian, Chris, and Tom. From what I can gather, Tom is Jason's father, and it explains a lot as far as Jason is concerned. Tom isn't a bad man from what I can tell, but he was either born a little slow or whacked with a floor nailer when he wasn't expecting it. Because they are of an older generation, Lounge Bob and Slow Tom are an inseparable twosome. I admire that even when Tom is at his stupid best, Bob sticks with him. Swears at him, but sticks with him. Ritchie, it seems, won't be making the trip. Wage resentment got the better of him and he stole one of Floyd's nail guns. I can't blame him; Floyd treats us like dogs and he hates to relinquish his money. Friday evenings we wait at his back door like dogs for table scraps, hoping to get paid with enough time to make it to the bank. Floyd knows better; he stalls so that we have to cash them another day. I couldn't wait him out last week, and everyone thought I had quit.

"Didn't think I'd see you here," says Ray. We sit on the six-by-six CCA rails that Joe and I spiked together for the driveway enclosure last week, listening to the neighborhood roosters wail.

"I couldn't wait. Had to pick up my wife at the train station," I explain.

"Yeah, I missed picking my kid up at school. Shit, man, his mother was *pissed*."

"That sucks," I say, not knowing what to say. "Kid's okay though?"

"Yeah. I took 'em both over to my house and cooked dinner." He becomes suddenly animated. "You know I make this amazing pasta sauce with gugootz."

"Goo-what?"

"Gugootz!" he says, emphatically. He stands up, "They're like a squash, grow about this big." He's holding his hand about waist high off the ground.

"Like zucchini?"

"*Better!* I grow 'em in my backyard. My pride and joy."

Okaay, I think, and am relieved for the first time ever to see Floyd. He won't be accompanying us, so he gives us directions to the house in Remsenburg. We leave and make an immediate stop at Dunkin' Donuts. Then Remsenburg. The house is a massive Italianate number on the water, opposite the Moriches inlet. It feels good to be back at a real house, the size of the place conferring an illusory worthiness I didn't suffer from at Floyd's house. But there's a catch. We're not starting in the house: we're starting in the garage. Not that this is a minor endeavor by any stretch. The "garage" could swallow my house whole and still have room for dessert. The structure boasts room for ten cars, servants' quarters, a game room, and two full baths. The trim being used on this garage is superior to the material I've seen used in many homes I've been in. Floyd's for one. Mine for another. If we conduct ourselves professionally on the garage work, we will be promoted in time to work on the house. It all feels a little Balzacian.

The overseer, the developer, of this lavish estate is a tall bald Yul Brynner stand-in. We immediately dub him Mr. Clean. He looks positively carcinogenic, though there is no evidence that he smokes. He simply fumes. Unlike Floyd, who yells and screams to browbeat people into obedience, Mr. Clean never raises his voice. The silence is terrifying to everyone, especially Rick the redhead, who has been appointed by Floyd to lead our crew, a decision simultaneously stupid and fitting.

Seeing that Rick has his hands full puppying after Mr. Clean, while simultaneously trying to marshal ten carpenters who don't believe in him, I sneak out early on the first day for more pressing business: photocopying. The final revisions to the revised, corrected, stamped, and signed survey have been completed, and we have to rush them to Sybil the Dread with six complete copies of my entire application to the Zoning Board of Appeals. Susan had bused out today, a Monday, just to help with this task. If we miss it, there's another month delay.

Nevertheless, it is going to be a photo finish. The deadline was noon—despite the building department being open until five—and it is now three-thirty. Susan brokered an extension until four with what must have been superhuman persuasion. Or she held a gun to Sybil's head. We are stretched so tight by this whole process that we are thoroughly, comically, bizarrely grateful for this smallest of gestures. And still we might blow it.

I'm standing in a sweltering second-floor copy shop on Main Street as some proprietary bearded photocopier, who doesn't want me touching his machines, does our photocopying for us. Susan is running the copies—one by one—two blocks down to Sybil. Three are with Sybil, three are in the bowels of his machine. I hand another copy to Susan and she's off. The clock reads three-forty-nine. I press Mr. Copy to speed up, *please*. He raises an eyebrow over his horn-rims, like I'm crazy. I *am* crazy, if I think about it. But I don't. Instead I keep strong-arming the Xerox jockey. Then he announces the machine just jammed again. "The humidity," he says.

"It can be fixed, can't it?" I say, pressing again. I know how lenient Sybil is going to be, and I'm convinced we're screwed. Susan returns and we wait for three agonizing minutes and watch Mr. Copy tinker. Finally the infernal contraption rumbles back to life. We stand and sweat, waiting for the last two copies. The clock now reads three-fifty-nine. I would like to say that I am of a stronger mien, that Sybil's impersonal (where's the small town when you need it?) and dastardly insistence that we make it to her by four doesn't phase me, but that would not be true. I am nervous and panicked, not to mention sweaty, infuriated, and obsessed. We toiled to get our survey and plans in order and simply can't afford to wait "another month," as Sybil so cheerfully chirps.

I once complained to Dexter about the circus atmosphere fostered by the multifarious meetings and deadlines of the building department, zoning board, and Architectural Review Board. He cut me a look like I didn't know the half of it, that if I had his job for a living, ushering applications for clients, I would really know what nightmare means. I was convinced that some clients could circumvent the process if they knew which wheels to grease. Heck, for the right price a bribe makes good economic sense—if your property is sitting undeveloped while you pay taxes, mortgage, and utilities, but can't live there. "Surely there's a faster way," I joked to Dexter. "What would it cost?" He smirked like I had no idea what I was talking about.

"A lot of people think they're corrupt," he said, "but if they were corrupt something would actually get done."

We make it to Sybil at one minute after four, winded and determined to leave the copies in her hands. She doesn't seem happy to see us. "This is all of them then?" she asks in a way that strikes me as strange. Deflated. Sour almost. What the hell does she care? Then I remember Dexter's comment, about things getting done. It makes me wonder if the building department isn't about building so much as not building, if the department is there for *arresting* development. In that vein, it makes perfect sense that Sybil is less than obliging to us renovators. We bring change. Like all home improvers, we are a threat to old Sag Harbor, to life the way it used to be. Sybil isn't prepared to go vigilante and burn down developments, but meddling does enough to delay change. On the other hand, my stress is probably fostering hallucinations that she even cares. She's just doing her job. I've simply reached a point where it feels personal.

"What time ya got, pal?"

I lace my boots and answer Rick without compunction: "Seven-forty-five. It was one hell of a long drive."

"Come here," he says, signaling for me to follow him upstairs, where I was working yesterday with Ray.

"First of all, who told you to nail off these trims?" he asks, red faced, pointing to a small and delicate piece of milled casing that fits around the window crank in a casement window. They had been tacked into place with brads at the Anderson Window factory. I had to remove them to do my work yesterday with the extension jams. I then tacked casing back over the window crank with a couple sixteen-gauge nails. Not a good idea, it seems.

"Now they're jammed, and you are gonna have to find a way to get them unjammed without breaking them . . . and they are very breakable."

I'm alarmed, doubly so because I was only able to complete

two windows yesterday. What's the big deal? Then I learn that *all* the trims have been nailed in place. Someone came behind me, followed my bad example, and then blamed me for all of them. Rick, terrified of Mr. Clean, is anxious I won't be able to fix them. I'm not so sure myself. It's one hell of a start to the day.

To make matters worse, Rick then wants me to work on the jam extensions for the semicircular, eyebrow windows above the square casements. These are very difficult to get into place because of their shape and tough to make flush with the interior. Thick highways of Spackle stripe the drywall and I feel firsthand what it is like to inherit someone else's sloppy work.

The work is painstaking for an experienced set of hands, and my hands have no experience with this at all. I glean as much as I can from Ray, who I feel won't turn state's evidence on me both because he doesn't care and because he's trying to fly under the radar for his own reasons. I'm staring at the window opening like it's going to divulge some secret when Mr. Clean walks by. He makes periodic trips from the main house to check on us in the garage. He never speaks, only confers with Rick, the mad foreman, out of earshot from the rest of us. The air of secrecy keeps everyone on edge. Suddenly I miss the no-head-games demands of the monkey hut.

The days pass in the Remsenburg über garage with low levels of dread and paranoia. The delivery of fresh building materials slows to a trickle during the week, then stops completely, making everyone wonder if we're through, and not going to the big house after all. Even Mr. Clean is circling with reduced frequency. Rick, more paranoid than ever, repeatedly tells carpenters, who are vigorously employed, to *do something*. He's becoming mentally unstable. Late Thursday afternoon, Ray and I are eyeballing an outbuilding in need of repair. Out of nowhere, Rick pounces on us. "What is this, a secret discussion?"

"The center beam is cracked, needs to be replaced," I say, unmetaphorically. Rick glances up at the beam, then back down at us. He turns on his heel and is gone.

"That guy is cracked," I say to Ray.

"That second hit of pot must have hit him wrong."

The what?

When I arrive Friday morning, Rick is even crazier than he was the night before. I can't imagine that he's on the Cheech and Chong at six A.M., but who knows?

"I fuckin' quit last night," he announces to me, almost amiably.

"You what?"

"I don't want to be a leader, just want to do my thing. I don't want to oversee no one. I'm getting an ulcer." I'm absolutely elated. He's been riding me all week like a draft mule, and now it's finally over. Yet it is also a little sad, for here's a guy that obviously knows carpentry but years on the job have taught him nothing about management. He couldn't lead his urethra to a urinal without guidance. He stammers around theatrically for a few minutes more, making a show worthy of a Floyd understudy, then heads toward his blue panel van. He punches the accelerator, spitting gravel all the way down the driveway, leaving with a cartoonish flourish.

The rumor is that Chris will be assuming the foreman position, and when he arrives at seven-thirty it is clear before he even says a word that he is. You can tell by his shoes. As Rick traded his worn work boots for a pair of running shoes, Chris has swapped his tan glue-smeared Merrells for a clean pair of black ones. His ascension to management is also signaled by the lack of a tool belt—the trappings of the working man. Again I'm paired with Ray: We're assigned to fix the patio roof, which had been knocked out of square, squished really, when they hauled Sheetrock across it to get into the upper floors. We try to pull the columns back in square by attaching a come-along to the headers. It seems like an ingenious solution, pulling the opposite sides of the hexagon in with a winch, but as the striated cable begins to fray I see one of us getting decapitated pronto. Ray suggests we construct a spring system to pull it in and I oppose him strenuously. I don't know what I'm talking about but what he is suggesting flies in the face of everything I learned in college physics. Plus Ray is an idiot, so I feel emboldened.

First we position a two-by-ten from the floor to a ceiling joist, and then nail another two-by-ten from the point where the first board meets the floor to the header we want to pull *in*. Lastly, Ray situates a board perpendicular to the second two-by-ten, the hypotenuse if you will, and starts hitting it with a sledgehammer. I'm convinced the header will press out and the roof will collapse, but that doesn't prevent me from staying underneath to help. It feels like volunteering for the *Kursk*, misdirected male ego and duty plunging me toward death. Against all expectation, the header gets pulled into place within seconds, and we secure it. I'm amazed. So, too, is Mr. Clean. All week Ray's recklessness has made him an object of regular supervision, and more suspicion than the rest of us. But now he is Mr. Clean's star pupil. His elevated status lasts for a whole three hours, until we are back inside constructing a soffit. We cut our required boards, then glue them to the ceiling with construction adhesive to be extra sure. The ambient temperature is a perfect 98.6, it would seem, for Ray doesn't feel a thing as the glue repeatedly drips from the ceiling and onto his shaved head. Mr. Clean, who you would think might look out for his bald brethren, eyes Ray's dappled cranium and walks off without a word.

In an act of desperation, a thirst for contact with my former life, I quit the day early to drive into the city. Excusing myself with another manufactured dentist's appointment, I wash off in the ocean—I wouldn't have time enough to drive all the way home—then backtrack into town. A friend's indie movie screening lasts from five-thirty to seven-thirty and I don't want to be late. Could I skip it? Sure I could, but I am starting to feel so isolated in Mayberry, any pretext to get into the city is one that I will leap at.

The traffic on the Long Island Expressway is, of course, stacked up. An accident slows things further and I make it to the screening as people are streaming out. Susan gives me a *where have you been?* look, which I defuse with an aggressive *that friggin' traffic* grind of the teeth. With that out of the way, we say our hellos.

We bump into our friends James and Camilla and we all decide to get dinner together. It is the perfect topper to three and a half hours on the hot island expressway, as James enumerates the string of million-dollar deals he has closed in the last month. Camilla is somehow able to interrupt James's soliloquy long enough to mention her promotion to Global Group Director—whatever the hell that means—for an amalgamation of beauty lines. It's a bracing experience, given that they know what is going on in my life and my stalled career. Together the two of them make for an excruciating evening, and it starts me wondering if they've always been this way and I have just somehow missed it. More than see them socially on a semiregular basis, Susan and I have vacationed with them in Peru without incident. Could both of us have been blind to their radioactive personalities even under the duress of shared foreign leisure?

The snowstorm of self-celebration continues over the main course and I begin to sink lower and lower. Rather than dull the festivities with dolorous recitations of recent interviews and hiring freezes, the string of leads that have amounted to zilch, I instead make supercilious remarks about how well things are going, how my career diversification in real estate development is really starting to pay off, that I can even afford a hammer now. Superbly, my cutting remarks are either disingenuously laughed at or, worse, completely unnoticed. To aggravate things further, Susan tries to prop me up by mentioning what amazing work I'm doing on our house. I want to sink into a hole. The trip into the city has had the exact opposite effect I had hoped for. Indeed, the whole evening is an affront to my former knowledge of James and Camilla. And to my stupidity: Couldn't I have found an easier way than job loss and renovation-hell to decipher who my friends were?

Susan picked up the check.

Susan I and spend the night in the city, testily discussing what we should be packing and what we should be throwing out of our New York apartment before the move. We have just two weeks left in this apartment—the apartment where we were engaged, the apartment where we spent the first months of our married life together—and it seems we are going nowhere, off a cliff. I mention that it might be nice to know where we are moving *to*, but this editorial remark is received icily and boomerangs back at me with a glare. Like, what have I secured in Sag Harbor, a finished home? No, nowhere near. We are still flopping in East Hampton, staying well past our welcome at Pam's house. The lack of any one abode to call home makes us crave one all the more strongly.

We get up Saturday morning, do some incidental throwing out, but the pull of the project is greater. We both want to head back to Sag Harbor and make some progress rather than stay in this apartment and feel glum. The July sun is already hot, baking the Long Island Expressway, so we drive fast with all the windows open, since the car's air-conditioning died months ago.

As we pull up to Union Street, Joe from Gang of Four Electric ("NO JOB TO [*sic*] SMALL") is pulling his things out of the house.

"I didn't know he was coming today," Susan says enthusiastically.

I'm braking and exiting the car at the same time. "Neither did I."

"Hiya," Joe says, smiling widely. "We got the rooms you wanted done. I hope I got them the way you want it."

"I really wanted to be here, Joe," I say, panicked and a little pissed off. "Why didn't you let me know you were coming?"

"I said Saturday last time we talked."

"You also said 'if you could' and that you'd call." I start for the front door, worried about what he wired, where he wired, how he wired.

"I left a message," he says unconvincingly. He reluctantly follows me inside, where Susan is already checking the interiors.

"Is this a switch?" she asks.

"Switches," Joe says. "For the front porch, the overheads, the wall outlet—"

"Isn't the front door opening this way?" she says, sweeping her left hand from right to left.

"Yes," I say.

Joe stares at the switches, hard.

Susan throws up her hands. "Then it's wrong, isn't it? Otherwise we have to walk in, and go around the door to turn on a light." Clearly it's wrong.

"You can't open the door the other way?" Joe asks, like it is no big deal.

"We could," I say, "if we had ordered the opposite swing door. But we didn't."

Joe's mood is sinking fast. "Well, if you had spelled it out . . ."

"Joe," I say, "we did spell it out, and I said I'd be here for questions." We walk through the rest of the house and identify several more problems. Wires pulled across studs that will be in a new doorway. Switches on the wrong side of the bathroom. It's frustrating, and I wish I could just do it myself. Yet I'm reluctant to work with something that can kill me as quickly as electricity can, and decide to concentrate on the telephone and cable lines. This foray into Joe's domain is already making him a little nervous. When I mention that I want to run the service line underground, and that I am willing to do it myself, he starts manufacturing obstacles.

"That's gotta be down a good five feet, you know, not a simple Ditch Witch job. And there's the riser fee from the electric company." I ask him if he checked on that and he says "seven hundred bucks for the riser, two thousand for the whole job." I'm in disbelief. The electric company would supply overhead cable if we wanted to move the line to a different pole, but if we want to move it underground we have to pay for it.

"You're kidding," I say. "We make the neighborhood look nicer, save them potentially downed power lines and tree trimming, and they want to ding us for seven hundred dollars?"

"That's the way it is."

Actually, that's not the way it is. I go into Long Island Power Authority myself that afternoon and talk to the rep, who says three feet down is plenty, and learn that the riser fee is only two hundred dollars. Obnoxious, yes, but not as offensive as Joe's game playing. He's clearly getting miffed with a pair of rogue home owners who want to usurp his authority. He starts acting out. When Susan, contrary to her nature, drew plans for the electrical layout of the home, Joe ignored them and wired the way he wanted to. It's war. I rent a Ditch Witch, wrestle the demon machine for a backbreaking day, and get service cable underground. The whole job done for $350. Soon thereafter, Joe abandons the job, leaving it half done. When I see his business card he tacked to the corkboard at the bank—GANG OF FOUR ELECTRIC—I add: STINKS.

Send in the Friends,
There Must Be Friends

As welcome as our Sag Harbor neighbors have made us feel, with repeated offers of house-sitting and dinner invitations, we are also feeling more and more cut off from our old friends. It's a separation with more behind it than simple geography. In our first year of marriage we have witnessed the disappearance of countless friends. Poof, gone. Weddings are going-away parties, plain and simple. Friends and relatives gather to crack a bottle of bubbly on your bow and that's it, bubbaloo, bon voyage, you're outta here. The honeymoon in Tahiti is the metaphor, a short trip symbolizing the big trip, the one without room service. It is a move to uncharted lands, for every marriage is a country without maps. Others may advise you of the general terrain, what to expect, how to handle the hostile natives, be they domestic or foreign, spouse or in-law, but the fact of the matter is you are on your own. It is a going-away party because you can't take them with you, and they wouldn't come along if you invited them. How could they?

Susan and I look back on our wedding day with an admixture of emotions: delight, gratitude, and out-and-out bewilderment. The day was resplendent in its meteorology. A sunny seventy degrees with the requisite single cloud from central casting. We were married on the decks of a waterside restaurant on Three Mile Harbor, in East Hampton. Susan looked fantastic and I was, well, marriageable. The ceremony was an undeniable triumph. Innumerable people made great sacrifices to be there and many made great efforts to ensure the weekend was a success, handwriting menus, arranging flowers, hosting and decorating a backyard clambake, singing home-composed songs, and giving humorous toasts that, in their bighearted narrowness of focus on our good points, veered toward eulogy.

Which only makes the event that much more bewildering. Looking back, Susan and I ask ourselves, who *were* those people? And more to the point, where have they gone? Where have *we* gone?

Imagining rewriting the invitation list today, Susan and I joke that we could cut the list in half. "Why did we invite him?" "What was she doing there?" Heartless? I hope not. Frank? Undeniably. Not all friends are meant to be yours for life, I suppose, and crossing from single to married ensures that some of those will fall away. The rules of engagement have changed, the reasons that you hang out, and your tolerance for smoky bars with beer on the floor changes. That, and after getting married I no longer wanted to chase a dream, I wanted to build one.

That Susan and I chose to build a dream home, not a dream apartment, on the east end of Long Island no doubt exacerbated our loss of prenuptial friends. It was that much harder to keep up friendships while living in a condition and locale that is profoundly distant from those city singles. And as if we had moved to another country, half of our wedding/going-away party invitees drifted away, quickly or slowly, and we were left with only our closest friends—and, of course, our families. Though we can't imagine why none of them are returning calls.

More material, *much* more material, has arrived on the Remsenburg site, tacitly approving our last week's work. Not so tacitly, Mr. Clean's demands are getting increasingly complicated. Chris gathers half of us in the massive living room. It stretches from the large vaulted vestibule into a rectangular space that feels like a football field; the entire ocean-side wall is made of sliding doors, some of which don't slide. The previous crew, which got tossed for a whole host of visible (and now invisible) mistakes, did not sufficiently frame this massive wall, and the weight of the upper floors is pressing on the sliders. But that's not what Chris wants to talk about. He is getting us set up on an intricate coffered ceiling, a network of interlocking beams that will run from one end of the living room to the other.

The "beams" in a coffered ceiling are actually faux beams constructed out of three visible pieces of trim, nailed in a U shape, that are attached to a nailer, a piece of lumber that is attached to the ceiling with nails (at the joists) and heavy-duty construction adhesive. Crown molding finishes off the edges, making an elegant networking of apparently interlocking beams. It is a big job, and one that is easy to screw up since everything must be kept religiously square, lest one mistake in one square affect every other on the ceiling.

Bob and Tom begin by snapping chalk lines on the ceiling to map out what we are going to build. Chris noodles over the blueprints anxiously before we start. As the Mexicans haul in the lumber from the front yard, Ray and I rip it down to size on the table saw. Our first task is cutting the dryboard, a microfiber engineered board that will be glued to the ceiling, and to which everything else is eventually attached. Top of the line construction would use finger-jointed stock as the support lumber, attached to the ceiling, but we're cutting a few pennies on what will be invisible.

But that's not an issue right now, cutting medium density board is. On the table saw the stuff positively explodes into great snowstorms of dust. After a half dozen sixteen foot lengths, Ray, who is manning the downwind side of the saw, looks like Mr. Freeze, covered head to toe in pale sawdust.

Notwithstanding the dust storm, the morning's work is un-eventful, pleasant even. I reflect that this is hard work—some of it drudgery, some of it dangerous—but it is also uniquely reward-ing. I resist the easy cynicism. Sure, at the end of the day, I'm working for some rich mogul who probably mistreats his staff and benefits from the deplorably low wages Floyd pays me. Instead, I concentrate on the fact that I am building something real, concrete, visible. One hundred years from now it will still be here.

This work is different—and not only because I risk killing myself doing it. At the end of any day I'm tired, filthy, and sore, but there's a satisfaction in that that I haven't felt in any white-collar job. For whatever reason, spilling fax toner on myself is not the kind of filthy that tells me *I'm workin'*—but pulling splinters out of my finger or brushing sawdust out of my hair does. Though I am only six months into my rookie season, I have advanced hugely from the guy who started tearing apart his house with a kiddie crow bar. Now I can look back at the house (or pigsty) I've been working on and realize I've probably used more of my physics, math, and logical problem-solving knowledge than I have in years. Even better, I can appreciate the building's design complexity, the skills and innovative materials I employed to build it—and then be able to confidently say, "I just kicked Thoreau's ass."

A stampede in the upstairs hallway gets our attention, and Ray flips off the circular saw so he can hear what is going on. The Mexicans, Julien, Didier, and Markus, hit the landing first. Alex, his jaw clenched and face reddened like a squeezed tomato, comes after them. I see a broken trail of blood snake back upstairs before it occurs to me that it is Alex's blood. He holds his left hand tightly in front of him, low. "He shot himself," Didier announces for anyone who hadn't figured it out already. Alex throws him a look.

Alex is obviously pained, but also embarrassed. "Is there a first aid kit?" he asks. Chris says there's nothing on the truck, a fact that is already well known by everybody. Floyd's legendary cheapness extends to job-site health care: There is not so much as a Band-Aid on the tool truck. "I have a small kit in my car," I say, wondering if it's still there. It's been some time since I've even looked. It is a very rudimentary kit that came with the car when I bought it.

We walk out to my trunk and I get a first look at Alex's hand. It is a ball of red by this point, with a dark red spot where the finish nail entered his index finger.

"It hurts like hell," Alex says, "hit right to the bone."

"Jeez," I say, cringing, but curious.

"I had to yank it back out." The finger is plumping like a Ball Park frank, blood rushing into the injured area. I swab it with an alcohol patch and Alex sucks in air through his teeth. "Man," he says, exhaling. I dress it with some gauze and first aid tape as Alex explains how much more it hurt than when he shot himself with a framing nailer.

My Florence Nightingale moment has made Chris suspicious of me all over again. "Where'd you learn to do that?" he asks. Rather than mention my college flirtation with premed or my time volunteering in a hospital, I say simply, "Used to be an MD."

"Probably were," he says, shaking his head.

But I soon learn what has really set Chris's mind working. "Mr. Clean seemed all worked up this morning," I say, as we walk back toward the house. "I thought he was gonna bust a gasket, never seen him like that."

"He was asking about people's experience levels."

This doesn't sound good. "Why?"

"Said he was paying for all experienced hands."

Gulp. "What crew doesn't have apprentices?"

"That's what I told him. But he was pissed about some of the screwing around." I think how hard I laughed, seeing Markus Gorilla Glue Julien's hammer handle when he wasn't looking. Another favorite prank of theirs is to nail each other's tool belts to the sawhorses during break.

"He's hardly here, how would he know?"

"I don't know, but he knew things I know he wasn't here to see."

That made it clear. A spy. "Gotta be the clean-up guy, it's always the clean-up guy." He laughs as I parrot his own line back to him. With the Mr. Clean conversation fresh on his mind, Chris calls Ray aside and says he wants the two of us to work on some of the single-bead window casing that has just arrived. And he wants the pace to quicken. Ray growls his agreement, but says he's going to lunch first.

"That fuckin' guy."

Ray and I are sitting in the front seat of his red Acura, parked at the beach, eating our sandwiches. He's still fuming about Chris's admonishment, and the larger fact that he holds rank on him.

"I used to run crews. Big ones, twenty-five guys."

"Yeah?"

"I don't know where the fuck he gets off telling me to move faster."

"Well, pressure from . . ."

"I mean, what the fuck? He thinks he knows how to get this done."

"Why don't you run a crew now?" I ask him, trying to change conversation.

"I dunno." He stares out across the chaotic surf. "I could . . ." Then he trails off. He reaches for a lighter. He takes a hit, holds it, and silently offers the joint to me, fighting to keep his breath in.

"I don't smoke, but thanks."

"Not even . . ."

"Not even. I'd be asleep on a couch for the rest of the afternoon." *Or I'd cut my thumb off*, I think.

By the time we make it back to the house Ray is sailing. The pot has energized him inexplicably.

"Call me a number!"

"If you want I can cut," I offer. There's been enough bloodshed for one day.

"Fuck it, let's go. Gotta pick up the pace." He's mockingly bouncing on his toes, like a prizefighter.

"Sixty-five and seven eighths."

"Long point?"

"Short to short."

"Gotcha." Ray grabs a sixteen-foot length of preprimed finger-jointed single-bead pine, propellers it around the room and cuts two forty-five-degree cuts. He passes it to me with a lateral football toss and I slap it up against the window jam. It's several inches short. I pull out my tape.

"I said sixty-five and seven, Ray. You cut fifty-seven and five."

"Fuck. Gimme that." I give it to him, but it's pointless, he can't add inches to it. He tosses it under the sawhorses out of sight. He cuts another. "There!"

There nothing. "You cut the same thing."

"Fuck."

"Sixty-five and seven eighths, okay?"

He cuts aggressively, angrily; the line on the board is rough. "Here."

"Better, this is sixty-five and five eighths."

"Man you're fucking me up," he says, grabbing the board and tossing it under the horses. We are in a faraway corner of the house, but Ray still does his best to hide the piles of miscut trim. *That's* a professional.

The afternoon goes on like this, with Ray refusing to cede the saw and destroying lumber in a pot-fueled offensive. My worry is no longer that he will hurt himself, but that his bad habits will torpedo me. My romantic reflections on carpentry this morning seem distant and malformed, like something I'd read long ago and idealized in the remembering.

"How's it goin'?" Chris is doing a pass-through to check on our progress.

"Great," Ray growls, "we're crankin'." I look around and see we've completed a window and a half. Chris catches my disbelief.

"Keep at it, okay?"

"Yeah. Hey, just wanted to let you know, I gotta pull out a little early tomorrow," I say.

"*Again?*" he bristles.

"Doctor's appointment," I lie.

"Jesus. Kojak is all over me. I need people here, *working.*"

"Sorry, man, last time."

In truth, I have to race up to Connecticut to meet Susan. Now that the lease on our apartment has officially expired and nothing to replace it has been secured, we are moving our belongings from Manhattan to her parents' garage. It's mildly embarrassing for both of us. Maybe more than mildly. We're not moving home, we tell ourselves, we're house-sitting. Susan's parents are leaving the country for an extended trip and we'll take care of the pets during August. We kid ourselves that this is economical, since we will be saving a month or two in rent—until we find something new—and we can dedicate that much more to the renovation. But honestly, it all has the whiff of failure to me. *I married your daughter, but do you mind if we camp in your house for a while?* It feels one mullet and two thrown chairs away from *The Jerry Springer Show.*

Driving from Long Island, I chew at the ironies of our life. We are home owners, but we are homeless. I feel isolated and alone, yet numerous friends and family are providing free places to stay while we fix up our dump. We are moving to the country for more simplicity, and yet are stuck in the bureaucratic hornet's nest of the building department. Working to make something we can enjoy is becoming more and more unenjoyable—the pressures and roadblocks and differences of opinion are tearing at us. The distance between us makes us yearn for each other all week, but by the time we see each other we are so stressed out that we carp at each other. We are pouring money into an investment, and we only feel poorer, that much closer to bankruptcy. We tied our lives together and in our almost single-minded dedication to build something together we are feeling increasingly estranged from everyone, including each other.

"How are you?" I ask Susan, as I climb out of the car.

"Good, you?"

"Good good. Hot."

"Tell me about it. The office air conditioner went on sabbatical today."

"Oof."

"Exactly."

"Alex shot himself with a Paslode. *That* was interesting."

"Oh, God," Susan winces.

We're trying to be bright conversationalists and loving spouses, but after the salutary kiss we descend into the end-of-week collapse. We drive to Kazu, a Japanese restaurant in South Norwalk, Connecticut, and sit and sweat bar-side. Returning from the restroom, I try to make light of our plight.

"Hiya, you from around here?"

Susan plays along. "Actually, no, just visiting."

"Can I buy you a drink?"

"I don't know, *can* you?"

It's a joke, but it's not funny to me. It hits too close to home. I know who will be paying for dinner tonight.

"Did Goodnough show up to finish?" Susan asks, quickly changing the subject.

I pretend a blank, you-know-that's-a-stupid-question stare. I don't mention that I didn't call, intentionally, because we're not ready for him until "other issues" are resolved.

"Jesus! Did you even call them?"

"I left a message," I lie, "but for what, to hear their excuses? Besides, to fix the subfloor in the downstairs bath—"

"We've gotta stay on them."

"Great, I'll phone rather than build. That'll speed things up."

The teppa maki and shrimp tempura roll do little to cool things off. Susan and I are barely fending off fighting with each other. Shouldn't we be conspiratorially planning the demise of the plumber, building inspector, and the entire Architectural Review Board?

"It just has to get done," Susan peals. "We just have to get it *done*."

A hot button, this pronoun slippage, using *we* to mean *you*, and I flare.

"This is madness. You want to sell the house? I want out. Let's sell the damn house!"

"We can't," Susan says calmly.

"Oh, I can!" I say. We're beat, and already too far in debt. We should cut our losses, regroup, and try a different house later. "I'm ready to sell the whole damn . . ."

"No, we *can't*," she repeats, firmly. "It's not legal to sell it in this condition. I already looked into it."

For six months now, Susan and I have been slogging along. Yet the "fixer-upper" we bought is so far from being fixer-upped that a tar-paper shack on Tobacco Road would seem like the Taj Mahal right about now. Despite the seemingly endless toil, we can still see every stud in our "house." Every rafter, every empty electrical receptacle. There is only the most minimal evidence of plumbing, a mockery. The house is in medias res, laid open to the elements; when the skies open, the floors get wet.

The more optimistic and big-picture-oriented among us (Susan) thought we would be planting rhododendrons beneath the picture window last month; the more pessimistic and process-oriented among us (Lawrence) is developing a really, *really* bad habit of dwelling on all the obstacles that stand in our way.

Even worse, in stark contradiction to the fact that we *own* the house (for the moment, let's shelve the distinction that the bank truly owns it, lest we really get depressed), it feels as though we have no control or ownership. We are held hostage, not in our house, but outside of our house. Like a cork floating atop a stream with no control of its own progress or speed, we are the playthings of the plumber who won't show up, the electrician who has walked away from the job, and most often the building department's shenanigans. We are but renovation sinners in the hands of an angry god. And now that we have decamped to Connecticut for a few days, we actually have time to decompress, look at things in perspective, and appreciate how mad we've become, and how totally insane the process is. From this safe distance, suddenly I don't care. At least not as much. I'm ready to take a new approach: push back.

"What? What's the matter?" Susan asks nervously, pausing to

finish buttering her bagel. I hold my hand up to silence her. *Wait.*
I'm picking up our telephone messages.

"An 'urgent' call from Sybil the Dread, who says there is a
problem with our plans, and wants us to call as soon as possible."

"What problem?" Her tone startles the dog.

"I have no idea. She didn't say."

Susan's knife is down, bagel unbuttered. "So what should we
do?"

"Eat."

"She said it was urgent."

"I'm going to finish my breakfast, then we're going to take
Sundance for a walk. Time for some push back. I'm tired of
leaping every time they say jump."

"But if there's a problem . . ."

"There's always a problem with them. When hasn't there been
a problem? Hello, *six inches!*" I say, referring to a slight erratum
on the plans for the first building permit. We had submitted a
survey that said our house was actually six inches closer to the
Division Street side lot line, eleven feet rather than eleven and a
half feet. Perfectly legal code wise, and more or less in the "town's
favor," but incorrect nonetheless. Since we were both in the city
at the time of that urgent call from Sybil, we asked that she
simply put ".5" next to the "11" on the plans. "No," she said, she
didn't have time to correct applications. In terms of unhelpful-
ness and petty tyranny, Sybil could teach Italian train conductors
a thing or two.

"You do remember the six-inch episode?" I repeat.

"Remember? I'm the one who drove two hours to correct it."

"Exactly. Pass the jam."

A few hours later, after walking the dog and taking a hot
shower, I call the alarmist in Sag Harbor to see what's what. I tell
Sybil that we are nowhere near Sag Harbor at the moment,

staying with friends since we are homeless, and that I don't think I'll be able to make it in for some time. A curveball to be sure. She pauses audibly.

"Could you send your architect in then?" A laughable suggestion since we don't have one. I certainly can't send in the mad draftsman.

"I wouldn't feel comfortable with that," I say.

"This has to get resolved."

"What is it exactly that needs fixing?"

"Well . . ." For the first time it dawns on me that she doesn't even know. "Can you hold for Mr. Smothers?"

I hold for all of five seconds, the time I imagine it takes Mr. Smothers to move his feet, careful so as not to knock the talking fish—"Get off your bass!" "I got a haddock!"—off the side of his desk.

He answers, laughing, "Ha-ha, so you're homeless, huh?"

Did he really just say that? "Out rattling a tin cup," I reply, trying to keep it light, though I desperately want to reach through the line and clock him and his bass.

"And you're not comfortable with your architect?"

"Not exactly, I'd prefer . . ."

"Well, this has to get straightened out."

"What is 'it' that needs straightening?"

"There's a discrepancy in the south elevation, makes the addition look like it is three feet too close to the Division Street side."

"That's impossible."

The bear is waking up. "*Huh?*" he says, like I just called him an idiot.

"The addition goes *straight* back from the house. For it to be closer, it would have to curve or jut out. It doesn't. The house is one simple rectangle."

"That's not what the numbers say. When are you going to be out here next to look at this?"

"I don't know," I say, marshaling my best push back, "things are at a standstill. Have you seen the house lately? It is one big plastic sheet." I say this thinking there is an implied responsibility on the building inspector for buildings to get built, that *my* abandoned property will reflect badly on *him*. Ice so thin has never been skated upon.

"No, I haven't."

"Well, it's a dump. And until we can get approval to move ahead on the rest of the project . . ." It's a veiled threat, and a pathetic one, but it does soften his strident tone.

"Do you have a fax? If you can look at this maybe we can get this straightened out."

"That would be great," I say, thinking it would be easier to get a trio of glass pyramids built within the center courtyard of the Louvre.

Susan and I spend the rest of the morning researching and planning—the cheapest way we know how, calling toll-free help lines. In addition to the Internet, which provides a wealth of options hitherto unimaginable, toll-free advice is a great building tool, especially considering that the question you need answered is *never* one of those damnable FAQs.

Today's specific task involves resolving our heating issue. Now that we have ripped all of the cast-iron baseboard heating out of the house, will we be able to move it around according to our new plan? Or is there another answer that will efficiently and afford-ably permit us to have heating and air-conditioning? We have ruled out the deli-nouveau aesthetic as an option, and we're heartened to hear from another heating contractor that we could duct the house for both. Matz-Rightway—"We install the best and fix the rest"—sends out Brandon to give us a bid. Matz-Rightway is successful enough to have a Brandon, someone who exclusively meets with builders—from know-nothing knuckleheads like me to exacting contractors.

Brandon is pencil necked and nerdy, and I immediately know this is going to be trouble when he starts measuring everything to the inch. Most heating and air guys will come in, eyeball the cubic footage on the job, and give you a rough number. Not so, Brandon. He lectures me on latent cooling (removing moisture) and sensible cooling (reducing temperature); he inquires about the R value of the insulation of every wall and every ceiling; he measures windows and doors to know exactly how much heat is going to escape; and he drives off *without* giving me a quote. "I will have to do some calculations," he says, tapping pencil to clipboard, "then we'll see where we are." I have visions of huge walls of old IBM computers, tapes spooling left and right, churning out Brandon calculations and Matz-Rightway bids night and day.

Brandon calls three days later with his prognosis: two air systems divided into three zones "with their own trunks and branch lines, of course," five tons of air power and *two* outdoor units. It occurs to me that he has confused our house with another quote he is working on. "You recall that our house has only 1,600 square feet?" I say, thinking it will jog his memory, make evident his mistake.

"Oh, yes, I remember. The calculations are what they are." To me the system seems massively overpowered, as if our tiny Cape Cod is going to be transformed by Matz-Rightway into one enormous Sub-Zero refrigerator crossed with a high-powered Viking stove, a Frankenstein of air-handling. I foresee walls being blown out by the force of it. "What is all that horsepower going to run me, Brandon?" I ask with trepidation.

"The number I have is twenty thousand, plus or minus."

"That's the number you have?"

"Yes."

"Does anyone else there have a different number?"

He laughs and tells me to consider my other bids. "Let me know if we're within shouting distance."

You can count on it.

"Just so I'm clear, Brandon, that's the traditional system, right?"

"Yes. The other would probably be an additional nine or ten."

Thirty grand? That's the Massive-Wrongway.

The "other" system is something Susan read about in a home magazine article: high-velocity air-conditioning. Initially I resisted the idea, not on any careful merits, mind you, but on the simple decision-making consideration that *it's not her area.* Never mind that she's making the mortgage payments, what does a wife know about ducting? Finally I read the article, when she thrusts it in front of me for the fifth time, and damn it if it doesn't seem like she is on to something.

This morning we are calling the manufacturer, Unico, aiming to deal directly, cut out the Brandon, and secure a solution that works within the tight confines of our house. The added bonus—but by no means a fiercely held belief—is that for the first time, ever, we will stay within the budgeted costs for one of our tasks. Well, we can't be faulted for hoping, can we?

A high-velocity air system works like a conventional system with trunks and branch lines, but there are a greater number of them and they are smaller. Capillaries instead of veins. Small insulated tubes, roughly three and a half inches in diameter, snake numerously throughout the house and get warm or cool air to each room. Rather than one box vent, there are several small openings the size of a half-dollar at opposite sides of the room. Due to their number and the increased speed of the traveling air, according to the sales rep, circulation is increased and a room's temperature from top to bottom and left to right is more consistent. This sounds good to me, but I honestly don't know why. I don't recall the last time I complained of living room wind shear, or harsh atmospheric variations in the dining area. Nevertheless, someone at Unico has been giving this some serious noodling and I'm the gladder for it. Similarly, when I am told that a high-velocity air system does a better job of latent cooling, I tell the rep, "I would have expected that," thrilling in my surface knowledge of home heating and air-conditioning.

Our next step is to find someone who can install the system for us. We find a guy named Krantz in *Dan's Papers*, the local circular. Krantz is huge. I'm not talking in the business huge, I'm talking Incredible Hulk huge. Massive. He fills the front doorway. When he gets inside, the joists creak, the stair treads groan in lament—I literally fear for our house. He walks around to learn the layout, tilting his head, bowing his shoulders in every doorway. Understanding that this guy has to bend, twist, and squeeze into tight spaces to get his job done makes me think someone gave him some very cruel advice on career day.

In addition to being the world's largest heating and cooling professional, Krantz is an endless repository of information. For this reason we will come to refer to him as Mike "Bad News" Krantz. He would drive us crazy if it were not for the fact that he is so consistently right. He's also the most enterprising and committed person we will work with.

"I called your guy," he says, referring to the Unico rep we had spoken to about ordering the high-velocity system for our house.

"Great, we—"

"But then I did some research. An engineer from Unico left a while ago to start his own company, improve on what he had designed for them. His company is called SpacePak."

"No kidding," I say. "Were they in that article you read, Susan?"

She shakes her head. "Only Unico."

"So I called them up," Krantz continues, "was on with the guy for two hours. It seems like the better system. Improved insulation on the tubing, longer dampeners at the end to minimize noise."

I'm sold. I'm astounded that you can talk about air-conditioning for two hours, but I'm sold.

"That sounds great," Susan says, "but what is it gonna cost?" She clenches her jaw, preparing for the worst.

"Should run about eight grand."

"The system alone, or with your installation?"

"Total."

I look over at Susan and she's beaming like we just won Powerball. It was the first item in our loosely organized budget that was on target, the one we wouldn't have to lose sleep over. Even better, we'd be able to install in our house something called SpacePak.

Four Square

The tighter our finances become, the touchier we become when any cavalier subcontractor seeks to separate us from our diminishing funds. Some tasks scream for money well spent. Insulation, for one, is deplorable work that is relatively inexpensive. In other words, a good job to farm out: Anyone we hire will do it more quickly than we ever could. Shingling the house is another laborious task we think will be more intelligent to give over to professionals. It's tedious, complicated in spots, and time-consuming.

Then the quotes come in. When a representative from Martin's Roofing and Siding, a local specialist in all things cedar shingle, blandly informs us, without even bothering to measure our house, that it will cost twenty-five thousand dollars, I am incredulous.

"We have a lot of windows," I suggest, but he shoots me down almost before the words exit my mouth.

"Just more to cut around. A wash really."

I ask how many shingles he thinks we'll need and he answers, "Forty squares." I roll the number around in my head, unsure whether that is a lot or a little. All I know is twenty-five thousand dollars is a hell of a lot, an insulting amount of money. Does he really think I'm going to hand over that kind of money to *shingle?* If it means putting two nails through each shingle while lining them in course, any idiot could do it.

That is how we become those idiots.

It's a beautiful day, in a way that screams for outdoor work, and Susan and I are ready to shingle. We have already pulled out all the old windows, reframed the walls, and installed the new ones. Shingling is the next logical task to tackle. We're going to save a bundle, we tell ourselves, and I figure it's a great piecemeal job to keep Susan occupied when she starts talking about design considerations. Idle hands are Martha Stewart's playground and all that.

We race down to Riverhead Building Supply to get some supplies. I order a few pounds of galvanized shingle nails and four squares of shingles. Four seems like a good number to get us started, and the most I figure we can squeeze into the trunk and back seat of the BMW. There are great towers of red cedar shingle in the yard, and we pore over them like we are picking out floor tiles.

"Why does this say sixteen?" Susan asks.

God, will the meddling and second-guessing never cease? "Why does what say sixteen?"

"It says, 'Sixteen bundles of cedar perfections.' "

"It doesn't say that. I ordered four."

She gives me the what-I-can't-read? look and holds out the ticket.

Sixteen bundles. Four bundles in a square. Four squares. She starts to chuckle.

"Shit," I say, laughing, pretending to do the math on my fingers. "Four of these bundles make a square. I ordered twelve too many."

"What do we want to do?"

"Let's squeeze them in," I say, like they're made of marshmallow. I cram several in the trunk, four more in the backseat, and a couple in the passenger seat. It's a real pain because the bundles are soaked and heavy from the rain, and I have to pass the shingles in from the driver's side.

Something dawns on Susan. "Where am I going to sit?"

I look at her. I look at the car. I look at my wife. I look at my shingles.

"Hmm."

"Hmm."

"Guess we'll pull some out?"

She nods.

I pick up the ticket and head back to the counter with my tail between my legs. The idiot who doesn't know bundle from square.

Miraculously we make it home intact and in good spirits. Attaching cedar shingles to this house, we both know, will create a miraculous transformation. It will also enter our humble little house into a long history of the venerable wood. King Solomon constructed his famous temple from the cedars of Lebanon. American Indians of the Pacific Northwest used the wood for totem poles, canoes, and tribal longhouses. Despite calling cedars "trees of life" they also used them for coffins. Today, we'll concentrate on the longhouse metaphors.

We unload the bundles and I put on my tool belt. Even more of a neophyte than I am, Susan works with a hammer in one hand and a brown paper bag of nails in the other. We have decided to start on the back side of the house, well out of sight, to get the hang of it. But it's not the nailing that worries me, it is the leveling. Since shingles wrap around the entirety of a house in courses, it is imperative to keep them level lest they begin to look like rolling waves and haphazard lines. This is always most noticeable at the corners when corner boards are not used. Corner boards are, simply put, boards that cover a corner, thus necessitating that shingles only run up to them, rather than up to each other. Some call corner boards a better solution, others call them a cheat. I call them a cheat, because I want to make life hard on myself and "weave" the shingled corners. Weaving refers to the fact that in each course one side of the corner has to overlap the other, so when you alternate the overlapping—the only sane solution, really—it has a weaved appearance. A stretch perhaps, but if anyone can come up with a better name they are guaranteed immortality in the most minor of ways.

The next matter is how to line up the shingles: where to start, how to keep them level, and how to prepare for obstacles like windows. A course of shingles is typically five and half to six inches high when you overlap them, and it is aesthetically preferable to avoid courses of very small increments around windows, doors, or at the top of a wall. One option is a "story pole," where the courses are marked, after deciding on the exact level of the first course, and then checking them around the house with the pole. It can be adjusted slightly up or down to accommodate for short courses.

A more antiquarian and painstaking method, the one proffered by Bad News Krantz, is to wrap a clear plastic tube around the house. The tube is not entirely full of water, so water bubbles act as a natural level. Logical yes, but the whole contraption seems so ungainly to me as to be laughable. I've seen people do it, but I can't testify to their mental state. The results, however, are flawless.

Susan and I have a last-minute huddle on just how the hell we are going to approach this, and how we are going to keep things level. I'm apprehensive about getting started and want a third or fourth opinion, since what we start in the back is going to influence the rest of the house. Then Susan's action plan wins out. She had spoken to Dexter about the shingling initiative and he gave her a quick lesson. This lesson was quickly forgotten since no notes were taken. So Susan's action plan is: We're gonna wing it.

Cut from the heartwood, the best part of the tree, cedar shingles are beautiful in a rustic way, and aromatic enough to beat moths into submission. As the scent envelops us, we start to feel like serious home builders. We get our six-foot level in place and start nailing our first course. Once this is set, we can measure an additional six inches up, snap a chalk line to guide us, and nail away. Only occasionally will we have to double-check level.

We also need to check the *contour* of each shingle, examine each for cupping. Shingles have two potential faults: checking (splitting) and cupping (rolling of the shingle toward the center). It is preferable to have any cupping occur toward the house, rather than away (which would look flared), and we begin examining each shingle as if we are forensic specialists. Needless to say, CSI: Cedar Shingle brings our progress to a crawl.

My head begins to spin, and I ask Susan's opinion on every shingle. "Is that the right side?"

"Lemme see." She holds it up, angling it slightly to divine its line. "No, I think it's this way. See that curve?"

I don't see a damn thing. "Are you looking at the bottom or the side?"

"Which one is the one we are looking for?"

"I dunno, the bottom I think." At least that's what *I've* been looking at.

She gazes at me expressionlessly. "Nail it."

"I like your style."

Once we find our rhythm we begin to move fast. Susan nails along the length of the house and I fiddle with weaving the corners, marking the specific widths and ripping the shingles freehand on the table saw. We are meticulous in our approach, giving just the right amount of space between shingles and alternating the widths to make it look natural.

By the end of the first day Susan has completed most of the rear wall. It looks magnificent, flawlessly put together and attractive. We think it wise that we got our practice here, and will move methodically around the rest of the house. Months later we will realize that no other wall received the same care, nor can claim the same result. That said, all four walls keep the rain out just fine.

The Parent Trap

Months later, as the leaves begin to fall, my parents make a journey out to the east end to stay for a few weeks and help us with the renovation. Their arrival has been delayed repeatedly by us, to the point that they were getting a little offended, like we didn't want them here. We *were* eager for their help, but we simply had no place to put them. After Pam rented her house for August, we decamped to Connecticut, then moved down the street to Mark and Gary's while they were away on business. Subsequently, we stayed on Shelter Island while friends, Joe and Sue Hine, traveled in Indonesia. It felt like circuit training for Bedouins. Our moving from house to house was also hazardous, for each home was larger and more expensively appointed than what we hoped to build ourselves. Residing temporarily in nice homes filled us with cabinet covetousness and tile envy. Staying for free was filling us with grander ideas and getting very costly. Each time my parents called to arrange their arrival we were in a new place, and when Sue and Joe's trip was cut short we were briefly back at Mark and Gary's. Something had to change, or we would need to hire a scheduler. Thankfully, Norm and Ellen rescued us, offering the Sag Harbor home they don't use in the off-season. Finally, after months of embarrassment, we could tell my parents that we had a borrowed place where they could stay. We are so eager to be in our own home, we promise ourselves—no matter what—that we will be out of Norm and Ellen's and into our own house in two months. The upper floor needs some moldling and paint, but it could be liveable in an extremely rustic sort of way. The ground floor is schizophrenic: The front living room is almost finished, the kitchen and addition still show their studs. Susan and I just installed the insulation, trying to conserve capital on even the most onerous of tasks.

The arrival of my parents promises not only easily exploited labor—given their enthusiasm for home renovation work—but genuine expertise as well. My mother has transformed a late-career foray in design consulting into a full-fledged contracting business. She uses all of her five-foot-two-inch frame to boss around temperamental (sexist?) professionals and meat-headed lunks five times her body mass. So far she hasn't been slugged. My father's résumé boasts not one basement renovation, but two, suggesting he's keen on this stuff, stupid, or my mother was honing her foreman skills at home first. My childhood recollections are of him going downstairs one color and coming up another, either dusted white from drywall dust, or with streams and tributaries of blood coursing down a forearm. Seeing blood we would recoil, fear for his life, and wail piercing lamentations. Then he would deliver a characteristically diffident summation of events, "Think I caught my thumb with the hammer."

Jazzed to show them nothing but the most considerate welcome, we tell them to meet us at Home Depot Expo in Commack. Expo has a wealth of items that are not at an ordinary run-of-the-mill Home Depot. For whatever reason, Susan is determined. My forces of "push back" are powerless against her. We race through aisles of tile and on to the lighting department, darting like a prodded and very confused herd. My parents give their own additional good advice, doubling the decision-making joviality. And, let me tell you, I am doing one hell of a job of jovial, convinced that we are squandering time shopping when we could be *building*. In the space of less than fifteen minutes my parents are transported from "good to see you" to "how do we get away from here?" I snip at Susan, whose broad-mindedness toward porch lighting is bordering on the pathological—the latest attractive piece being the *most* attractive one. Then we turn a corner and discover lock sets.

"Oh, we should look at these," Susan enthuses.

"Or we could put the door in first," I snap. My parents both take a step back.

"We're going to need locks," Susan says.

"True. But today the back end of the house is completely torn open and there is *nothing to steal*."

"God, I was only trying to help."

No doubt she is. She is working from a good place. But, at the same time, our basement is getting cluttered with stuff that either has no known use or was bought in a fit of fancy and is now less usable than a claw-foot tub. Worse than unusable, it will take another trip—time wasted—to return it. The finish line for our project recedes farther and farther away with each passing day.

"Wow, look at these lights," Susan says.

I glower.

"You don't like them?"

"Why would I buy crap just to cross that item off the list? 'Cause that's what that is, crap. And we'll buy it today then decide in four weeks that it is junk and we will go all the way to friggin' Commack to return them."

"Jesus, what's gotten into you?"

By this time my parents, who are staunch midwestern non-confrontationalists, are entering the early stages of shock. They do their level best to deny what is taking place, looking to the walls, to the floor, over at that lady pulling her kid off the pile of Persian rugs, anything to politely avoid the scene in front of them. Less than a year ago they witnessed Susan and I profess our eternal love for each other, and now they stand in averted-glance disbelief as we carp at each other in front of designer lighting knockoffs. It gets so bad that I have to make overtly jokey remarks to calm the waters—ha-ha-ha—and let everyone know that the whole lighting fiasco was just a misunderstanding, and ages ago.

My mood brightens as we head out the front door. Until I look into the cart. Somehow Susan has smuggled four carriage lights, two pedestal sinks, and a Baldwin lock-set past me.

We make it back to Sag Harbor late in the afternoon, just as the light is beginning to fade and a chill is entering the air. We give Barb and Cliff a quick tour of the premises—since a longer tour would require a larger house—and wind up in the basement.

The atmosphere has unmistakably changed. With a sympathetic tone ordinarily reserved for wakes and fallen soufflés, my mother looks at us and says, "I had no idea."

"What?" I ask.

"I just had no idea. That things were this ba—. . . that you had taken on so much."

I joke with the contractor, "Didn't we say 'gut job,' Mom?"

"Yes, but I just had no *idea*."

"What do you think, Cliff?" Susan asks, teasing out his unvarnished opinion.

"Well," he says, "you've definitely got some work here."

"Then let's get to it," I suggest, corralling everyone back upstairs.

I huddle us in front of the project at hand: the side door. I've been fixated all day on getting home and getting this damn door in so that we can cross it off the list. It is progress, and I want to nail it into place before Susan reconsiders which way the door should swing. As we maneuver the door from the living room to the kitchen area it dawns on me, for the first time, that I don't know how we are going to accomplish this. Dexter gave us advice on windows, but doors? Nothing. Nor have I done a single door installation while working for Floyd. And this case is a little tricky, since the ground elevation outside the door is six feet down, and the side stairs have not yet been built.

To make matters worse, we measure the door jamb and the rough opening and discover that they are the same. Exactly the same. There is no way that that door is going to get into that opening short of some celestial force elevating and sailing the door into place perfectly plumb and perfectly level. With no margin for error there will be errors. Everyone looks at the guilty party, the one who roughed the opening. Me.

"Um, well . . . ," I say, thinking aloud, "we can't really cut into the floor, especially since we're putting new wide-plank pine down. The sill would be lower than the floor. I guess we could shave a quarter inch off the header . . ." I let the idea dangle there, hoping someone, anyone, will say *Good idea*. No one does. Instead we all crowd into the door opening like the answer is mysteriously hidden within the archway. But we're not finding anything other than how to get four vaudevillians stuck between a couple two-by-fours. My mother, who is apprehensive about appearing to take charge of the project or offer too much unsolicited advice, offers an oblique suggestion. "I've never heard my guys wanting to cut into a header."

"I don't *want* to cut into the header, I just don't see another way."

"What is that up there?" Barb says, studying the header.

"A two-by-twelve. Beefy." I could have gotten away with a two-by-ten, even a two-by-eight for the span of three feet, but since a two-by-twelve landed where I needed it to, it was a fast and strong solution. A trick I had picked up from Dexter.

"I suppose it wouldn't hurt to cut off a inch . . . ," Barb says, with a toss of the eyebrows. That's good enough for me.

"Let's do it. Sawzall!" I call out, like a surgeon, to no one in particular. Though actually, I will use the Sawzall second, to clean up, after I have trimmed the header with a circular saw.

Once the rough header is ready, we move on to the business of getting the door into place without dropping it out onto the lawn six feet below. It is decided that Cliff and I will tilt it out sideways, muscle it into place, and tilt it back into position from the bottom to the top. Susan and my mother will be on ladders on the outside, guiding it into position and, should we drop it, getting squished. Cliff approves of the plan heartily. The sun is setting and light is getting scarce as we lift the door and move it outside the house. Once in place I check for plumb and level. It is neither.

"Can I nail it?" asks Susan, who holds the Paslode finish nailer and wants to tack the door framing into place against the house. Unlike a window, for which this is a good procedure, it is actually preferable to nail first through the jamb (stabilized with shims) into the header and jacks. But I don't know that yet, so we are nailing the thing off as if it were a window. Susan and Barb hang onto their ladders, approaching hypothermia, judging by the grumbling on the other side of the door.

"Not yet," I say. Cliff and I are trying to figure out why it's tight on one side and not the other and, worse, why when we shim the lower left corner it gets tighter in the upper right corner, against all expectation. When the jamb is level, the door won't open; when the jam is out of plumb, it swings open of its own accord. The damn thing is turning into the Devil's rhombus. We try the shim on the opposite side, which helps plumb, but has now thrown it back out of level.

Susan is getting impatient. "Can I nail it *now?*"

"No."

"It's dark, Lawrence, and it's getting *cold* out here."

"Nailing it when it's crooked won't make it warmer, I promise you." This is not received well by Susan. Mom, meanwhile, is curiously quiet, either frozen or fallen off her ladder and dead. Then someone—all I know is that it wasn't me—suggests we screw the jamb through the door hinge, into the stud . . . gently. This will pull the door into position and give greater strength to the whole apparatus over time. It works like a charm, save for the fact that I have only one brass screw long enough, and it strips easily as brass screws do. We look at our work, improved but not perfected, and decide that there will be time enough tomorrow to buy more screws and really have at it.

When we return to the job site the following morning it is revealed, in the light of day, as a real mess. Always eager to build rather than clean, Susan and I have not done an estimable job of removing excess dust and wood scrap, organizing lumber remnants, or putting all the tools and supplies in a fashion that is remotely thought out. Indeed, I have veered on tantrum more than once searching like a puppy for his tail when I cannot put to hand the particular tool I need. Thankfully—or so I think—Barb is going to take this upon herself. "A clean work site is a safe work site," she intones, sounding motherly and foremanlike simultaneously, and fires up the Shop-Vac.

Susan, Cliff, and I stand in front of the large picture window, finished with our job site breakfast of cream-cheesed bagels and coffee. The high-pitched drone of the Shop-Vac adds to the freakish vision we have out the window. A faux-wood-paneled station wagon glides down Division Street, driverless. Fishing paraphernalia is strapped to the roof racks. "D'you see that?" Susan asks.

I'm not sure what I just saw. "The headless scalloper?"

Cliff shakes the remaining sleep from his head and leans toward the window to watch it pass. "And it's pulling into your drive."

We move around the back to get a better look. Sure enough, it's pulled in. A door opens slightly, then flings open all the way with a kick. Still all we can see are a couple of legs, the side of a buttocks, and a magnificently rotund belly, which is heaving. The gut pitches, rolls, and flops like an electroshocked grouper, until finally a beefy hand grabs the door frame and yanks the entire torso upward.

Arnie Smothers, the building inspector, pops up red faced and winded. He's here for the framing inspection, to check that we have restudded the house according to code, before we insulate the place.

He enters magisterially, smelling like a lobster trap. He walks with show confidence, unintentionally mimicking the Great Oz. "Morning," he says, not so much to us, but to the subflooring. He peers at the top plates and the rafters, making it clear he is already on the job.

My father's sincere curiosity stops him in his tracks. "Having some trouble with that car seat?"

"Darn thing's shot. I'm practically riding in the backseat."

"Yeah, we saw," Cliff says. "Maybe we could prop it in place with a two-by-four." I think of making some crack that it wouldn't be up to code, but I resist. If he's as humorless as a cop, I don't want to risk it. Instead, I signal that I'll show him what's going on, what we've done. He asks about the large hole cut in the closet, under the stairwell to the second floor. I tell him that's where the original stairs were and where we are going to put them back. "Gonna be tight," he says gruffly. We move to the living room and he studies where the rafters land on the top plate. At least I think that's where he's looking. "Gonna need some hurricane clips," he says, and I scribble it down on the notepad I brought just for this purpose, and chirp, "Will do."

We travel around the rest of the house without incident and he heads back to his car. Cliff is standing nearby, proudly waving good-bye as Smothers cruises off bolt upright.

With the morning's excitement out of the way, I enlist Cliff to help me with the deck footings. A crap job to be sure, but he doesn't care, he's happy to help. We are putting a six-by-twenty-foot porch on the front of the house, and we need to sink some concrete footers at five-foot intervals, far enough out (five feet) from the house to support the majority of the deck, but back far enough from the front of the deck so as not to be visible once we attach a trellis to the bottom of the whole contraption. We dig holes large enough to accommodate twelve-inch Sonotubes (they look like giant toilet-paper-roll tubes), which will contain the cement in strong cylinders. A twelve-inch tube three feet in depth demands a lot of concrete, and mixing it is a real chore. Cliff and I alternate fighting the stuff with a garden rake and a spade and hauling more eighty-pound bags of Sakrete from the backyard. I wonder if there is anything heavier than wet concrete. From the feeling in my back the answer is no. Meanwhile Barb vacuums incessantly, so much so that I am beginning to wonder about the electrical bill. Her "clean work site" ethos is off the charts: We're dustless; the power tools are arranged alphabetically on the living room floor; the tarps are folded and stacked like bed linens.

Working in a bent position, Cliff suddenly pops up, attentive as a prairie dog. "Who is that guy?" he whispers.

"Who?"

"That guy," he repeats, trying to point discreetly with his temple.

A nondescript guy, maybe five-eight and 175 pounds, wearing khakis, soft-soled tan shoes, and a blue windbreaker, walks down Division Street away from town. He has mousy brown hair and thick glasses that from the side hide his eyes. He stares straight ahead, androidlike. A manila envelope is clutched under his left arm up high on his chest. His right arm hangs almost motionless by his side.

"That's Norman," I say.

"Probably the third time he's walked past."

"Just getting started."

"Who is he?"

"Neighbor, I think, from a few doors down Division Street. We call him Disorganized Norman. He walks back and forth all day long. I swear to God I think he goes to the dry cleaners to pick up his pants, brings them home, and then goes back for the shirt."

"He never looks over here."

"No. Rumor is he's got tunnel vision. That's why he doesn't drive."

"How do you know his name is Norman?"

"We don't," I concede, guiltily admitting we named him after Norman Bates. I look up and a red Kia Sportage zips up High Street. The driver cranes his neck severely to see us with his good eye; the other is behind an eye patch.

"And then there's that guy," I say, as the Kia accelerates out of sight.

"Who was that?"

"Previous owner. Schwartz. Drives by a couple times a week to see what we're doing."

Cliff asks, "Does he approve?"

"He never stops. Actually speeds up if he sees us."

"Sounds like a nut."

"One of many, Dad. Keep your eyes open and you might see Witchie Poo."

"Who the *hell* is Witchie Poo?"
"You'll see. Start mixing."

That afternoon, I run to Riverhead to pick up six more bags of Sakrete, and when I return I find that Cliff has completed another entire footer. The man is in his mid-sixties and he's a wall of steel. I wonder if his football days, his success on Rose Bowl squads for Michigan State University, contributed to his unstinting work ethic. Perhaps I am blocking incidents out, but I don't ever remember him grumbling about physical labor. This I see as a character flaw: Why in God's name squander an opportunity to rhapsodize about how bad you've got it? I know I have inherited (or learned), some of his reckless work ethic in terms of home improvement, but there is plenty about my father I don't understand. Initially he was going to visit alone, in a Disneyesque father-son home building and bonding scenario, that I looked forward to. Perhaps, over sweat-producing labor, I'd unlock some of the secrets of his life, how he has viewed his journey from bicycle polo on Detroit streets, to playing football in college, getting married, raising three kids, and then watching them swim out of the shallows into their own realities. Maybe he'd crack and talk about his life in an unedited way, forthrightly, like I've never heard him.

As things turned out, though, our twosome blossomed into a foursome. Susan was able to take the week off work, and my mother's projects at home were on hiatus. But it is not this population surge that interrupts me from learning more about Cliff.

He is scootching out the front door opening. From his seated position, Cliff pushes forward, hopping to the uneven ground. He lands badly, something goes crack, and he falls like a sack of grain, almost crushing Susan, who is trying to catch him. I run over. He looks both pained and on the verge of laughter, like he just wet himself.

"Uh-oh," he says, "I think something popped."

"Are you all right?" Susan asks.

"My ankle. I think I'm going to need help getting up."

"Just sit," I say. "Don't get up until we look at it."

Hearing the commotion, my mother runs over to meet us and we all stand over Cliff, staring at his feet.

"Oh my God, Cliff. Look at your ankle." Susan points to his swollen left ankle, the foot slightly splayed.

"That's the good one," Barb says. From years of running and really bad ski boots, neither of Cliff's ankles are ready for their close up. Now this right one juts out weirdly and looks even bigger than the left, bloated and reddened, like a grapefruit with a drinking problem.

"Oh, my G—" Susan begins, but I cut her a look.

"Help me up," Cliff says.

"Cliff!" I shout. Suddenly I'm the parent.

Two hours later, we are in Southampton hospital, and my father's nightshirt flutters behind him, revealing his bare back and a droopy pair of Fruit Of The Looms. I am helping him into the bathroom, holding him firmly by the arm and thinking, *I'm not ready for this*. One moment my father is besting me in concrete production, and the next I have visions of his later years, infirm or in a nursing home, with me struggling to be patient with his deterioration. I am not ready to acknowledge that he is no longer the pillar of strength I grew up with. He looks over to me, "Put the seat down for me, would ya?"

It does not help our apprehension that we are in Southampton hospital. Its reputation is less than sterling. Some say the hospital is responsible for killing Roy Lichtenstein, the artist, who lay in one of their beds with pneumonia and was so passively cared for that by the time they determined what he had it was too late. Thankfully Cliff does not have pneumonia.

After the initial concern about his welfare, and after the fear that the hospital would graft his ankle into some mongrel nightmare, we sit in his hospital room breathing sighs of relief and eating pasta imported from the local spaghetti emporium. His pain is subsiding, the surgery to screw his ankle back together went off without a hitch, and he will be discharged tomorrow. With death averted, I slide back into selfish sentiment: This is really going to slow things down. Thinking that my parents' visit would kick into gear a project that was already loathsomely behind schedule, I am suddenly confronted with not only trying to renovate a house, but with dealing with the loss of a worker and helping to care for an invalid. I recall hearing once that Eskimos would place their elders, when they ceased being productive, onto an ice floe and then nudge them away from shore. We prop Cliff in front of the television. The pain on his face is obvious, not from his ankle so much as being unable to contribute to the progress, and guilt about slowing things down. We console him the only way we know how: cold beer. That, and we promise that by the time he is healed and off his crutches he can come back and do some work.

It is not an empty promise. Not by any means. If anything, the workload is growing.

Change Orders

It is becoming clear to Susan and me that we are no longer the people we once were, nor the couple we used to be. Marriage has changed us in ways I would have thought unimaginable just a year ago. Where we once were accustomed to corralling friends for an afternoon of touch football, enjoying an evening in a Greenwich Village bar listening to Latin jazz, or blowing forty bucks on a bad movie and a bucket of popcorn without regret, we now have a monomaniacal focus on home renovation. Tearing down walls, razing rooms, and visualizing ways to rebuild, redesign, and furnish them with furniture we don't yet own—this is what motivates us. It's our Dungeons and Dragons, our Pokémon, our crack cocaine. We talk about it constantly, over every meal, in every restaurant. Every lunch and dinner we are eating out, talking about what we might like to destroy and rebuild.

We have also become the kind of people who steal spare moments, at all hours of the day and night, and watch porn. Home porn, that is. Whenever there is a spare minute we stare at home shows on the Learning Channel and HGTV with the same glazed-eye dedication that other people reserve for SpongeBob SquarePants. I can't remember how it started exactly. Maybe an uninhibited moment with the channel clicker in hand, stepping one wicked toe over the line of propriety. Getting a first lusty eyeful of Lynette Jennings, the madam of the makeover. Or maybe we saw something irresistible advertised from Martha

Stewart's adult toys section at Kmart, and later had it discreetly tucked into a brown paper bag at the register. From there it was a slippery slope to the hard stuff: *This Old House, HomeTime,* and *Trading Spaces*—the kinkiest couples indulgence since key parties. We learned the hard way that there is no turning back. You can't unwatch *Debbie Does Decking.*

"Go back a sec!" Susan exclaims, almost raising her head off the arm of the couch.

"What? For *Designer's Challenge?*" I'm incredulous, like it's softcore and beneath us.

"Yeah, I started watching this one last week. They do this amazing bathroom redo you should see."

"We've *ordered* the bathroom tile," I say. We need new bathroom ideas like we need a third septic tank.

"Still . . ."

Still nothing. This can lead to no good whatsoever. Susan's persistent enthusiasm for new ideas is tougher to contain than a radioactive spill. It is always the most recent idea or suggestion she comes across that magically transforms into the best one, the one we will be going with. This fearlessness of change attracted me to Susan when we first started going out. If the Italian restaurant was packed, we'd go Malaysian; if *Mission Impossible* was sold out, we'd go bowling. Roll with It Susan, I called her, admiring her unflappability and ease with quick turnarounds. Spontaneity, impulsiveness, readiness for change—these are good things when you are dating a person. When you're married and renovating, I've come to learn, they're admissible evidence in the divorce hearing.

"Look at that," she enthuses, "it makes the room bigger." The designer had put mirrors on one entire wall, cutting out holes where necessary for lighting. "Do you like that?"

"No," I say hastily, preemptively. I'm not even sure if I like it or not, I just know that their bathroom redo is not going to become my bathroom redo. This process has no doubt made me more negative, quick to shoot down ideas. As much as I dislike this new trait in myself, I fear what a little enthusiasm might bring, mostly because I know what a little enthusiasm might bring: change. "I'm flipping," I say.

"Fine." It's delivered with a hint of resignation, a hint of this is no fun if you can't muster any enthusiasm.

"Well, would you look at that?" I thrill, attempting a return to the good mood.

"What?"

"Paige got a haircut." Paige is Paige Davis, the host of the home renovation hit *Trading Spaces*. The premise is simple: Neighboring couples trade homes for a weekend, and with a budget of one thousand dollars they completely redo one room in each other's home—with help from a professional designer and carpenter.

"She needed a haircut."

"Totally."

"I like it," Susan says, and settles comfortably into the couch.

The people on *Trading Spaces* have become our extended family on weekend mornings. Paige, Ty, Frank, Genevieve, Doug, Amy Wynn, Vern. We have opinions on every last one of them. My personal favorite is Hildi, a statuesque brunette with a sharp tongue. Stylishly turned out on every show, Hildi handles floor sanders while wearing high-heeled strappy sandals. If you ask me, that's just better TV than John Madden on NFL Sunday. She reminds me of Susan—before a year of renovation and months of grouchy husband.

It speaks to our fatigue, emotional distance, and our draining addiction to design consideration that we are sprawled on this couch rather than back in bed thrashing balletically through the percales. That and our fear. More than once we have asked,

"How difficult can it be?" only to learn from *This Old House* that the answer is: "Plenty. Plenty difficult."

On the other end of the home show spectrum, the cold shower if you will, is Envy TV. You don't see people working on Envy TV; you see people workin' it, flashing their bling bling and big livin'. Defined by shows like *MTV Cribs*, E! Television's *It's Good to Be* . . . , and BET's *How I'm Living*, they are adept at turning viewer jealousy into Nielsen ratings. It takes about a nanosecond to see how they're living: better than I am. A *lot* better than I am. I stare in wonderment that anyone would want to watch these shows and be reminded how comparatively lousy they have it. And yet I stare, amazed and in awe. How did those dimwits— these Vanilla Ice wannabes—amass the sums to buy such garish homes stuffed with obtuse furniture? How can I be more like them?

The envy leaves a bad taste, though, momentarily damping our enthusiasm to fix our own insignificant igloo. Then the reality of the anvil around our necks sets in; if we don't get off our fat asses and fix our shit heap we will never get out of our emotional and financial straights. It's the only way to change things. We could flee, divorce, knock the place down with a wrecking ball, but that wouldn't change a thing. We're in deep, and the only way out is through more digging.

After months of anticipation, the guys from Chesterfield Excavation are due to dig out the back of our house in preparation for phase two: the addition. I can hear their arrival from blocks away, as a huge 550-horsepower Mack truck growls loud enough to make the asphalt shake. A massive excavator, with a long extendable arm and huge toothy bucket, crawls down Division Street and positions itself on what is, for only a short while longer, our driveway. The machine dwarfs our house. Dexter is on site to lend his expertise and prevent disaster. "You got measurements for this?" he asks, referring to the precise depth to which Chesterfield should dig.

"Yeah," I say, though not too confidently, remembering last night when I was scrambling around the back of the house in the failing light, like a student cramming for the test the next day. In desperate ignorance, I was scraping away at the plate on the existing house floor to get my dimensions.

In my defense, it's a complicated measure to take. The existing floor will continue back from the house, establishing the ceiling in the added rooms. Since we are also adding a deck past the kitchen, I need to accommodate for a slightly different floor elevation on the deck: we want that surface to be slightly lower than the sill of the back door lest the water come screaming across the deck and into the dining area. To further confuse matters, I need to establish an eight-foot ceiling height in the added rooms, rather than the six feet ten inches that exists in the basement. After all, without an eight-foot ceiling, why bother going to the trouble of building an addition?

The question then is whether or not—while accommodating for the eight-foot ceiling, ten-inch floor joists, three-quarter-inch subflooring, flooring, and sleepers above the concrete slab—the grade of the lawn will be above or below the basement slab. If this is calculated incorrectly, the added rooms will be lower than grade. Heavy rainfall won't drain toward the street but right into our house. Is there enough room? I think there is . . . barely. So when I say, "Yeah, I've got measurements," to Dexter, I am secretly hoping he will ask to see them and confirm that I am right.

He doesn't. He walks off instead, disappearing to make phone calls.

*   *   *

Randy, the Chesterfield guy, rips away at the back cinder-block wall, the asphalt driveway, the cinder-block back stairs, and the excess dirt with alarming rapidity.

"Where's Dexter?" Randy asks. "He should be here, I don't want to take responsibility if that thing comes down." The chimney hangs onto the back of the house precariously. The brick spire almost floats in space. One miss-dig by Randy could send it toppling.

"Haven't seen him," I say. Where the hell could he be? It dawns on me that he doesn't want to be held responsible if the chimney falls either. It makes me think of Dexter's mantra, *You gotta get that worked out*, in a whole new light, not simply in terms of logistics, but in terms of limiting exposure, responsibility.

Everyone wants to be a part of it, but no one wants to accept responsibility if it fails. Like marriage, I suppose.

Deepak Is My Foundation

Of one thing I am certain: I am happy not to be a mason. My first foray into cement for the front porch footers left my back sore, my hands drier than salt, my eyes burning, and my chest with a vague indefinable aching. For several days afterward my lungs hurt when I breathed deeply. Too much dust. I'd cemented inside and out.

So it comes as a great surprise, to say the least, that the sunniest subcontractor we hire is a small, stout, muscular mason named Sam Bolivar. He looks like a rough-hewn gnome with a tuft of curly gray-brown hair and rows of rocky teeth. In his mid-fifties, the years of hard work are apparent on his face and hands, but not on his attitude. From the minute he arrives he is shoveling, shoveling, shoveling. Making the final trench for the foundations, revealing a layer of undisturbed soil, Sam pitches hundreds of pounds of dirt with mechanical efficiency. Only occasionally does he stop to refresh himself with something to drink.

"You're doing a nice job with this house. I like the detail you cut in the front," he offers.

"Thanks. It's taking a little longer than we wanted."

"You don't want to do it wrong."

"I guess."

"I did a house like this once, in Wainscott."

"Is that right?"

"With my first wife." Sam tells me the story of his first house, his first wife. Not unlike our home, Sam and his wife's needed a lot of work and, being handy, Sam was just the man for the job. Sam's wife, though, was not handy. She was a bossy Brazilian bombshell who wanted the best of everything. The best fixtures, the finest tile, the most exquisite flooring. Sam toiled to make her happy. He worked when he returned from a day's labor, and worked the weekend long. Still, she wasn't happy. She wanted more. More improvements to the house, more beautiful materials. "Then one day I realized," Sam says with enviable equanimity, "that it wasn't about the house. I can't make her happy, only she can make herself happy. And if she can't, well, that's her problem." Even after his epiphany Sam continued to work on their home, not wanting to leave a job half finished. It was giving him pleasure to make the house better, and the more he worked the less time he had to spend listening to the Brazilian.

I suggest to Sam that his thinking is pretty evolved, and if anyone else were in his shoes, myself included, they might not be so level-headed as regards the Brazilian. "Might even," I suggest, hoping not to overstep any bounds, "tell her to go jump in the Amazon. Go suck a piranha." Sam laughs and confesses that he used to feel that way, too, but he has been reading Deepak Chopra over the years and decided it wasn't healthy to get mired in resentment. "She was trying the best she could, you know? And if she is imbalanced, well, I can't let that imbalance me." I look at Sam in utter amazement. It cannot be a coincidence that he has come to work on my home. It must be destiny or kismet or really great eavesdropping technology. Clearly he knows *(how? from whom?)* that my marriage is strained, and he was sent here, to *tell* me something. But what, swami, what? What knowledge have you come to impart in my time of need? That I am trying my best, and Susan shouldn't think I'm such a schmuck? That Susan is trying her best, and I shouldn't vilify her voracious appetite for more paint samples? Or that it will all work out, that the house will be completed and I will transform from Evil Lawrence, the angry, impatient thrower of tools, to Good Lawrence, a thoroughly centered, considerate, and Deepak-quoting husband with a deep respect for masons?

I ask for the rest of the story, thinking it will hold the key to Sam's teachings. "So what happened?"

"The day we got the C of O," he says, referring to the Holy Grail of construction, the Certificate of Occupancy, "she filed for divorce."

Two days later, Sam has all his forms in place. A series of interlocking plywood boards stand upright to accept the concrete slurry. Sam sprays down the forms with a light oil so the concrete doesn't adhere to them too strongly, and he is ready. On schedule, a large ready-mix concrete truck rumbles up Union Street. Large red and white isosceles triangles rotate on its big drum mixer. The concrete-truck driver climbs down to work the controls. He looks like a slightly pudgy Billy Bob Thorton, without the wildness in his eyes. A spray of brown hair pops out from under his baseball cap. After he gets his gloves on and the cement flowing, he has time to talk. He too has a story about first marriage and home renovation. Amazingly, it is the *same* story. His wife hectored him into fixing their mid-Island ranch home, never leaving him a solitary Sunday to watch football in peace. Upon completion, which is to say the C of O holy grail, she announced she wants a divorce. He is decidedly less circumspect than Sam about it, and avoids any Deepak-like equivocations.

"A real bitch."

"Sounds like you had a handful," I say noncommittally.

"Boy she could holler. I thought things were going good, but then she just got crazy. I was readin' something, it has something to do with the hormones.''

"Hormones?''

"Yeah. Women, it makes 'em crazy at different times. Men don't get that.''

"We got other things to make us crazy,'' I say.

All in all, a very successful day—and a terrifying one. I call Susan later that evening to tell her about the progress, and let her know about these mad Long Island wives driving their husbands into the ground. She laughs a little too forcefully if you ask me.

The interior of Chase Bank in Southampton is a wide-open affair with soaring ceilings. Romanesque revival, maybe. It is not a big bank but because of its airiness and charming lack of security it feels big, unlike those Plexiglas Habitrails in Manhattan. I could, if I wanted to, walk right up and touch a teller; there is nothing separating the two of us. In the rear I can see the vault, an impossibly large round door with twelve independently tumbled locks. They will require some extra ingenuity in the bank-heist flick you could film here.

Today there is a cheerless four-foot-high Christmas tree by the Deposits Only ATM and an unlit menorah atop the information desk. I'm sitting in that back section of the bank, the part reserved for client services, where people discuss mortgages, home equity loans, investment "vehicles,'' small business loans, and other financial arrangements that point to the future.

I, on the other hand, am here to liquidate my retirement account. Miriam asks me to wait a moment while she retrieves the necessary form. For some reason she doesn't keep a stack of them in her top drawer. I stare at the back of the head of some guy at the next desk. He's asking how he can transfer money, "Just fifty thou,'' to his wife's account in a different bank so she has it handy when she's in Aspen. I hate him. I hate her. I suddenly hate Aspen.

"Okay then," starts Miriam, settling back into her chair, "how much of the account would you like to disburse?"

Disburse. Bless her soul, what a caring individual Miriam is to ask how much I would like to disburse, to allay my misery with a euphemism.

Every goddamn penny, Miriam. "All of it," I say.

"Well, if you remove everything, the bank will have to close the account."

"I see. All of it less a buck, I guess."

I can only imagine what Miriam is thinking as I sit there in my stained and dirty work clothes, taking out my last pennies. Whatever it is, she is treating me with the utmost solicitude, like I have terminal cancer. Something about her niceness makes me sadder and more desperate than when I sat down. I want to grab her forearm, tell her not to worry, that I'm gonna be all right, that all the signs are pointing to the end, that I am undeniably at the end of my financial rope, but, damn it, I'm a fighter, Miriam, a fighter. This money will help me hang on a little longer, keep the credit card sharks that have been phoning regularly at bay. I know it's stupid to pull out retirement savings, but I have no choice. To be utterly honest, Miriam, I need the cash to take care of some essential business, otherwise life will grind to a halt and I will look like an utter failure. I'm sure you can appreciate that. What's so essential? Well, Miriam, I have to buy a new exit line to the septic tank—I cut through the old line with the Ditch Witch, burying electric cable—and some Christmas presents. I mean, really, I can't ask my wife for money to buy her a gift, can I? What would that make me? But I'm gonna bounce back, Miriam, I swear it. Then I'll be back here, you'll be here, we'll be back here together and we'll stretch that account past the one dollar amount again. Just you wait. Just you wait. Please wait.

"If you could sign here . . . and here, next to the X . . . I'll put this through today and the funds should be available in your account by the end of the week."

"Not today?"

"I'm afraid not. It's not like a simple withdrawal." Miriam has instantaneously become my nemesis, my tormenter.

"I don't understand. It's my money."

"I'm sorry," she says. But she is *not* sorry; I can see that. "This paperwork has to go through three departments since it is not regular funds."

"Well, I wish you would have told me," I say for no reason.

"Would you prefer not to disburse the funds?"

Oh, you and your goddamn disbursing, I think to myself. I consider it for a moment, but what is there really to consider?

"No, that's okay," I say, and pick up the pen.

I guess the septic line can wait until Friday.

The Bastard in the House

In terms of assessing mistakes we have made, one of the largest has to be doing things in two stages: renovating the top-floor dormer and first-floor living room before moving on to the extended kitchen and the lower ground-floor addition. It has doubled the number of trips for every step—plumbing, electrical, insulation, Sheetrock, flooring, painting—and increased the waste. An undeniable blunder, it was one more or less forced on us by the building codes and zoning board application process. We couldn't wait to start, but we didn't have permission to start everything. As a result our desire to have just one clean room, one clean corner that we can call home, has been perpetually frustrated.

It is that frustration, more than anything else, that sparks the most arguments, arguments that are beginning to wear on us like sandpaper, to the point where we are both too raw and depleted to care for our deteriorating marriage. Now the biggest issue is money. I estimate we could finish in two months if we can maintain our current pace. But with empty savings accounts and maxed-out credit cards our progress is slowing. The romance of renovation has long since died, and we are tired of living in other people's homes, house-sitting for vacationing friends. Small issues turn into big issues, and big issues torment us daily.

"Can we just spend five minutes organizing?" Susan asks.

"Can we maybe get something *done* first?"

"You always say that. I don't know why we can't clean up for five minutes, make the place a little civilized."

"Because you're constantly moving things around . . . I couldn't find the flat bar—"

"Downstairs. Next to the Shop-Vac."

"Yeah, great, but how am I to know that when it was on the windowsill half an hour before. I spend the whole goddamn day looking for things."

"It wouldn't be that way if you organized them."

"It wouldn't be that way if you didn't keep moving them. They're always in a different fucking place."

"I can't live like this!" Susan yells, her voice cracking.

"*You* can't live like this? I live like this all week long."

"Half our shit is at Pam's, half our shit is at the Hines', half our shit is in storage, half our shit is at Norm and Ellen's! Look at this place!" she shouts. "Look around you! Look at how we're living! We're living in bags. *We're living in fucking bags!*" This is no time for a refresher course on fractions. Forlorn Hefty bags full of wrinkled clothes circle around our feet, having just been moved from one borrowed bedroom to another. The reality of it is unbearable. What have our lives become in the name of this old fucking house?

"I don't *care*," I scream back, angrily, "we can't get this done by cleaning."

"You always say you don't care!" Susan is now shouting at the top of her lungs, her breath heaving and eyes beginning to water. "And that's just *not fair!*" The midwesterner in me takes over and I hurry to close the bedroom windows. Our screaming is at a point where we risk deafening squirrels and squandering our nice-young-couple reputation among the neighbors. My heart is breaking. For her, for us. But more than that I am mad as hell, thrashing around within my own thoughts. No solution is clear to me, all choices I can imagine will just make things worse.

"You know what really gets me? What really pisses me off?"

"What?" Susan says between her teeth, not wanting to hear anything from me right now.

"What really gets me is that some fucking day in the future, God only knows when, someone is going to see the finished house, and we'll tell them our pathetic little tale about how difficult it was, how hard we worked. And then they're gonna say, 'Well it's all been worth it now, hasn't it?' Right, like we're supposed to go along with this charade that the journey was tough, but *boy-oh-boy* we made it through? And you know what I'm gonna say? You know what I'm going to say?"

"What?"

"No fucking way. No fucking way is this worth it. Because that's how I feel. Look what it is doing to you, to me, to *us*. This is fucking worth it?"

"Do you want out?"

"What?"

"You heard me. Do you want out?"

Do I? God knows I've been thinking about it, every way imaginable. Getting in the car and driving nonstop to Tempe, Tijuana, even Toronto. Diving deep, deep into the ocean and floating to where it doesn't matter anymore. Running off with that cute Mexican deli counter girl in Noyac to start a new life; we could move to Chiapas and live a simple existence without credit card debt, close to the earth, knitting ponchos and raising goats.

"Are you going to answer me?"

"I'm thinking."

"If you are taking this long to think it's pretty clear . . ."

"*You* know? You can answer that easily?" I say it like an accusation. A tear streams down her cheek.

"Yes."

I breathe audibly, theatrically. I don't know if I am punishing her or me with this behavior.

"I want in," I say finally. Coming out of my mouth it sounds more like concession than affirmation. And maybe that is what it is. I'll let her try and pull me up from the depths for a little longer, God only knows why she wants to try. I have turned into a glowering, short-tempered asshole. If I were her, I would leave me.

With divorce averted, for the time being, we get back to work. In cosmic irony, today's task is to get the shower stall tiled in the upstairs bathroom. The quarters are tight and the work is painstaking and difficult, especially considering our choice: glass mosaic tile. Many glass tiles can be exorbitantly expensive, especially larger tumbled glass tiles, but we found a manufacturer, Bisazza, that was within our budget. Okay, not within the budget exactly, but not so far outside the budget that we felt gut-wrenching compunction about it. Besides, we reasoned—again—that if we are going to so much trouble then we have a right to construct something that we will enjoy. Perhaps that is the greatest lesson I have learned so far: Don't build anything you want to like. Start to care about it, try to improve it, individualize it, and you are on a downward slope to dementia.

Susan had seen a tiled wall in a Manhattan store that had three bands of glass tile, dark, moderate, and light blue ascending a wall. This was our initial inspiration. So we bought *six* different shades of glass tile from sea green and aqua blue at one end to white on the other. Our plan was to use the darker shades on the floor and intermix them, climbing the walls. The shower floor will recall the sea, the upper reaches the sky. I swear to God we thought this was a good idea. And it would have been . . . if we had nothing else to do in life for ten years and no cognitive brain activity whatsoever.

As soon as the tiles arrived, we realized our mistake. The mosaics came in sheets, hundreds of tiny glass lozenges face mounted on paper. Entire sheets can be affixed and then the paper is damped with a sponge and removed. We thought of laying them out in stripes, but we hadn't ordered equal numbers of each color, and there would have been incomplete stripes. Susan's ingenious solution was to randomize. Mix up all the tiles and make an arbitrary pattern on the wall. Easier said than done, Susan quickly learned, as it meant she had to peel all the tiles off the paper backing and reattach them to sheets of clear contact paper she bought at the hardware store. This took *weeks*. It is complete mental asylum work, and I half-expected to walk in on her diving head first into a wastepaper basket to escape the repetitive and meticulous nature of the work. I've never seen this kind of mad commitment to the projects on *Trading Spaces*, I'll tell you that.

Now we are ready, I think, to realize the dream shower stall. The painstakingly randomized sheets cover the bedroom floor staging area. Susan prepares to mix the SuperFlex thin set. This is the mortar we will trowel onto the shower stall wonderboard walls to secure the tiles. Sound professional? Hardly, we still have a headache from reading some typically impenetrable tile in-structions: "Fully vitrified porcelain tiles should be installed using a latex modified thin set or basic (nonmodified) thin set mixed with an acrylic latex additive. But, for installing ceramic or glass tile over vinyl flooring or wooden substates you will need a high quality latex modified thin set mortar." Huh? I ache to read some tax forms, just for relief. Susan calls the counter help at Max's Brick and Tile to bail us out. Because we don't have a mixing paddle to attach to a power drill, Susan hand mixes the thin set. The cementlike mixture calls for very little water and she tires.

"It's difficult. Do you want to try it?" she asks. I'm still seething from our argument.

"Do I *want* to try it? No."

"Would you? It's killing my arm."

"I'm fixing this floorboard," I say stubbornly. *Boo-hoo-hoo. Just stick with it. You seem to think you can do everything else without me, Miss Independent.*

"Lawrence, can you help me with this thin set. This has to get done to*day*."

"Say the magic words."

"Please."

"Words."

She looks at me. Thinks about it. Rubs her arm. Looks at the bucket of thin set in front of us. I start to walk away.

"Okay."

"Okay, what?" I say.

"I need a man."

"That's more like it," I say, laughing for the first time today. Clearly she'll say anything to get her house built.

Once the thin set is mixed and ready, which is to say it has set up or slaked, we get to work. Susan read the *Working with Tile* handbook and tiled the floor in the downstairs half bath, so she's the pro, the tile guy. "What first?" I ask, and she starts to bring in the tile sheets. She smoothes thin set on the concrete wonderboard that we have sheathed the stall with, and then scrapes with the toothy side of the hand tool, leaving an even distribution. She puts the first square in place, pressing lightly on all the tiles, and removes her hands.

"How does it look?" she asks.

"Great," I confirm.

Then the sheet begins to slide. I smell disaster in the offing.

Susan is—or at least *acts*—unfazed. "Grab the glue in the other room, would you?" I do, and she mixes some Weldbond (the Universal Space-age Adhesive) into the thin set for greater holding power.

It works. She moves laterally and up. As she reaches the curb I cut tiles with the snips to make them fit where space is tight. This may sound precise but it is not. Glass shards shoot in all directions as the snips bite the tile in half. Worse, as we tile upward, problems arise from the fact that the reconstituted sheets do not have the same dimensions as the original sheets. It looks like hell. We are losing our patience, and the thin set is thickening. The task that Susan found so pleasantly simple on ten square feet in the downstairs half bath is proving very difficult when working with much smaller tile and on three walls and a floor. Mosaics slide, flip, and even break. It is like tying your shoes while wearing winter gloves, the goal so flagrantly familiar and the materials so aggravatingly cumbersome. We pull down a few sheets in frustration. Okay, *I* tear down the sheets in frustration, while Susan watches in mute horror. And then not so mute. We realign them and try slapping them up again and move on.

In a few tortuous hours, we have one wall completed. Not a speed record by any standard but we're happy to be done with that much. After a couple sandwiches from Madison Market, we dive back into the penury, trading jobs just to spread the pain around. It is getting increasingly difficult since the available space to work in is diminishing. We bump into each other frequently, getting thin set over ourselves, the wrong side of the tile, and just about everywhere else. We get half the stall tiled, but the greater accomplishment is surviving this day. I don't know how many more days like this we will be able to get through, though. "Is it too early to drink?" I ask.

"It's never too early to drink," Susan replies, dropping her safety glasses on the floor.

Maybe I did marry the right woman after all.

On Monday morning, Susan heads back to the city to make money to support us in the fashion to which we have become lamentably accustomed. And money will be needed, for we somehow underbought on the tile. I spend the day working on the pine floors in the upstairs bedrooms. We want an old-house look, so we purchased random-sized tongue-and-groove pine: six, eight, ten, and twelve inches. After I tack down a layer of construction felt (tar paper) to eliminate squeaks between the flooring and subflooring, I calculate how I can run the boards from the front bedroom across the upstairs landing and into the back bedroom in one long line. I don't know why this is important to me, but I want to achieve it.

Hours later, as the sun is setting, Bad News Krantz shows up to make a couple cutouts for his tubular SpacePak ducting. I walk him through my work upstairs on the floors, quietly proud of what has taken me all day to accomplish. I show him the random lengths; the long stretches of pine traversing the length of the house. After using a power nailer on the tongue side of the board—securing the planks in place—I am also top nailing with wrought-iron nails (which look rough-hewn like mini–railroad spikes) to give "old house" character. I've learned from experience that it is better to predrill holes for these nails, complete with a countersink, since the wrought-iron heads are so big and can split the boards. Krantz gives the floors an approving look, says they look nice. Then he drops the hammer. "Did you use polyurethane glue in the joints?"

Ahhhhhhh. "No. Is that necessary?" I ask, thinking I've just nailed the living bejesus out of these boards from every angle.

"It can help reduce squeaks between the tongue and groove."
As is turns out, he's right. I knew better than to use typical wood
glue since when the joint shrinks and swells with the humidity,
the glue can crack or snap when you walk over it. But polyurethane glue is more elastic, quieter. Absolutely necessary? No.
But the best possible method. Yeah.

Fuckin' Krantz.

We're sitting in the living room. Or, rather, one year into the
project, the only *livable* room—the porch we slapped on the front
of the house. Everything else has a quarter inch of sawdust from
cutting window trim. Money has become so tight that some days
we have to lobster claw for spare change between the car seats,
just to buy two pizza slices and a Coke. Today we splurged for
sandwiches, but I fear I'll still be hungry.

"You need to get a job," Susan announces, unwrapping her
tuna fish on whole wheat.

"I've been looking for a job." The post–Internet crash and
post–September 11 job shortage are persisting. Moreover, trying
to find a job back in the city while trying to renovate a house in
the stress-filled country is downright crazy making. Prioritizing in
an environment when no one shows up on schedule—but can be
counted on to show up when they're not scheduled and mis-
interpret how you want something done—is a veritable catch-22.
What is more important: the scheduled (but unlikely) delivery of
twenty yards of three thousand grit concrete, or losing a day going
in for an interview with no job at the end of it? Since quitting
Floyd's months ago I've had no steady source of income, just
infusions of capital from cashing out retirement accounts and
sheepishly borrowing money from my parents. We've tried
everything to keep this project afloat, to stay out of bankruptcy,
and avoid losing the house. Combined with Susan still paying the

mortgage and other large bills, I'm sitting on the porch eating my Turkey BLT feeling like a world-beater.

"No, I mean a *real* job," Susan persists.

"A real job? A *real* job! Let's see, I was putting roofs over heads—never mind for the moment that they're vacation-home roofs—and you do what in PR? You *influence* the media?"

"You know what I mean."

"I certainly do."

"Imagine if the roles were reversed, if you were paying the mortgage, the taxes, most bills, and I was working only on the house. How would you feel?"

"Like a traditional family."

"That's not fair."

"Fair? Marx, Engels, *and* Mary Wollstonecraft are all twisting in their graves. Working at home isn't work? My God."

"It's not like we have a child."

"I don't believe it. I break my back on this damn house seven days a week, but that's not work unless I'm changing diapers? You're an à la carte feminist!"

"For God's sake, Lawrence, I'm working twenty-four/seven in the city and then out here on weekends."

"You think this is all my fault, don't you?"

"Look at the way we're living," she said.

"I'm not having a whole lot of fun either, you know."

"Well, I didn't sign on for this."

That's a real conversation ender. I think to say that we vowed for better and for worse, and this is the worse part, but I don't. Why underline the obvious? I stare into the distance, over our beat-up construction-assaulted lawn, and fume. We have come this far, worked so hard, and it is all falling apart. I feel unmoored. Desperately uncertain and afraid to say so. And I'm angry. Angry with myself, angry at Susan's fulminations. But can I blame her?

Maybe the stress is finally getting to her the way it has gotten to me.

Worse, maybe my persistent melancholy has flipped a switch in her mind. Many days I feel nothing save for a hollow desperation, convinced that there isn't a way out and any actions I take will just cause greater frustration, larger obstacles. I feel embarrassed and deadened by my stretch of bad luck. It multiplies when I see it on Susan's face, too; clearly she is wrestling with the thought of whether she can live with a man like this. We both know what the answer is; the only question is how long.

"I just don't understand it," she says, in an attempt to bolster my spirits. "I don't understand why this is happening to you. You're one of the smartest people I know; you're talented, funny, you have a graduate degree . . . it doesn't make sense." Hearing this, I know that I have infected our marriage with gloom, and that my despair is taking the breath out of both of us.

Yet Susan soldiers on, trying new tacks to be upbeat and supportive. On Sunday she clips a "Lives" column out of the *Times* magazine entitled "Survivor." The author relates his family's painful legacy of Huntington's disease and its debilitating effects on the brain and central nervous system. After losing a husband to it, and watching three sons suffer terribly, the author's mother went down to the nursing home to visit her older sons and shot them, ending their misery. I put the magazine down, stunned. Stunned that a mother would go to such lengths for her sons at such great personal cost, and stunned that Susan is implicitly telling me it could be much worse. In her mind's eye, I have reached bottom. Something needs to be done about my depression, and Dr. Phil isn't returning calls.

The next day, frustrated and in need of cash—and certain that the city would be a bad move for the moment—I look for a job doing what I know: carpentry. Plus, our house is getting to the point where we need to install trim and I need some skills in finishing work.

Walking into the offices of Corinthian Contruction I know immediately that I'm in a different league. It's not just that they are looking for carpenters with five to ten years of experience, when I don't have ten *months* under my belt. It's the mood of the place. First, there's the receptionist: Tiffani, a strawberry blond Alyssa Milano/Shannen Doherty. Buxom, wearing tight-fitting everything, she clicks around the office in strappy sandals. "Have a seat," she winks, "first we have a little test for you." I immediately think pee cup, but no, she hands me a six-page horror.

The first page asks for the names of twenty different rooflines. Staring at it I go completely blank, unable to even identify hip roof, like the one we have on our front porch. Is "Bad idea" a roofline? "Terrible taste"? "Suckered by the architect"? I scribble in a couple and turn the page, too embarrassed to hand the thing back to Tiffani and just walk out. Next, I'm asked to name the component parts in cutaways of stairwells, basements, attics. I marvel at the fact that almost every board in a house can be called a stud or a joist. This *can't* be right. I breathe a sigh of relief when I can specify stringer, header, and ridge plate. Finally, I move on to the multiple-choice portion, exercising the skill we all learned in high school: Look for the answer to one question in another part of the test.

Cheerfully, Tiffani tells me that I can go upstairs when I've finished. Am I taking too long? I worry. Do people usually finish by now? I nod and quickly scan through the pages again, guessing that it's best to give everything a name, even a wrong one, since so many items in construction are called different things by different people. And blanks would look conspicuous. I stuff spaces with any word that comes to mind from my own experience. Flitch plate. Blocking. Furring strips.

"Like high school again, huh?" Tiffani muses, looking up from filing her nails.

I go upstairs and meet Jef—with one *f*—who is dwarfed by his desk. He grandiosely rests his feet on the corner of the enormous wooden desk, nearly dragging his butt completely out of his leather chair. As he flips through the test, he bites his lower lip and mutters softly. Occasionally he "hmms" for effect. And then, abruptly, he puts his feet on the floor, sets down the test, and delivers the one question out of all possible questions I know is coming. "You got tools?"

I get a call back and two days later I am meeting One-F Jef's partner, Nick Bigfatgreekname, a boxy Greek guy who plays the slick schmoozy role, the salesman, the guy who wants to get to know you. What made you move out here? How long have you been out here? How do you like it out here? I confabulate some story about having friends who live out here—as if—and they spoke so highly of the area that I thought I would give it a try.

"Who are they?" Nick asks on cross-examination.

"Ah . . . Steve Moss. He writes for the *New York Times*." Stupid thing to say, I think. "And James DeMartis," I add. "An artist and metal worker. He works for John Battle at Battle Iron."

Nick brightens at the mention of someone he knows. "Good metal work," he says, "but too slow."

"Yeah," I concur, "they call him Slow-Motion John."

"Well," One F interrupts, "we'd like to try you out on Monday if you're not busy."

"What else could I be doing?"

"Great. It's kind of a try out system, for the first week. We assume that all will go well, and then in a month we have a review and will try and bump you up a little."

Up from fifteen dollars an hour? Wow!

The prospect of a job, even a fake one, an assumed occupation, is enough to instantly improve my mood and outlook. Strictly speaking, a second jump into carpentry in terms of dollars and cents can't stand up to much scrutiny, not being a major revenue center. But some income, *any* income, might begin to reassemble my recession-shredded self worth.

Lately, I've come to feel that all my previous convictions about sex roles and money making are not well thought out. I had eagerly embraced some politically correct axiom that either Susan or I could be the main breadwinner outside the home, either of us could work in the home, and it wouldn't matter. But nothing could have mattered more.

It's not that I feel emasculated—to use another cliché—but I do feel bored and resentful working alone on the house all week long. I'm hammering away on some rashly conceived and repeatedly redefined dream, and my brain is going soft in the process. I might learn to appreciate the isolated drudgery that the prototypical 1950s housewife endured, but that doesn't mean I feel rewarded in my latter-day approximation of it. Needless to say, bored and resentful are not good moods to confess to someone who is paying the bills. We are both so busy running to keep ahead of the bill collectors, working to get the house built that we never see, truly, what the other is going through, nor take the time to recognize each other's endured stress, quality-of-life sacrifices, or continuing and expanding efforts to get the damn thing done.

In spite of this we have days of miraculous teamwork, echoing our early enthusiasms for the renovation and reminding us that we've been married two years, not twenty. By the time we set out to lay the floors in the living room, we are no longer naïvely charging ahead as we did with the twelve-foot sheets of drywall. I've gotten over my proprietary attitudes toward the power tools and Susan, more impressively, now knows the difference between eighths and sixteenths on the tape measure. Two weeks ago we stood in the Riverhead lumberyard, freezing in the cold and individually choosing the boards that would become our downstairs flooring, selecting planks with just enough knots to show character, but not so many as to become problematic. We got them home and stacked them on two-by-four kickers to acclimate before nailing them down.

I call for a board, "Nine five and five eighths."

"Got it," Susan says. She grabs one of the eight-inch planks, cuts one end square, then roundhouses the board and cuts the other end to length.

"Perfect." I powernail the thing into submission on one end and pull in the other end, which is slightly warped. With a square of tongue-in-groove cut diagonally, I screw one triangular piece to the floor temporarily, then hammer the other piece between the plank and the anchor. The floorboard moves into place, eliminating the gap, and I nail it into place. While I'm doing this, Susan is cutting another piece of construction felt to slip under the next rows to minimize squeaks. On occasion we even employ a little polyurethane glue, just for Krantz.

"It looks amazing," Susan says. And it does. The entirety of the living room is completed, and more than half of the kitchen area is covered in a buttery expanse of pine. The floor looks a little light, but with the polyurethane the boards will darken and mellow in tone over time. Walking on the new boards feels good, but better yet, it *sounds* good, each footfall being less pronounced on the increasingly sturdy floor.

"It almost looks like a house," I say.

The floors are nearly complete, the walls in phase one are all Sheetrocked, taped, spackled, and primed. Wires, copper and PVC piping poke out of the walls for electrical receptacles and plumbing. Soon we will be ready to install kitchen Sheetrock and then the cabinets. It would have been faster to do it all at once, I'm reminded, but I'm content that the floor in this room will be knocked out and we can do the rest of the kitchen next weekend. I call for another board and Susan is back with a twelve-inch plank in seconds. It makes me think I should let her start at Corinthian on Monday and I can go into the city.

A dark blur out the front door catches my eye. "There goes Hannibal."

"That wasn't Hannibal."

"You weren't even looking," I protest. "It was definitely him. Hannibal, Harris, whatever."

"How do you know it was him?" Susan asks. More than likely she is wondering why I really care. Lately I've taken on the small-town sport of attending to everyone's comings and goings.

"It was a Town Car."

"Did you *see* him?"

"Not really, but the car just . . . looooomed," I say, hunching my shoulders, curling my fingers like claws, and sounding for no reason whatsoever like Vincent Price. Susan looks at me like I've lost it, tells me to stop watching the street and get back to nailing. I do, and soon we are finished, having laid the entire living room and kitchen floor in roughly five hours—with no arguments.

Before top nailing the whole floor off with the wrought-iron nails, I suggest we break for lunch. Susan offers to secure supplies at Riverhead, the lumberyard, while I call and harangue the electrician on the phone and get us sandwiches at Madison Market. Before we knew how to get things done the two of us would go to the lumberyard, but we've learned that it is much more efficient to send Susan alone. Together, we're ignored. Alone, Susan is catered to with the sort of solicitude you can only read about in Michelin guides. A single—which is to say unescorted—woman in the lumberyard sets off alarms, it seems, as phalanxes of yard helpers materialize in seconds. They tie lumber to Susan's roof; they load shingles in her trunk; they give her yet more paint samples. I should be concerned about sending her into a tsunami of testosterone, I suppose, but damn it, there's a house to be built.

"Anything else?" Susan asks before leaving.

"Maybe some kind of metal cleaner?" I propose. "For that hardware Mark dropped off."

"Saint Mark," she reminds me, chuckling. Mark became Saint Mark about a month ago when, unannounced, he filled our basement with boxes and bags of renovation loot. An embarrassment of riches: door hardware, lock sets, plumbing fixtures, hinges, tiles, a set of French doors, and what must be forty pounds of latches for cabinets, the metal kind that need to be turned to open. They were exactly what we had in mind for our kitchen, but having checked prices made them simply out of the question. Now, thanks to our patron saint, the one Susan has told for the past two years that we'll be done in two weeks, we'll have the kitchen we want.

When Susan returns a little while later we take our sandwiches—the same damn 105 and 7 that we always get—settle on the front lawn moss, and casually engage in some neighborhood surveillance. The local traffic today is intense. Norman, who I saw heading homeward on my way to the market, is doing his best Mr. Roboto back toward town, a crisp manila envelope under his arm. Witchie Poo races to and fro three times in the space of one sandwich, pedal-pumping like a mad rabbit. By the time we're getting up to leave, Norman is lurching homeward yet again with a brown paper bag. In the two years we've been toiling, I've never once spoken with him.

He's never even looked over in our direction or acknowledged anything has even taken place on our property. The house could be burning down and his eyes would be fixed forward. Today, I decide to dare a hello as he passes by.

"Hello," I say.

He jerks his head toward me, startled, but rapid fires out a near shout, "HI!" then promptly redirects his gaze toward the center of the street and marches off. It is one of the more peculiar encounters I've had in life, much less in Sag Harbor. I glance over to Susan to see what she thinks, but she missed it. Her eyes are focused on the mailman.

"What could this be?" Susan asks. The postman has left his truck and is walking toward us with a large package.

"I don't know," I lie. He tramps across the mossy expanse and hands it to Susan.

"Thanks."

She studies the label, which is addressed to her. "I didn't order anything from L.L. Bean." She's incredulous.

I stand back and let her open it.

"What's . . . what are these . . ." Susan is pulling one, two, three large canvas bags out of the box.

"Bags," I say, "they're bags."

"Ye-ah," like I'm the idiot, "but I didn't order them." It's not yet sinking in.

"Well, *someone* did."

A smile crosses her face, perhaps less from the windfall in sacks so much as from seeing me make an effort. A glimmer of life, of playfulness, returning.

"Honey," I say, "I can't change the fact that we're living in bags, but at least we can live in *better* bags."

She thanks me with a kiss, and asks, "Could you also order a working bathroom?"

Operation Biscuits

If Floyd's crew was the Bad News Bears, Corinthian Construction is Special Ops. Everything is done with a military precision and a regimented emphasis on appearance (uniforms!). On my first day, I report to the office to fill out paperwork for Tiffani, and she gives me a dossier emblazoned with the now familiar Corinthian name. Inside I find a list of current projects, phone numbers, a detailed map with directions to Lot 5 (my job site), and time sheets. Everything is emblazoned CORINTHIAN and complemented with an architectural rendering (blueprint blue and complete with dimension lines) of a Corinthian column capital.

Driving onto Lot 5 is like entering a private resort, a Club Med of construction, with large white signs that stand sentry and show the way. I strap on the same worn tool belt bisexual Ritchie found me so many months ago and meet up with Dirk, who has a walrus mustache and a ticklish temperament.

After observing that I can cut wood without killing myself, Dirk starts to put me through the paces, asking me to work on a complicated door and two window combination that has to be trimmed out. Significantly, my project is on the back side of the house. My first day with Corinthian is a lesson to prospective home buyers: If you want to see how well a house is built, don't examine the entryway or the living room—check out the back door or the basement. That's where the untested workers go. (The quality of workmanship on a house is revealed in an infinite number of unexpected ways: I can now surmise the dedication behind a builder by merely touching a towel rack his crew has installed.)

On most homes, rough openings are framed and then windows and doors with preattached exterior trim are inserted into those openings. The interior trim is completed later, after the Sheetrock installers (the "rockers") are done. On high-end or custom construction—which is to say, Corinthian Construction—the exterior trim is also done on site. Think about that for a second. If you put a window in a space larger than itself, how do you nail any trim to the window without it toppling over?

Dirk shows me a back entryway, a set of French doors and two windows. Since the distance between the door and each window is not great, a single piece of preprimed lumber must trim out both the window and the door above, and then only the door at the lower part. It's a tricky set of cuts made trickier by the fact that the window jam is flush with the rough opening, but the door protrudes out from the building by an additional eighth of an inch. To avoid water seepage, the board must lay flat against the house, the window, *and* the door.

"You're gonna have to dado out the back," Dirk explains, "so it catches the door jamb right. Rabbet it out, okay?" Is he looking at me suspiciously?

"Sure," I say flatly.

Dado? Rabbet? Dirk used the terms interchangeably. I'm not familiar with either one of them. I collect my materials and take my measurements slowly. When Dirk is off somewhere I ask Jaime if his door frame gave him problems, fishing for insights on just what to do. Reprising my act from Floyd's crew I ask him where the dado is on the tool truck. This is a misstep, since a dado is not a tool, but a type of cut that channels out excess material so that adjacent pieces of wood fit together snugly. Jaime looks at me quizzically and says, "Just do it on the table saw." I mull this over until it comes to me, how cutting on the table saw with two shallow cuts will make my piece of trim sit flatly against the house.

Dirk swings back to check on me and to remind me, in case he forgot to mention it, that the door frames have to be biscuited. *Will this torment never cease? What the hell is a biscuit?* "Yeah, I assumed," I say, looking over his shoulder to keep track of Jaime's movements. I'm gonna have some questions.

When the time comes, I ask around for the biscuit cutter. "You seen where it got to?" I ask no one in particular, in my by now well-honed techinique. It's on "that sawhorse there," Jamie points, and I lament having fostered more bad English. I grab the tool by the handle, but can't for the life of me figure how it works. There are two metal pieces at a ninety-degree angle to each other, but they are unmoveable. I press the trigger, reck-lessly, and hear a blade but don't see it. I stand back, pretend to remeasure my board, and wait for someone else to use it.

Jaime mercifully walks over, and asks me, "You done?"

"It's all yours."

He holds the cutter flush to his trim piece, presses the trigger, and forces the biscuiter toward the board. Wood shavings fly out the sides. Finally, I get it: The retracted blade is spring-loaded and cuts out a thin wafer-shaped biscuit in the edge of the board when the tool is pressed hard against it. Jaime walks off without knowing he saved me.

Used in both mitered and butt joints, biscuits help form a superstrong connection. The biscuit itself expands from the moisture in the glue and locks two boards in a tight joint. As I'm finishing, I'm confronted by Mr. Johnnie, the world's best blind carpenter. He is spoken of reverently by Nick the Greek and

One F, as his skills are superhuman and exact. He owns every tool ever made. He's not really blind, but his eyewear lenses are thicker than the shark-tank glass at SeaWorld.

"What dimensions is your dado?" he asks. I'm momentarily stymied by what he's asking me, and also I can't help staring at his left eye, which ricochets left and right in its socket like a billiard ball. How the hell does he hammer a nail?

Recovering, I recall how I got the window trim to work. "I've cut three eighths out one quarter deep."

"Sweet," he says, and launches into Mr. Johnnie patois, a numbingly rarefied carpenter speak. "Then rather than rip it twice on the table I can set my three-eighths flute route to channel it out."

"Hey, if it works for you," I say, and watch his wide frame, accentuated by the wide-body L-1011 of tool belts, rattle back to where he was working. I go to start on another window that needs to be trimmed out.

"Aw, fuck!" I say, after cutting the wrong edge of some one-by-ten trim. I turn the saw off, put my board down, and ponder what to do. And then it dawns on me: I'm the only one swearing on this crew. These guys are positively clean-cut. No swearing, no drink, no drugs. Everyone is weirdly dedicated, even cogent. The severity of purpose extends, I'm shocked to learn, to a policy of no breaks. We're working a punishing ten-hour day in the sun and get only twenty minutes for lunch. There will be no Roach Coach today, nor any day.

Amazingly, no one is complaining about it. In addition to Mr. Johnnie, I'm surrounded by Hilario, a kid from Mexico who stylishly wears a cotton rag like a bolo tie; Doug, a mild-mannered Opie look-alike; Claudio the Tornado, whose rapid pace of work is staggering; and Magnus the Mute, a thirty-five-year veteran of the carpentry trade who is far and away the most talented craftsman I've ever met. Magnus's last job was doing custom window installations, a magnificence that costs somewhere in the neighborhood of three quarters of a million dollars. For windows. Interestingly, Magnus doesn't own his own home. Never has.

Announced by an advance party of aftershave, Nick the Greek roars up the dirt driveway in a new Chevrolet Avalanche, a truck/SUV that looks positively interstellar in its design. Jumping out of the cab he is already talking before both feet touch the ground. "How's it going, guys?" he asks. "Lawrence, how ya doin'?" He works the place like a brilliantined Mafia capo in a social club. He says hello to everyone, gleefully taking in the progress. His pride is obvious, that he is in charge of this large crew, that he is responsible for erecting this superb and superbly massive home. I envy him that.

Everyone appreciates the attention, even as they occasionally wonder how much his truck cost. That afternoon I do a rough survey of the vehicles this company has amassed: I see two matching 2002 Chevy Avalanches (Nick's and One F's), an emerald green Dodge 4×4, a white Dodge Ram Sport 4×4, a Ford XLT Lariat, a Jeep Laredo, a maroon Nissan Pathfinder ("Painting Division"), and two white tool trailers. They are all emblazoned with the Corinthian name and architectural rendering. These guys may know building but damn it, they *really* know branding.

Perhaps the most startling turn of events is that I am surviving on this crew, while others more senior are being shown the door for poor work. Jaime, a veteran with twenty years experience, gets fired on my first day. His habits were a little lax, I am told. If their standards are so high, I worry I could be next. So I'm startled when word gets back to me, two weeks later, that Dirk said about my work, "He's a little slow, but it's the cleanest framing I've ever seen." Nick repeats this pronouncement as encouragement, and I take it, simultaneously proud and fighting not to betray myself with laughter.

"Is that Cynthia Nixon?" Susan asks, looking stunning in a long black dress. I don't look half bad myself, though it's been so long since we've been out for a classy Manhattan evening that I feel like a kid the first time he's in a suit. I left work early to be here. Susan's father, Ray, sensing how desperately we needed a break, invited us as his guests to the Gala Benefit for City Center, where he is chairman of the board.

"I wouldn't know Cynthia Nixon if she slapped me with a mackerel," I say, handing her a glass of Perrier at intermission. I order a stiff glass of champagne.

"From *Sex and the City?*" Susan prompts. Clearly I haven't been keeping up with my gossip-column reading. Tonight there is plenty to keep up with. The lobby sparkles, and the crowd does, too. A dazzling array of New York luminaries are scattered throughout the crowd, from writers Tom Wicker and Tom Wolfe to actors Alec Baldwin, Joanne Woodward, and Paul Newman. We are joined by Monica and a friend of hers. I pocket my scarred and glue-stained hands.

"You all right?" Monica asks Susan. "You look a little pale."

"Fine, just tired," Susan says, not wanting to alarm her during the festivities. In truth, she has been feeling terrible and lethargic for days. I worry that the entire renovation has finally, undeniably become too much. Ulcerous. She grips her stomach as we go in for the second half of the *The Pajama Game*. She's a fighter and slow to complain, so I know whatever it is might change everything. As soon as the final curtain falls we squeeze down the aisle.

"How's *This Old Fucking House?*" asks Peter, an acquaintance who works tirelessly as a war correspondent.

"Good," I lie. "How's your book coming?"

"*Done!*"

"Must be nice not having a full-time job," I quip, "plenty of time to sit home and write!" He chuckles and we say goodnight. Susan is feeling worse, and we both reluctantly insist on skipping the after party and the chance to chitchat with celebrities and pretend they are just like us. I hurry to get Susan into a cab. Get her home, get her some rest.

The following morning the bulldog in Susan is inclined not to bother going to the doctor's, feeling moderately better and hoping the abdominal pain will continue to subside. I implore her to follow through, what can it hurt? She promises, and I kiss her good-bye to head back to the job site.

The whole drive back I wonder if she'll bother to go, and am moderately anxious that she might not. As much as I love her strength, I also have difficulty with her refusal to listen to anyone else, namely me. I count the ways—or start to—that we have refused to back down in the past year. Two equally stubborn nutcases, steadfastly arguing that we wanted black granite or green marble for countertops when, in point of fact, neither of us had really given it any thought fifteen minutes previous or harbored any real countertop convictions.

Perhaps it is too easy to suggest that illness or disease or unforeseen circumstances can change people, relationships. Perhaps the relationship is not changed, but restored; monumental news has a way of clarifying what is essential. That, at least, is what I experience when I finally track Susan down that afternoon, not at her normal doctor's office, but at a specialist. Every unhappy thought and quibbling argument wasn't eradicated but put aside, put aside in a way that helped me escape the momentary pressures of our renovation and helped me recapture my love for my wife. Everything, and I don't care if it sounds like a cliché, was changed in two words. Two words that added more pressure, more financial stress, more excitement, and one huge goddamn deadline.

"I'm pregnant."

Getting Plastered

Brain surgery was invented to give employment to those people who don't have the patience, the dexterity, or the fine motor skills to spackle. Anyone who has ever finished off a room of Sheetrock, or frosted a cake, knows this. And yet the two trades do share some similarities: When performed admirably, brain surgery, like good spackling, is invisible. Conversely, bad spackling, like bad brain surgery, is obvious. Smooth walls take on a freakish appearance when marred with huge taped sutures and pustules of plaster. The evidence of a hack, a pretender, a neophyte.

After my parents' unscheduled early departure, thanks to that broken ankle, Cliff and Barb were overtaken by pangs of guilt, having come to help and, instead, barely achieving a good vacuuming before being vanquished. Feeling terrible that they had to leave before we were able to accomplish the one large task we had set for ourselves—Sheetrocking phase one, the upstairs and the living room—they generously offered to pay to have it professionally done. To say we didn't hesitate would be understatement.

"So we would like to . . ."

"Great!"

"pay for the Sheetrock."

"Thanks. We never imagined you would have offered but, wow, it'll be a big help."

Our eagerness was fed by that morning's Waterloo. I had rented a Sheetrock lift from One Source rental in Southampton, convinced that Susan and I could pop things up like professionals. Since our living room is eleven feet ten inches wide, I figured we could slice two inches off a twelve-foot piece of Sheetrock and winch it above us as effortlessly as a cloud. It was a ridiculous approach, as the tight space combined with my misplaced drive for perfection caused the board to pinch in every direction as we raised it. The lift, properly used, will make getting a twelve-foot piece of Sheetrock screwed off above your head relatively simple; without it, Susan and I wrestled the thing above us, clumsily propping sagging sections with an elbow or head while holding screws and drills in our hands. We pushed at it wildly, looking like we had been set upon by vultures. Nothing would get it into place for us. Pushing, pulling, hitting, swearing. None were of any avail. Susan suggested we align the Sheetrock in the other direction, lengthwise in the room, but I was adamant. It would look silly with so many seams. On our subsequent try, with redoubled effort and increased swearing, the board buckled, cracked, and toppled down onto both of us. What wasn't broken then was broken shortly thereafter, when I threw the remainder across the room in a fit. "Fuck it! I'm taking the thing back."

"We could try it the other way . . ."

"I'm done. We'll hire someone for this crap. Goddamn it!"

I was at work the day they came, but I returned home to a staggering amount of progress. The studs, heating ducts, electrical wires, phone lines, and insulation had all disappeared. All that was visible was a smooth skin of Sheetrock. Strangely, however, a multicolored trail of candy wrappers snaked through each room, even up the stairwell. Skittles, Mars bars, Mike and Ikes, Sour Patch Kids; phase one was either Sheetrocked by a bunch of alcoholics in need of a sugar fix or a group of exceptionally skilled seven-year-olds. The second group of Sheetrock substance abusers—the smokers—arrived the next day and commenced the spackling. With remarkable speed they had the seams taped, the holes patched, the rough spots sanded smooth. How hard can that be?

Once phase two comes around, we are older, wiser, and disinclined to repeat our mistakes with the drywall lift. It had damn near killed us, and then we damn near killed each other. Susan has another idea, and it doesn't mean traveling to Southampton to pick up any tools: She is thinking Dan and Cyndy.

"We can't do that," I protest, "we barely know them."

"We do too know them."

"Not Sheetrock know them."

"It'll take ten minutes to get these three pieces on the ceiling."

"Should you really be lifting?" I ask. Susan is feeling a reprieve from her abdominal discomfort, and is eager to get this done.

"Why not?" she asks, knowing very well why not, but dismissing my concerns as prematurely overprotective. "They'll help us get the pieces on the ceiling, then you and I can do all these walls, see?"

I did see. I saw disaster. If we were lucky we could get *one* up in ten minutes.

Then again, some progress is better then no progress. Besides, the Sheetrocking candyholics had proved Susan right, and me wrong, about the direction in the living room. This was an opportunity to even the score. Two Sheetrocking wrongs, evenly distributed, would make us both right.

When I look out the window and spot Dan and Cyndy walking up Division Street, I almost feel sorry for them. They're so innocent and unknowing, so trusting. Susan focuses on them like a hawk on field mice. *Oh, Jesus.* She runs out to snare them and I follow behind reluctantly, raising my eyebrows in a way that says this wasn't my idea.

"Hi guys," Susan calls over the front nonlawn.

Dan shouts, "What's up, Chip?" using the nom de guerre they assigned Susan after seeing her paint each bedroom three times, then promptly pull out more paint chips to consider whether she should go for a fourth. Like we need more work.

Cyndy the Atlanta spitfire asks if we want anything from the deli. "We're going to grab a bagel."

"I'm good," I say, "but you can tell Rich I'll be better if he doesn't sell out of his pastrami special again today." Susan says she's good, too—though I guess she's not talking about her intentions.

Then Dan walks right into it, asking, "What are you guys working on today?"

I hunt around for a tree to stare at.

"The kitchen," Susan says.

"Wow, that'll be huge when you get it done. You guys are so . . ."

"We were wondering . . ."

I wasn't wondering, I think. I most emphatically was not wondering.

"If you guys could help us on your way back. Just for ten minutes."

"Sure," Cyndy says. I'm not sure she knows that she is agreeing to heavy lifting.

"We just need help getting a sheet of drywall on the ceiling," Susan explains. "The rest we can handle."

"Yeah, we can do that," Dan says in a much more measured tone.

I'm hoping my silence is communicating that I had nothing to do with this.

"Great!" Susan says.

Miraculously they return, and we show them the one piece of drywall that we have to get up. Forty-five minutes later all four of us are atop overturned spackling-compound buckets, struggling to keep sheet number *two* aloft. Dan, Cyndy, and Susan are in charge of holding. I am in charge of drilling—and getting everyone caught in the extension cord. "I could go get another drill," Dan offers. "I've got a cordless."

"That might be a good idea," I say.

I catch Dan and Cyndy exchanging a glance and I feign an apology. "We'll reroof your place next week," I offer. We all laugh vacantly. We're not going to be reroofing their place because *they* are not going to be reroofing their place. They are smarter than we are: They will hire someone to do it.

Several hours later, four of us frosted with a light Sheetrock dusting, we are sore and winded. I'm not sure how, physically, an emphysemic sugar addict can do this work on a daily basis. Dan and Cyndy are surprisingly good humored about the affair, but they are smart enough not to walk by our house again during working hours. For weeks they run their errands using the other end of the street.

Without extra lifting power, there is no way we are going to get the rest of the Sheetrock up. And to hire another crew is simply too expensive. We decide instead to take the middle road, hiring unskilled semiprofessionals, and for the first time enter the Hampton's skin trade. Seven days a week, groups of Mexicans and Central and South American immigrants collect in front of Riverhead Building Supply to get work as day laborers. Builders, landscapers, pool cleaners, and home owners circle like grocery store habitués looking for a red-light special. More often than not they find it.

On Sunday morning, Susan and I pull onto the opposite side of the road, careful not to give away our immediate intent lest we be descended upon. "Are we sure we want to do this?" I ask, sounding like I need some affirmation before I go score us some heroin.

"Why? It's not illegal is it?"

"I dunno. How can it be if they're all out here?"

"Well, we need to get the kitchen done." True, the work isn't getting done, and it is already close to ten. We can't squander the day.

"That one looks strong, has broad shoulders," I say, as if assessing a passing parade of Vegas-strip hookers. I step out of the car, closing the door quietly.

"Go talk to him," Susan says. "And ask that guy in the orange shirt."

"Why him?"

"He's got a nice smile. Probably a good attitude."

I crane my head back in the car door to look at her squarely. "He's not going to buy you a drink. He'll be hoisting gypsum over his head."

"Exactly. You need a good attitude for that."

"Maybe you do," I say, rolling my eyes.

I walk across the street and suddenly I'm more loved than Shakira. Everyone circles around me, eager for work. I talk to Edgar and Rudy, two Ecuadorians, but they want fifteen bucks an hour cash. It occurs to me that, considering taxes, this is better than I make working on a legitimate crew. It's a buyer's market so I haggle, "Eleven and I'll buy lunch."

They practically carry me back to the car. Through my fractured Spanish I explain that they both have to get in from the driver's side of the car, and they look at me like I'm some kind of weirdo.

Of course, the expertise Edgar and Rudy so eloquently professed—*si, si, si*—at the lumberyard melts to bald ignorance by the time we're back at the house cutting the first piece of drywall. To make up for their utter lack of knowledge as drywall professionals, they move very fast. In all directions. I try to calm them down, saying that doing it once slowly is better than twice fast, but my Spanish is about as good as their Sheetrocking. They enthusiastically agree—*si, si, si*—no matter what I say, and race ahead. Somehow, almost inexplicably, we get the stuff up by quitting time Sunday. Ragged, yes, but that's why God invented Spackle.

As blown sideways and tired as the pregnancy is making Susan feel, it is energizing me. Realigned, I am working with renewed vigor, feeling that she—*they*—are depending on me. Which is why it is midnight and I am spackling. Badly. I can't get the hang of it, and I have tried every technique I can conceive of. Doing overhead tape, I apply the speed-is-everything approach, balancing a two-by-twelve board on two Spackle buckets and running the length of it, Spackle paddle aloft, smoothing plaster compound before it dries. Rooster tails of white compound fly behind me like I am hydroplaning. This can't be right. Then again, I don't have time for right.

When the speed-is-everything approach leaves specks, trails, and bald patches, I convert to the more-is-more approach, smearing on great thicknesses of the stuff, then scraping off what doesn't fall naturally from the force of gravity. This too has its drawbacks, as the elevated board I am treading on grows increasingly slick. I modify my methodology again, settling on the slap-and-tickle: spanking a good pound of compound over the tape and drawing it along softly with a wide blade. One-thirty in the morning rolls around and I put down my tools and admire my work. Overspackled? That doesn't begin to describe it. I am in the world's largest meringue.

Susan and I are sitting across from my parents at the Beacon restaurant on Water Street in Sag Harbor. The June sun is sliding over Long Beach and into the bay. Susan and I are on pins and needles, not having told anyone but Monica and Ray about the tiny knot of cells in Susan's abdomen that are racing to divide, replicate, and become someone. We're not sure if we are ready to tell anyone, but we can't *not* tell them, considering Susan is entering her late first-trimester sleepies. Besides, we figure it will cheer them up: While driving out to visit us they got word that their dog died.

My father grins a grin I have never seen cross his face before. He looks childlike.

"That's great. When's the due—"

"December Sixteen."

Our attention pans right, to my mother. She looks like someone punched her.

"That means you won't be home for Christmas."

"Probably not," I say, avoiding the less measured *"Duh!"* out of respect for her bereaved state. First the dog, and now *we* are abandoning her is how I imagine she feels, and that's what came out, however badly.

Cliff brings it around. "This is more important . . ."

"Of course, of course," she says, catching herself. "But you should really tell your brother and sister, too."

Huh?

"We will," I say, "but it's early. We're telling you because you're here."

"And we appreciate . . ."

Appreciate? We're not RSVPing.

"I mean, it is wonderful news. It is so . . ."

"I'm glad, we're glad . . ." Mom tries one last time, then collapses.

Oh shit. Where is this tangled conversation going?

"Did you hear the specials?" I ask, trying to change the subject.

"Halibut, I think he said," Susan answers, in a tone I know well by now, a tone that says she doesn't know how this visit, this celebratory dinner, got off to such an odd start so quickly and so irretrievably. A tone that also says she just wants to go back to sleep.

After dinner we head home and camp at our house. At least my parents do. We had planned to give them the one operational mattress in the house—ours—but Susan's state has changed all that. Instead, they sleep in the back bedroom on an inflatable mattress that they seem to take with them everywhere, just in case. The next morning they are up punishingly early, seven A.M., my mother already vacuuming and my father sanding. It's clear why they have survived so well together for all these years.

By the time Susan and I make it downstairs, my father looks like the abominable snowman from the Rudolph the Red-Nosed Reindeer special. Thanks to his still-healing ankle, he walks a bit like him, too.

"Jesus, Dad, you should be wearing a dust mask."

"That's what Momsie just said." He calls her Momsie, which I think she likes, except when she doesn't and she says, *I'm not your mother.*

"That's what I told him," she pipes in from the living room, where she is painting the front door with forensic care: sand, vacuum, sand, tack cloth, prime, sand, tack cloth, paint, sand, paint. We all have a quick breakfast and Susan goes back to bed, destroyed with fatigue. For some weeks this is, and will be, her schedule. Wake, eat, then promptly go back to bed until lunch or dinner. Susan's mother was the same way, apparently, during the early part of her pregnancies. Anything other than sleep was simply not an option. Interestingly, my mother was not at all this way during any of her pregnancies. I may be imagining it, but this seems to be a source of friction between the two of them. Perhaps Susan feels guilty—however wrongly, but *you* try telling that to a pregnant woman—that she is sleeping while everyone else is working. Or does my mother feel, hey, we traveled halfway across the country to help, and you're going to sleep? Where did the antagonism start? Is it even real? I have no idea, but this much I know: I am stuck in the middle and parse every statement like an independent counsel.

My mother amps up the palm sander to smooth the door for a second coat, then remembers someone is sleeping in the house. "I hope I'm not being too loud," she says.

Was that a dig?

If it was, Susan's nascent maternal intuition is some dangerous mojo: She's downstairs with us minutes later, willing to pitch in.

After hours of continuous sanding, my father succeeds in getting all Spackle off the walls and onto him. The surfaces are once again flat but he has clearly shaved years off his life. The four of us huddle in the kitchen and survey the cabinets. There are nineteen cabinet cubes that have to be assembled like a three-dimensional puzzle against the back and side wall of our kitchen. This is easily the most complicated project we've taken on, because differences of even a sixteenth of an inch will affect how the cabinets join together and how the granite countertop rests atop them. It is also, easily, the most high stakes, given the price of the cabinets.

"Which end are you going to start on?" my mother asks. I sense she has an opinion, given her experience, but she doesn't want to come off as bossy.

"I think the right?" I say, looking at my father.

He scowls in concentration.

"Right?" I say, looking to Susan.

She looks again at the cabinet layout in her hands. "I don't know; it seems that the left corner is the most difficult." True, three pieces come together as the cabinetry turns the corner from back to side wall. It would make sense to get warmed up elsewhere, save the toughest for last. But if all the other cabinets don't line up perfectly the slight variations will accumulate and become grossly apparent in this corner where there is no room for error. It bears mentioning here that the wall is not completely straight, as the studs have twisted, turned, and bowed slightly over the years as they have dried out. I should have used a power planer and a six-foot level to make the wall completely flat, but I only learned this trick after we put the Sheetrock up. An even better trick, when money is plentiful, is to use studs made of engineered lumber—which remains straight—for kitchens and bathrooms. This trick is even more useful today, as highbred woods are grown rapidly for quick profit, resulting in trees with fewer growth rings, which results in lumber more susceptible to twisting and bowing as they dry.

"Screw it," I say, "let's work up to the corner." Everyone assents halfheartedly. "What the heck," Cliff says. We wrestle the first few cubes into place, shimming behind the cabinets where necessary, then screwing them into the walls. Susan, against our protestations, moves cabinets around the kitchen as we need them.

Once we make it to the corner we make some calculations. Then some more. Cliff sighs, "Let's remeasure the cabinet."

"Great idea," I say, hoping that it varies from what the specs say it should be. It doesn't; it's exactly twenty-seven and thirteen-sixteenth-inches. As we figure it, there will be a quarter-inch gap between the left wall and center cabinets. That is huge—a gaping hole that can't be corrected with a liberal amount of phenoseal caulking.

Cliff and I trade glances like defeated running backs after the homecoming game. "Damn," I say.

"Well . . . ," Cliff starts.

"Yeah?" I jump at the chance he might have a solution.

"We could just force 'em together. A couple really big screws . . ."

We both know this will split the wood, making an even more unsightly situation. "Or we could hold them in place and see what we are dealing with, outside of the measurements." We recruit Mom and Susan to help with the fiasco. We strain to keep the cubes aloft, squeezed together in place.

"Not bad," Mom says as encouragement. I throw Cliff a look, masking my surprise. He's smirking and might explode into laughter, giving us away.

"Here," Susan says, handing me a power drill with the swiftness of an operating room nurse. I screw them into place and can't believe the result. The imperfections in the bowed walls cancel out the quarter inch gap we had created installing the other cabinets. Cliff and I smile a pursed lip promise not to say a word, then share a high five.

"They're perfect!" Susan yells with glee.

I feign offense. "You *doubted* us?"

Performance Anxiety

The first days working for Corinthian are a head-spinning series of different jobs. I suspect they are moving me into and out of as many environments as possible, testing me out, seeing what I am capable of. After working on the Lot 5 exterior trim for a day and a half I am pulled over to a job building a picket fence on a waterfront estate in Water Mill. I'm paired with Doug, a transplant from Missoula, Montana. Doug is a stranger in all senses of the word. When his temper flares he exclaims, "Boy howdy!" and when he's really disappointed with himself, he bellows rhetorically, "What's a girl to do?" But these outbursts are rare, since he rarely makes mistakes.

He is wrapping the posts with clear cedar, and I'm charged with putting the points on the pickets, known colloquially as "cutting the tits." Doug says that he wouldn't do any other job, though he came to carpentry after trying other avenues, including graduate school.

"No kidding. A master's degree?" I ask, unsure if I'm happy to be working with someone who will be able to carry on an educated conversation, or mildly piqued that my uniqueness has evaporated. Not that I'm confessing so much as a GED just yet. "In what?"

"Recreational therapy," he says.

"Recreational therapy," I repeat, turning it over for a minute. "Yeah."

"So what's that mean," I say, "you got a master's in playground?"

He laughs. "Yeah, I'm a professional camp counselor." It doesn't sound like the Doug in front of me. He is demonstrably dedicated to his career; he has more tools than a mad dentist. I'm mildly in awe of his commitment, as he exudes a northwest woodsy devotion when I see that his hammer handle, his square, and other tools are made from wood, not fiberglass or metal. In light of his obvious acumen, I am all the more amused when he calls me over to where he is working. "Let me ask your professional opinion on something," he says.

Is he kidding? No, it seems he is not.

After my two-day stint working with Doug, I'm asked to run a job in Southampton. I'm flabbergasted momentarily, then nervous at the responsibility. If my work collapses who is on the hook? Me? Corinthian? Soon I learn that the job is finishing a basement room and constructing a massive twenty-four-by-ten-foot table to hold a toy train aloft. No one is going to die. Maybe. The train enthusiast is paying somewhere in the neighborhood of fifty thousand dollars to watch his choo-choo go in meticulously planned circles. More tellingly, I am told that the job has become mine because all the veteran guys have begged off the job. On Friday afternoon I learn why.

"What's this?" asks Augusten, a precociously dangerous seven-year-old.

Oh, Jesus! "That's a nail gun," I say. "Please put it *down*."

Augusten's four-year-old brother, Broderick, is running loose and unsupervised, too. "Can I have this?"

"No, Broderick, that's toxic," I say, grabbing an oozing tube of construction adhesive out of his hand.

"What's tox—"

"Poisonous." I look over at my partner, my helper, my crew: Hidalgo. He can't believe we're building out the whole basement for "thees fucking train" and he can't understand why we have to work around these tiny terrors to do it.

He returns my look and just shakes his head, then points behind me. "*Cuidado!*" Augusten is chasing Broderick with a pencil—the pencil he snatched from my tool belt. Oh, God. I lunge to grab it, but it's too late. Broderick gets it in the side of the head. Screaming, he runs up the stairs. Augusten is mildly surprised at the noise level, then picks up a Jap saw—the trade term for a jagged-toothed pull saw.

"What's this?"

The whirlwind continues when I am next transferred to Lot 4, otherwise known as Nick's house. The boss's lair. One of the angles of professional contractors, whether Floyd or Corinthian, is to use the cheap labor on your own house. I am sent over with Ecuadorean Edy to frame gable ends on the entire second floor. Sitting atop a hill, I scout out the house. It's a large, if by this time predictable, Hamptons manse, with the required red cedar shingles, Marvin windows, and Belgian block drive. A distinctive twist will be the third-floor hot tub to watch the planes take off and land at East Hampton airport.

It is also the toughest and most hazardous work I've been asked to perform. Real man-sized construction. The gables soar four-teen feet from the second floor, and framing to code with two-by-six fir, the boards are long and heavy. To get the king studs into position, which is all but impossible from within the house on high ladders, we set a metal screened platform on a forklift and raise it high into the air. It rattles in the unseasonably cold wind that charges up the hill. I climb up first and get immediately vertiginous. The platform sways. I struggle to keep my balance, holding the Paslode gun and boards. Edy laughs at my struggles and continues in his stubbornly broken English. "Es too shorty."

"It looks too short to you?" I say, seeking confirmation.

"*Sí*, es too shorty." I can see him judging the plumb of the stud. "Need more longer."

I ask him to confirm plumb, before we cut more lumber. He holds the cheap "Contractor Grade" level I bought at Riverhead Building Supply.

"Es nivel," he says, holding the six-foot level to the board.

That's odd. I move the board an inch and a half to the right. "How 'bout now?" I ask.

"*Sí*, es nivel." Level again. Plumb. I look down at him and catch him snickering. "Pinche nivel." Fucking level. We laugh. I should have spent the extra money on a good level: This one would read the Tower of Pisa plumb. My boss has entrusted me to construct his home and I'm turning it into a fun house of off angles.

I put the last board into position and angle nail it. Perhaps from the cold, perhaps from an overaggressive angle, the nail skips off the board and hits my hand like a bullet. I've shot myself. There is a fiery throbbing in my hand and I almost lose my balance, getting a good look at the forty-foot fall beneath me. I squeeze my hand and wonder if I am worse off not having health insurance or not having life insurance.

Next stop is the Hausman-Tso home, tucked in the pine-heavy forests of East Hampton off of Swamp Road. An expansive green edifice, dark green board and batten siding, the place looks like a neo-Austrian sausage factory. Small square windows circle the second floor, and glass panes fill the entirety of some walls. It is a cathedral to the unnecessary expense. I spend hours installing bathroom fixtures, six-hundred-dollar toilet paper holders, one-hundred-dollar towel hooks, priceless door stops. The cherry wood floors have been sanded and tongue-oiled three times and they are getting ready for the fourth. If you hold your head horizontal, down low, and if the light is right, you can see some sanding marks left by the drum sander. I consider suggesting that if they let the sandy-shoed owners and their guests walk through on an ordinary beach weekend you won't be worried about the specters of a drum sander anymore, but I think better than to put my oar in. The biggest obstacle to completion—and this job is woefully behind sched-ule—is the missing kitchen cabinets. They have not yet arrived from Germany. Balthorp is the must-have brand in Manhattan, apparently, and these city dwellers must have them in the country as well. The cabinets will knock the kitchen price well over the two-hundred-thousand-dollar mark. I corner the foreman for more details and we fall into the bitchy superiority that you only hear from bored carpenters and the Bravo channel.

"Balthus?" I ask.

"No, Balthorp."

"Well, whatever. For that kind of money they must be fantas-tic. Inset, the whole shebang?"

"They're *overlay*, can you believe it?"

"I *can't*. Overlay. They must be solid wood, though?"

"*Veneer!*"

I hold up a hand. "I don't want to hear any more."

The following weekend, our new plumber, Paul Halsey, comes over to put in an up-to-date exit line for the downstairs auxiliary bath-room. When we bought the house this room was little more than a glorified outhouse, less commodious than your average truck-stop restroom. It was a bare toilet and sink, installed halfheartedly by the previous owner, and attached to a separate septic tank that was tougher to find than a lost ark. As I dug for the mysterious pool, the backyard began to look as though it had been attacked by a voracious pack of gophers. I called Schwartz, the previous owner, who insisted it was "just beyond the driveway" in the back. I gauged where the driveway had been before the excavators carted it off, then dug and probed repeatedly and unsuccessfully. Finally, out of frustration, I dug an eight-foot-long ditch where the line would have to pass, were it in the backyard. Six feet down and without result, I swore that I would either find the damn pipe or become a grave digger. I resolved to dig from the house, following the pipe as far as it took me, to once and for all determine if there was a septic tank attached to it and if it was usable. (Otherwise, it would be prohibitively costly to reroute the bathroom.) I heard a clink as I hit the steel pipe exiting the house. In minutes I had hit pay dirt: the septic a scant ten feet straight out from the side of the house—nowhere near the driveway. I was thrilled but confounded. Is Schwartz's memory that bad, or did he mislead me because, despite being on the zoning board, he never sought a permit for the new tank?

Downstairs, Paul is breaking up a section of the slab floor. I enter the cement-dusty cacophony with trepidation. Paul looks like he could be Hades' bouncer. Fierce green eyes stare out of his big blocky head. Lavishly tattooed arms, wider than my thighs, taper only slightly to beefy hands that look like they could crush concrete. To complete the aesthetic, his boom box spews a punishing and unrelenting playlist of Black Sabbath and Ozzy Osbourne. He says he never asked what happened to our first plumber. I tell him how close we came to murder, and wouldn't recommend Goodnough to anyone.

He smiles a crowded toothy grin. "What?" I ask.

"Lemme guess, they sent a couple guys. Solid work. Then they sent a couple guys who didn't know their ass from an Allen wrench. Fucked it up. You got pissed. Your calls got returned but nothing got fixed."

I'm stunned. "Yeah, how'd you know?"

"I used to work for Goodnough," he says, laughing. "I was one of the first guys. Got sick of other guys fucking up my work. He grew too big too fast, so now he's got all these idiots."

"No kidding."

He grabs his jackhammer and prepares to return to it, then stops short. "Where's Susan?" he asks.

"Sleeping," I say.

"Sick?" He sounds genuinely worried.

"No. Yes. Not exactly," I fumble, then make some stupid gesture like I've got an enlarged abdomen.

"Hey, congratulations, man. That's great. It's a trip."

"Thanks. It's pretty exciting." I can't help but smile.

"I wanted to be a delivery nurse."

"You? Really?" I'm having trouble visualizing newborns arriving to a Nurse Paul's workplace soundtrack of "Suicide Solution" and "Children of the Grave."

"Yeah, I really got into it. Birth and all that. Read everything I could. I wanted to study to become a nurse and they said men couldn't be delivery nurses."

"That's weird, there are male delivery doctors."

He shrugs and jerks his hammer over to a section of recalcitrant concrete.

I turn to head back upstairs, but catch myself and say, "By the way, nice haircut." It is cropped very closely, a change that makes him look even more severe.

"Thanks. Gotta look respectable." He draws a hand over the stubble on his crown.

"Did you go to Marty's?"

"How'd you know?"

Remarkably, Susan and I had landed on a superlative deal for our kitchen cabinetry. Searching through Home Depot and various cabinetry showrooms, we were aghast. The standard, off-the-assembly-line cabinets looked like something from IKEA, but shoddy and at five times the price. Our disgust turned to despair, that we might have to spend so much money to be so dissatisfied, like going to a four-star restaurant knowing you would contract food poisoning. Determined not to buy cabinetry that was going to fall apart in a year, we searched antique stores, but failed to find a workable solution, the slipper that would transform our kitchen into something regal. Well, not regal, but certainly not immediately combustible. Then we contemplated the unthinkable: *custom* cabinetry. The word alone is usually enough to scare any home renovator trying to maintain a budget. Custom cabinetry, so goes the received wisdom, would cost double. Maybe, if you buy from the same supplier who can sell you standard. But Susan, in her research, got a tip on Crown Point, a family-owned-and-operated cabinet maker in New Hampshire. They would sell directly to us, saving us thousands. We bought superior cabinets more affordable than crummy ones at Riverhead Building Supply. Indeed, when I mentioned our good fortune to a friend who was building a new house, she immediately called Crown Point and learned that a better set of cabinets would cost her five thousand dollars less. She sought to change, but was dissuaded when her contractor informed her that she would be installing Crown Point cabinets by herself. He must have been getting a hefty kickback from the lumber yard to push their wares.

When the Balthorp cabinets finally arrive at the Hausman-Tso compound they are accompanied by a pair of trained installers from the city. They have come out with dustless tools and hotel reservations, laboring for days to assemble the cabinets according to an indecipherable Teutonic strictness. Their music—an industrial circular-saws-cutting-trash-can-lids barrage—scares people. I'm intrigued by their work and would like to watch them finish, but I have an appointment with the bosses.

After the month-long whirlwind tour through all jobs Corinthian, it is time for my performance review. I'm sitting in the office, waiting for Nick to get off the phone, unsure of what to expect. I survived this long on their crew, but has my work been up to snuff? Will they cut me free today? Jef offers me a beer and I accept just to go along and seem at ease. Michelob Light. Jesus, I didn't know they still made this stuff. The crisp hopsy bite feels good on my dry throat. Nick hangs up the telephone and I prepare for a laundry list of suggestions, criticisms, encouragements, challenges to do better. Or else the big *sayonara*.

Nick starts the review. "How's it goin', Lawrence?"

"Good, all is good. I've really enjoyed—"

"Great," he says, "I'm glad you're liking it. Now, what we want to do today, what we want to talk about . . ."

Uh-huh?

Jef jumps in. "You need a truck."

I glance over at One F, the numbers man. "A truck?"

"Yeah, a truck. And it would be good if you got your own insurances, we could bump you up on your hourly." Jef is referring to my liability insurance and worker's comp insurance. They are big items on every contractor's bottom line, and like wily sharecroppers, contractors try to pass the burdens and risks of employment to the employee at every opportunity. I'm flabbergasted.

"I see," I say, "but I'm a little strapped at the moment."

"Sure, Lawrence," Nick says reassuringly, before driving further. "But most of these guys have a lot more tools and their own insurances. Those cost us a lot."

I do a quick mental comparison of what this "review" would be like in white-collar America. They'd be telling me to buy my own photocopier and fax machine. Some paper might be supplied, but I should count on myself to supply the toner. And while I'm at it, I should expect to bring my own desk, chair, computer, and phone. Otherwise it would just cost them too much for me to do work for them.

I try and steer the conversation toward something more obviously reviewlike. "Is there anything about my work you want to comment on?"

They look at each other in silence, like the question never crossed their minds. Eventually, Jef offers, "Everyone gets along with you. I mean, bad news gets back to us pretty fast, and there hasn't been any bad news."

I suppress a smirk.

"We really haven't seen a lot of your work," Nick adds, "you've been jumping around so much. That's kind of uncommon here." So much for my illusions of the grand plan, going through the gauntlet of variegated job-site tests. They haven't even been paying attention.

I tell them how eager I am to get more tools, even a truck—but I need to make more money. I push for twenty dollars an hour. Additionally, I stress that I want to take on as much as I can at Corinthian.

"But we can't go to twenty dollars an hour," Nick says.

Jef perks up. "We can go to seventeen, but if you want to carry insurances we could go to twenty." They are happy to pay me slightly more if I agree to increase my own expenses. I'm miffed at the thought. I hardly need another bill right now.

"How does that strike you?" Nick asks.

"Do you want the polite Lawrence go-along-to-get-along answer, or how I really feel?"

What can he say? "I want the truth."

"Well," I start, "twenty bucks an hour with the added burden of insurance strikes me as a joke. Frankly, even seventeen, though I appreciate the gesture—really, thanks—is a joke."

This is the first time I've seen Nick speechless. Jef looks riled.

Having nothing to lose, and thinking I should be concentrating on my own house now that bambino is on the way, I continue recklessly. "I mean, I'm glad there's no 'bad news' about my work, but I've got bills to pay: gas, phone, food, rent, shoes-socks-underwear, the occasional movie. Never mind health insurance, which doesn't exist. Never mind dental insurance, which doesn't exist. I'm running a negative at fifteen; I'll be running a negative at seventeen. And you want me to pay insurance at twenty?"

They look at me like it's a shakedown. I take a swig of beer before I say something stupid.

"Well, I've got to watch my money, too," Jef says, finally.

"That insurance for you costs us a lot," Nick confirms.

I put the beer down. "Are you blowing hot air up my skirt?"

Nick says, "No, I'm not blowing hot air up your skirt."

"You are," I insist, "you *are* blowing hot air up my skirt. You know how much you save employing me as a subcontractor, not as an employee." And I know he does, because his lawyer told him. Just a week ago, our Corinthian-emblazoned "Time Sheets" were replaced with "Subcontractor Request for Payment" forms, to skate on the right side of the law that states employers must insure their employees and can't force that expense onto them.

"Listen," I say, trying to bring the tone down, "I like working here, but I could make a lot more money waiting tables. I'd rather build a career in construction, but not if I can't eat at the same time."

"We want you to stay, too, Lawrence," Nick concurs. "And there's growth here. We have enough work right now for the next two years, no problem."

Somehow we settle on eighteen dollars an hour. I underline

that two years security is attractive, and I reiterate that I want to learn, to take on as much as possible.

"You mean like foreman?" Nick asks.

The thought had never occurred to me. "Sure," I say.

"You're definitely foreman material."

With pregnancy, Susan's desire to clean up the work site is no longer about imposing some order amid chaos, it is about nesting. One morning, I walk into the living room and catch her dragging the rattan furniture—the only furniture we currently have, two chairs and a love seat—from the front porch. She arranges the three pieces in a comfortable U shape beneath the picture window. The white outdoor table that goes with the Adirondack chairs has been repurposed as a coffee table in front of the sofa and is laden with editorial offerings: free glossy circulars like *Blue Sand* and *Hamptons Magazine* that litter the doorsteps of every business in town during the summer months. A collection of seven CDs rests on a side shelf, looking like a severely denuded, albeit sincere, media center. The arrangement itself is positively welcoming and homey. When they arrive shortly, Susan's parents might actually consider coming in and getting comfortable, sitting down for a chat. Once they enter this *House and Garden* coziness, however, they will quickly notice that there are no cushions on any of the rattan furniture, only half-inch plywood. But I don't interrupt. I have learned better than to get between a pregnant woman and her nesting impulse.

"It looks nice," I say.

"Thanks," Susan says, placing a bud vase on the coffee table.

"I especially like how you balanced the seating with that dorm room fridge in the corner."

She cuts me a glance, and we both smile.

Ray and Monica arrive at eleven-thirty, accompanied by Susan's brother David, who is visiting from Denver. We start with the requisite dash to lunch, but this time all of the customary lollygagging around town, peering in shop windows and eating ice cream cones, is cast aside. Things have changed. They want to work. On the house. I'm skeptical that this is how they *really* want to spend their Saturday afternoon, but they insist. The ticking clock within Susan's abdomen is turning us all into different people. We return to the house and they admire the progress we have made, but no one is denying that this house is one hell of a long way from any dwelling you would want to bring a baby into.

"Which is going to be the nursery?" Monica asks, peering into the two upstairs rooms.

"The taupe one . . . ," I say, letting Susan finish for me.

"But we're going to repaint it."

"I'm not handy," Ray confesses (again), "but, uh, do you want to go shopping?" The last time they visited Ray bought us a welcome mat, and I'm wondering if this is what he has in mind, a quick jaunt to Ace Hardware. He is relentlessly generous and we try our best to relentlessly decline—we're in our latter thirties for crissakes, struggling to maintain some modicum of independence, to keep our pride intact. But this is no time for pride. I half-heartedly beg off, knowing that I'll cave as soon as he presses the point. And he does. More surprising, though, is his offering to brave the lumberyard.

"Sure," I say, "let me get them set up, and we'll go grab some lumber." I show David where in the lawn we would like a downspout trench dug, so that I can bury a tube to lead water away from the house when we have the gutters attached. He's an unproven commodity, but he can't get into too much trouble here. Then I ask Monica to paint a door since she is careful and has a reputation for meticulousness. I ask Susan to take it easy, but that's like asking the tides to take five. I can see her eyeballing the shrubs she bought prematurely—a year ago—and now wants to get in the ground more than anything.

Ray and I race down to East Hampton and buy several hundred dollars worth of single-bead casing to finish trimming out all the windows in the kitchen and the downstairs addition. The fronts of the sixteen-foot boards rest on the dash of his Volvo wagon and the tails fly far out the rear, almost touching the road. I jump in the passenger side and he asks, "All set?" in a tone that says, *This can't possibly be legal.*

I glance back at the boards, then at him. "All set!"

Is he getting his first good look at the man his daughter married, or at the man his daughter's marriage produced? Either way, I'm a little more reckless, maniacally willing to take almost any risk to get the damn house done. We race back, slowly, to Sag Harbor.

Driving up to the house I feel like a foreman who has just walked in on his drunken crew: They are all on the front porch. Monica is pouring lemonade, having roughed up one door with semigloss latex. The thick obvious brush strokes in her workmanship will keep art historians intrigued for decades. David, who is six-foot-five, gym-ripped, and chiseled—indeed could be *the* David—is sweaty and collapsed into an Adirondack chair. I walk toward the house and can't resist unleashing my inner Floyd.

"Jesus Marylou, did you see this, David? Someone friggin' scratched my lawn!" I left him with a shovel, a spade, and a pickax thinking that they would be sufficient firepower to strike oil. Now there is a four-foot long trench all of three inches deep. I stare down at it disbelievingly. "We need this roped off; someone might fall in there."

"It's tough," David protests. "There are a lot of roots in there. And a stump."

I hold up a hand. "Not to worry. I'll have my pregnant wife finish it."

The funny thing is, she will.

Who's Your Foreman?

Several weeks later, as spring is sliding into summer, the rattan furniture has moved back outside. Inside, Susan is nurturing her nesting jones in a psychedelic fashion. The living room is becoming increasingly populated by "incredible" finds from flea markets, antiques stores, and the ABC outlet in Riverhead. Susan picks up nice pieces on the cheap, though sadly none of them go together. The living room has a large pillowed white sofa, an oversized black Chinese cabinet for the TV, and a red wing chair that needs to be recovered. Clearly my wife is suffering from some novel disorder; She's an Attention Deficit Designer. Upstairs is not much better. There are beds, yes, but the side tables are corrugated boxes and our storage units are still L.L. Bean bags. Susan's pregnancy is beginning to show, except in baggy clothes, and her energy level plummets more quickly, putting half our workforce on temporary disability. I am a garden-variety schizophrenic. In moments alone I swell with anxiety, feeling overwhelmed by an exponentially growing to-do list (sand and paint that wrought-iron crib) and my severely stalled career. Did I say stalled? Hell, the thing is up on blocks and rusting. When I am with Susan I am positive—sometimes falsely positive "for the cause"—but mostly elated that we will be three, that one project will definitely be done in a matter of nine months. And we don't need a permit for this one.

In an improbable but earnest attempt to get out of my career slump, I invent an excuse and take an afternoon off and go into the city for an interview. My teeth should look like George Hamilton's with the number of times I have used the dentist line. I am going in to see Michael Ellis, an acquaintance I met through Susan; Susan's father, Ray, is on Michael's board of directors. So I'm barreling into town in unair-conditioned BMW splendor on the packed Long Island Expressway, trying not to sweat through my suit, and wondering about this interview. Either it is a strong contender—"Hey, a personal connection is the strongest job lead"—or Michael is doing a sympathy interview, a favor to Ray. Skeptically, I'm leaning toward the latter interpretation, but damn it there's a bun in the oven and I need something—anything—economically viable soon. The road to hell is paved with diapers bought on credit.

Suffice it to say that my worst fears are realized in the forty-five minutes of banter and repartee. Michael politely asks about my résumé high points, and I answer with idiotic sincerity. I drove all the way in for this?

Afterwards, I meet Susan at a birthday party for one of her "close" friends who, I'll bet you dollars to doughnuts, we will never see again. Despite the jovial mood, I feel like I'm at a wake, mourning the death of our former social life. These people are all hooked in, advancing and flourishing; none of them have dust in their eustachian tubes. It is wonderful to see Susan, to savor her maternal secret (we have not yet told anyone other than our parents), and a stiff drink after the interview fiasco feels great. But I have to be at work in the morning, so I leave the party and start the commute back to Sag Harbor. With traffic permitting, I can be back by eleven-thirty and get some sleep before the five-forty-five alarm clock.

"License and insurance card?" the officer asks. I hand them over silently. I'm sober, having had only two drinks all evening, but doubtless alcohol is still on my breath and I'm not in the mood for any highway-side gymnastics.

He shines his flashlight over the documents. "This is expired."

"Yes," I say, "GEICO just sent the new one, but I neglected to put it in the car. I *have* insurance." This, thankfully, is true. I'm sure he can check it with his onboard computer or something.

"Hmm," he ponders, moves his flashlight around. "And your inspection is overdue."

Is he going to believe me when I say that the car was in the shop for brake work and I asked them to do the inspection, but they didn't? Should I lie, tell him I have an appointment tomorrow? Would it matter?

"You're kidding," I say. "*Really?*"

He throws me a look and says he'll be back in a minute. He's not. Nor is he back in fifteen. What the hell is he doing, preparing to arrest me? Jesus, my life is falling apart at the seams. I can't even keep my car up-to-date in my penniless state. How the hell am I going to raise a child?

The officer returns, but I don't hear a word he says other than "Here" and see him hand me something. I'm watching it happen to me, not feeling it happen. Three tickets. Expired inspection. Expired insurance. Speeding. I might have said thank you, or good night, or stick it up your ass, I don't remember. I just remember the unforgiving night heat, trucks careening past my open window, and staring up at the stars for a moment before driving off. Then things got bad.

Forty minutes down the road, the car darkens inexplicably. The music, once blaring, is now barely audible. It blares again, then goes all tinny and hollow. I wonder, momentarily, if in the annals of medical history anyone has ever simultaneously lost their hearing and vision. I seem to enter the Twilight Zone. It is unmistakable; things are going dark and quiet. *Whoosh!* Shit, save for that semi. So it's the car giving out, I decide, not my entire central nervous system, and I enter the initial emotional stages of a death: *denial, anger* . . . I punch the gas. The headlights brighten. The music returns. It works! Momentarily. In another hundred feet the dashboard and headlights are completely dark. Then *acceptance*. My car is dead. I'm coasting, gliding over to the shoulder and onto the grass. Goddamn it.

Pine Barrens is a stretch of Long Island where there is no development, no service stations, and no lights. I jog toward the last sign of life I saw a mile or so back. It's eleven at night and the air is still hot. I scale a cyclone fence in my best suit—my wedding turned *interview* suit—and hope to hell it won't rip. Something has to survive this night. Sure enough, there are lights but no one is home. I bang on the glass doors of a cinema until the security guard arrives to confirm that yes, everything around is closed. "There's no service station anyway." Am I in remotest Slovkia on an off night? How can there be no service station? He "knows a guy," the guard says. I'm not sure there are any words that can instill greater trepidation in a stranded fool than the minimum-wage movie hall security guard in front of you "knows a guy." The alternative, I'm told, is a beat down hotel three blocks away, but he "don't know what goes on there," implying prostitution, drug busts, knife fights. I call the guy.

The alternator on my car burned out, so I leave it on the side of the road with all the windows open. Supposedly someone is going to collect it in the middle of the night. Towing is one hundred dollars, and a ride home to Sag Harbor in the back of a Town Car is another hundred. The guy knows how to get paid, I'll give him that. With an additional $475 in repairs tacked on, my trip for an interview with no job on the end of it will cost me roughly what I make a week at Corinthian.

I get to bed at two A.M. and call Dirk in the morning to let him know of my travails. He sends Daniel, a clean-up guy, to pick me up. Once I get to the site, Dirk is decidedly less solicitous and levels me with a threat. "If this keeps up, we might not need you around."

The words just hang there. I think about the last days, my difficulty balancing work and simple tasks like getting the car inspected—the real source of which was fear of more expense. Suddenly my job is on the line, and I am not living up to my obligations. A lack of money and an abundance of pressure have resulted in bad decisions, and those bad decisions have put me on the wrong side of the law and in greater debt. My little construction crew experiment has become too real, it dawns on me, in all its comic and tragic implications. I have become an overstressed and underpaid carpenter. I have created a nightmare that I don't know how to get out of. I have turned into someone who yells at the heavens in frustration. It is all too reminiscent of my days working for Floyd. Put another way, I have become Dale.

After a hiatus, and days spent putting the finishing touches on the fifty-thousand-dollar train room, we are back at Lot 5. At least some of us are: Dirk is running a different job, so this one is overseen by the relatively new Magnus. Taciturn, in his midforties, with a long brown straggly ponytail, Magnus is a job-site anomaly: He turns the boom box to NPR if he gets to it first. Magnus doesn't believe in doing anything unless it can be done in the most tortuously complicated way. A real purist. We are putting together the back deck, an expansive affair with a central porch surrounded on all sides by a series of stairs, an outdoor shower, and small subdecks connected by walkways. Most decks built in this climate are made of pressure-treated wood (CCA or ACQ) or cedar. Depending on your budget, there is knotty cedar and clear cedar. For Lot 5 we are using tongue-and-groove mahogany.

After sinking the footers, constructing the framing, and building a massive network of stair supports, we start in on the mahogany decking. Magnus, Edy, Armando, and I make up the crew. We will start by creating the bull-nosed stock for the stairs, since it will be nailed in place first. The perimeter determines everything after it. To create this lumber we will route off the tongue on the tongue-and-groove stock, then take two more passes on it with a quarter-round router bit. I mention to Magnus that we could just as easily get rid of the tongue on the table saw rather than with a flush router bit and he gives me a look that says, *Hack*. He approaches Armando to ask if he is comfortable using a router. With an exposed blade as sharp as a razor and no guard to protect you, comfortable—and very cautious—is an important thing to be with a router. Armando shakes his head no. Magnus moves on to me. "Of course," I say, recalling that I have used one a sum total of once. Edy busies himself cutting one-eighth-by-one-fourth-inch splines, small boards that can be inserted between two adjoining grooves to reverse the direction of the flooring. He's become red with a covering of mahogany sawdust. Initially everyone laughed at me for donning a dust mask; after two hours of coughing, everyone is wearing one.

We, of course, biscuit all our joints and use polyurethane glue to keep things in place. There are different varieties, but we are using Gorilla Glue, which is supremely bonding. An added benefit is that polyurethane glue foams to three or four times its original size, forming a strong seal and a complete one. The excess can be scraped or sanded away, and water is kept out of the joints, which is especially attractive in exterior applications. The dangerous tendency is to rely on this foaming and to use too much glue in spaces where boards should really be brought tighter together. Our job-site culprit in this matter is Edy the Ecuadorian, who is a great framer, but less patient with detail work. When we return the following day, the section Edy had worked on looks like a series of mahogany planks with Cool Whip mountain ranges squeezing out between them. Magnus wants to talk to him. We start calling him Edy the Glue.

Becoming *Them*

After months of ignoring the inevitable, Susan and I decide to face the music and take on the most alarming item on our to-do list: shopping for baby stuff. The task before us promises to make our lives more real, less illusory. It will be even more challenging now to keep our anxiety under wraps, and to ignore the fact that we are halfway through Susan's pregnancy and there are still no locks on the doors. The nursery is painted yellow, but there is nothing in it.

Babies "Я" Us looks like any other box store, but its transformative powers are undeniable. After only a few minutes inside the front door, trouble is already apparent. Susan, who I had always thought of as a strong-willed, intelligent, and decisive woman, is a bumbling mess. A puddle.

"What kind do you want?" I ask. We are standing in front of the breast pumps.

"I don't know. There are *six!*"

"Should we ask someone?" I look around; she stares ahead vacantly. "There's someone."

"No, let's go look at mattresses."

Mattresses? I shrug, and we walk through the high-chair section, where there are no less than fifteen models with every accoutrement short of a sidewinder missile. We pass the changing tables, which can cost several hundred dollars, while appearing to be made of recycled toilet paper rolls. Then there is an entire arena of rocking chairs, which range from conventional to comfortable-though-butt-ugly glider, though *all* of them have been upholstered with fabrics rejected at the Hyundai factory. Finally, we make it to the mattresses. We need one that will fit into the wrought-iron bed that we refinished.

"What's better," I ask, "a firm mattress or a soft one?"

"I like firm."

"I know *you* like firm, but babies are soft. What's best for—"

"How do I know?"

"Honey, I have no idea either. Let's take a deep breath."

"Let's go get some diapers, we definitely need those."

"They're back by the breast pumps," I say calmly, not wanting to push either of us over the edge. As we snake back, past the rocking chairs, past the strollers (Yugo to Humvee), past the changing tables, teethers, diaper pails, bibs, onesies, walkers, and mobiles, I'm feeling our old selves fading, our new selves coming into befuddled relief. We used to play darts in smoky bars and shake it to David Bowie's "Fame" and Linkin Park. Now we are prospective diaper buyers. We look at the expanse of diapers in wide-eyed amazement, like we've just turned a corner and discovered the Grand Canyon.

"Not to sound like a broken record," I start, "but what kind?"

"Monica used to swear by Huggies."

I pick up a bag of Huggies. They are light purple. "I'm not buying anything with Barney on them."

"They don't leak."

"I don't care. Barney's not getting near my kid's ass." I check out the other packages and see that almost all of them are branded. Barney, Sesame Street, Tiger Woods. We put a bag of Pampers in the cart and conclude, with our new parental logic, that if we have diapers we will need something for diaper rash.

Abruptly, I'm ambushed by a profound sense of déjà vu. But I couldn't *possibly* have been here before. Then it strikes me that I have been in a parallel and less complicated universe to Babies "Я" Us: Home Depot. The proving ground, the test case, the junior varsity of box stores. With Babies "Я" Us the stakes are so much higher: You aren't deciding between forty-five tile styles, you're buying a diaper that could change a life.

We pick out butt emollients, cruise back through the stroller section, eye the breast pump alternatives, and then, unexpectedly, come face to face with the nipple wall. We stand speechless. The wall is ten feet high, it travels in both directions seemingly to infinity. There are short nipples, there are long nipples. Square nipples and round nipples. White, clear, and brown nipples. Some have an "orthodontic" bend, others jut straight out. I can tell that this is the last straw, that Susan isn't ready for this much this fast, that my suggestion to check out baby bottles was *very* optimistic. The variegation and sheer numbers are just too great. We need some sort of flow chart or decision tree or algorithm.

Finally Susan speaks. "Have you ever seen so many nipples in your life?"

I think for a second, looking up in amazement. "Not all at the same time."

The August heat has become punishing, and by eight A.M. we are already stripped to our shorts. It's even too hot to wear a tool belt. We're like bugs on a mirror, burning from above and below. The only water, to mix cement, is kept in plastic trash cans. Look closely, you can see mosquito larvae swimming. Magnus is dipping a Styrofoam cup into the water.

"I'm not sure they washed out those cans," I say.

He is sweating through his jeans. "I don't care," he says. Within an hour, we'll all be there with him.

This job is feeling increasingly remote, disconnected from the Corinthian machine, which is operating at full steam on other projects. Nick and One-F Jef rarely visit to check up, which is relaxing, but also disconcerting. Meanwhile, Dirk has absconded with all the tools from the tool truck. We are left with what we can cobble together. Corinthian keeps such a tight reign on supplies we often run out, and rather than be unproductive, we use nails and tubes of glue out of our own trunks. It dawns on me that we are helping to pay for some rich fuck's summer home. Magnus is starting to clue in to the fact that his job as supervisor means that he bring the most tools from home, and the other guys get to use them. He locks a six-foot-high JOBOX full of tools in the garage.

It's the same crew today—Magnus, me, Armando, Edy the Glue—with the addition of some gum-snapping Ecuadorean named Joaquin. I take his spirited delivery as a latter-day Ritchie, but I'm wrong. He's married and expecting his firstborn a month before Susan and I are.

We are almost finished with the stairs, which look magnificent, and are about to start on the porch floor itself. Joaquin is on his cell phone again, and for the benefit of the others I jump on him: "No mas mamando gallo, eh?" *Enough fucking around, no more strutting around like a rooster doing nothing.* Edy and Armando chuckle at my hijacked Spanish, especially since they think Joaquin is full of himself. Even Joaquin smiles at my faux assimilation, says that his wife is having some kind of trouble today at work. She's not the only one.

Magnus comes around the corner looking so riled that for the first time he might lose his Nordic cool. "You don't look happy," I say.

"Change orders," he says flatly. The words hang there as if he had invoked something overpowering and deadly that we can't control, like Sasquatch. He explains that the front entryway is to be expanded. To do this they will need to dig back down to the foundation, take out part of the concrete wall, and tie in new concrete walls to the existing structure—just so the owner can have a larger foyer. "And the porch has to change," Magnus concludes.

"I beg your pardon?" He can't possibly be talking about the porch and decking system we've been working on. There are untold thousands of dollars in mahogany, plus thousands more in labor sunk into this porch over the last weeks. Change it? It makes little sense unless you can add on to it intelligently. "How much more do they want?"

"Less," Magnus says. "Apparently the architect never signed off on the plan Nick gave us. It's supposed to be smaller. We gotta pull all this out."

Now I know my hearing is shot.

"Pull it? As in demo the whole thing?"

"Yeah."

Everyone is looking at each other in disbelief, like these fucking rich yahoos. I wonder if there is any way I can use this material on the back deck I have to build on my house, maybe something can be salvaged. But no, it is so well put together—nailed, glued, and biscuited—that the steps only come apart with sledgehammers and crowbars in huge ragged chunks. Theoretically we should be happy; we get paid to work, and we will obviously have more work. No one here is losing money because of this change order. Yet we all walk around despondent, angrily throwing boards into the Dumpster. Countless hours toiling under a hot sun to achieve these magnificent stairs, and now we're taking them apart with sledgehammers and crowbars. It's all being thrown away. It feels like cutting off your own working limb. We finish the demo and break for lunch. Joaquin jumps in his beat-up truck, mumbling about having to take care of something.

The morning's misery is replaced by the afternoon's hilarity. Once we are back on a forward course, everyone's mood lifts. The music is blaring some Mexican Top 40 station and Edy the Glue is atop a sawhorse playing air accordion to the merengue ripiado gyrating out of the boom box. Joaquin runs back and forth from where we are working on the deck to the kitchen area, where he has installed his pregnant wife for the day. She works as a nanny to a young girl, and because of some mysterious problem, has brought her to the work site today. They sit in plastic deck chairs, in moderate terror, as the sound of Magnus's power planer two rooms away squeals throughout the hollow expanse of the house. I try to shout to Armando Gallo to grab a chalk line so we can start the first course of mahogany on the new, diminutive porch, but my voice is drowned out by the afternoon air traffic. Phalanxes of helicopters, shuttling city slicks in their Sikorsky shares, swarm over East Hampton for their Friday invasion. I can almost hear Wagner's operatic charge "Ride of the Valkyries" as the flock screams over our heads.

"Lawrence, have you got a minute?" Nick asks, having shown up at the end of the week to check on progress. It sounds ominous.

"Sure."

"You can finish what you're doing, no hurry."

Great. I grab the handle of the deceptively heavy generator and drag it into the tool truck. After we are through cleaning up for the day, I start after Nick, who is now commiserating with One F.

"Let's go around the side," Nick says, leading me and One F out of earshot of the others, and then through the Bilko door into the basement. It feels like a cheesy mob movie and I'm either going to be a made man (foreman material!) or this is a hit. The three of us stand in a loose circle in the dank basement. A single hanging bulb gives light. Nick gestures to Jef to start, but he doesn't.

"What we wanted to talk to you about, Lawrence," Nick says, "is, uh, that we have to let you go."

"It's not a personal thing," Jef offers, "it's just a numbers thing." I immediately think that I pushed too hard on the insurance versus raise question weeks ago and now I'm the sacrificial lamb. But I don't feel like letting them off so easy.

"Let me go?"

"We're sorry," Nick says.

"I'm confused," I say, gathering my wind. "Are you not happy with that front deck I built?"

"No, it's fine."

"And the cedar shower enclosure?"

"That's fine too."

"Fine, Nick? Just fine? Is that why Jef was taking pictures of it a little while ago, because it was just *fine*?" I can't believe they keep a photographic record of the "fine" work on their jobs. I busted my butt on that shower stall, took pride in overcoming its unforeseen complications. Was my job perfect? No, but it was a damn spot better than fine—I've learned enough to know *that* this past year. "And what about that stairway we just walked down?" I demand.

"Lawrence, it's not personal," Jef repeats. "We just need to trim our numbers of people."

"Didn't you say you had enough work for the next two *years*?" I ask Nick.

"Uh."

"'Cause that's what I based *my* decision on, my decision to stay with you guys."

"Well," Jef cuts in, "a couple large jobs we were counting on aren't happening. One went to another firm, and the other is on hold indefinitely."

"I just think your decision is really shortsighted," I say with a flourish. I'm beginning to feel that this is the best turn of events, that I really do have to concentrate on our house again before the baby arrives, but I also want to make this difficult for them after lying to me. "Did I not tell you that I was willing to take on as much as possible? That I could run jobs, prospect jobs? Hell, I know a guy in Bridgehampton who needs something to invest millions in, and he's motivated on real estate development." This last tidbit is true, but I am hardly the go-to guy for moneybags just yet.

Then Nick levels the hammer. "Lawrence, you're a B carpenter."

It takes the wind out of me. A B carpenter. And to think they said it wasn't personal.

"I just think it's shortsighted on your part," I repeat halfheartedly. Then I thank them for the opportunity and head back toward my car to pack up. On the way I learn that Joaquin also got the boot. The fathers-to-be are both out on their ears.

"It really *is* hilarious," Susan says. We are sitting on the front porch watching the rain start to fall on Union Street and idly discussing what we are going to do for dinner. My firing keeps creeping back into the conversation.

"Yeah, what's so funny?"

"*B* carpenter!" She laughs again and shakes her head. Personally I fail to see the humor. Any firing stings, and being called second tier on the way out the door doesn't cushion the blow.

"Yeah, a laugh riot."

"Lawrence, how many were on the crew?"

"I don't know. Twenty, give or take."

"And how many were A carpenters?"

"Uh. Doug . . . Dirk . . . Magnus. Three."

"And how many Cs?"

"A lot. More than half."

I smile, discerning a little late what she is driving at.

She generously sends the point home. "And how long have you been a carpenter?"

"A year, maybe." I consider that everyone I worked with had at least five or six years under their tool belts. "Holy crap! Do you realize you are married to a B carpenter?"

Secretly, Susan is thrilled that my days as a B carpenter have come to an end, as forces beyond our control necessitate getting a lot done fast. Miraculously, our entire kitchen comes together in a few short days in the fall. The days of eating in restaurants are finally coming to an end, so too is grilling outdoors and washing dishes in the bathroom sink. The black granite countertop and island top are installed and the kitchen is transformed. Quickly we put in the sinks and faucets and call for our appliances to be delivered.

Selecting the appliances was a job in itself, with the variety and cost fluctuations inherent in such large-ticket purchases. We selected a DCS stove because we wanted commercial grade without the Viking price tag. Indeed, before Viking became the powerhouse in commercial quality stoves for home use, they asked DCS to make their prototypes. Now, playing catch-up, DCS is a superlative value. We also chose a Bosch dishwasher, which makes less noise than a contact lens cleaner, and a cheapo Home Depot floor model trash compactor. Lastly, after scouring the galaxy, Susan found a top of the line GE refrigerator at a liquidation center in Medford, Long Island. For weeks, she told everyone we met what a great find she landed. Less than half retail! Finally, we were convinced we had something that could impress Krantz.

"Profile Artica, right?" he asks, the doors of the fridge still covered in protective plastic.

"Yes, we managed to find one pretty well priced," Susan says, preparing to wow him.

"I just picked up the same one."

Susan grins. "I wish I would have known, we would have told you about the liquidation center in Medford. We paid only $2,200."

He raises his eyebrows. "That's pretty good. I got mine at Long Island Wholesale for $2,000."

If someone told us the foundation was crumbling, we wouldn't have been more deflated.

Fuckin' Krantz.

"I can help," Susan says.

"I don't care if you *can*; you're not," I say, trying to sound emphatic. Like a husband, like a *father*.

"Then how? We've got twenty people coming in one week. The house is a wreck." True. Because we are insatiable maso chists, a baby shower that Monica offered to throw at her completed, appointed, and furnished home is actually taking place at our house. It is a race to the finish. Again. The story of our home renovation has morphed into the story of our pregnancy. Like so many of our earlier decisions—cedar shingling the house, buying mosaic tiles, installing our own cabinets— deciding to get pregnant was entertained casually, discussed with the same "what can be so difficult?" false confidence. We had no respect for the scheduling, the time involved, absolutely no grasp of *the process*. Susan's doctor, the subcontractor on the baby initiative, suggested that we could reasonably expect, given our ages, to consume six months to a year just trying to get pregnant. We knew we weren't spring chickens, but it was a heavy realization. Indeed, since several couples our age had recently gone through the entire roster of fertility gymnastics, we took the doctor's advice to heart. With six months to a year's practice, then nine months of pregnancy, we would probably have a year and a half to two years to get the house finished, furnished, and ready for a newborn.

That was the plan, anyway. When we discussed it, we were still residing full time in Norm and Ellen's house, enjoying winter evenings by the fireplace after punishingly cold days at the work site. Unfortunately the project management skills we were learning the hard way on the construction site hadn't yet sunk into another, more pleasurable project: human procreation. With the first try, our casual plans became actual, and the clock began ticking. The comfortable two years we had allotted ourselves turned, overnight—once Susan saw her doctor—into little more than seven months.

"We could get Mark to help with the shower," I suggest, knowing full well that (a) he is out of town and (b) we have asked him for so many favors during our renovation that it's too embarrassing to ask for any more.

"He's out of town," Susan says.

"Oh. Well, Gavin maybe," I suggest lamely, knowing how reluctant he'll be to scuff his Gucci loafers.

Susan gives me a look that says Gavin would be less help than she is in her seventh month of pregnancy. She's right, but I put my foot down. "Absolutely not. It's out of the question, you're not lifting anything in your condition."

Forty-five minutes later, Susan and I are in the back of the Yard Couple, a local antiques boutique that looks like the vortex of everyone's unwanted and disgorged furniture. A rusted panel truck without wheels sits in the backyard with a stack of unloved love seats, ottomans, and sofas. We are wrestling an overstuffed white canvas sofa out of the truck and into the back of a borrowed van. I have one end and Susan has the other. I'm in a hurry to get the damn thing home, yes, but more important to get us—*her*—out of sight. What kind of man forces his pregnant wife to carry heavy furniture through a minefield of overturned birdbaths, rusted bed frames, and disintegrating bookshelves? Will gaping onlookers believe me when I protest innocence, saying, "It was her idea"? I can hear them returning home, recounting the misdemeanor: "Then the jerk tried to say it was her idea, can you believe that?"

We make it home and unload the sofa before anyone has a chance to alert the Sag Harbor police department. Then we move the sofa from place to place, engaging in our characteristic backbreaking dance—some couples tango, we redecorate—until, at last, we stand back to admire our work.

"It looks like shit," I say.

"Yeah, I was kinda thinking the same thing," Susan says. Rushing to get some furniture into the house, we have landed on a new style, a sort of U.N. Sanford and Son, junk from the world over.

"But," I say, falling into the cushions, "it's comfortable."

"I was hoping . . ."

"Come on, it's going to be fine. This is temporary." It's been too damn long for me to honestly believe the second part of that utterance, but I *am* beginning to believe the first. I'm just thrilled that after months and months of hard labor without normal creature comforts, we can finally live like our peers are living. We can sit in our house, on our sofa, and watch thoroughly disposable television.

*   *   *

Susan and I spend the rest of the afternoon putting the kitchen together. After installing and painting the kitchen cabinets we still have to attach all of the hardware. For what seems like weeks, Susan has been sitting at the kitchen island polishing bin pulls and flush catches—all the hardware that Mark recovered from the Southampton estate. We found a product called NOXON, which may be the only item we've used in months that doesn't have a warning for expectant and nursing mothers. With a time-consuming tripartite scrub-rub-polish procedure, Susan transforms the tarnished pieces so that they that look like new. When we see replacement pieces in a catalog for twenty-five dollars a piece, we feel as though we have won the lottery without even buying a ticket.

Now that the pieces are going onto the cabinets the kitchen is transformed. Finish work is the jumbo shrimp of construction, for it never ends, never seems to be finished. I recall Oregonian Doug asking me if I preferred framing work or finish work and I admitted that both held their charms. Finish work was challenging and engaging, but framing work showed big changes fast. Doug looked at me like I'd just confessed to being Democrat and Republican. It just made no sense, this ambivalence. Doug was decidedly high church: a stain-grade finish carpenter, one whose skills were so exacting he didn't need the safety net of caulking and paint. When I recount that conversation to Susan, she has a different interpretation. We are taking a break from kitchen installation to watch a rebuilt garage going up across the street, and I can't help but be impressed.

"Bang, it's going right up. They'll have it framed by lunch," I say, admiringly.

"That's so you."

"What is?"

"Goes right up. So male." Before I can even protest, I smile with the recognition that she has hit on something. Framing is the male carpentry yang to the finish carpentry yin. The latter is more mysterious and frustratingly deferred than the female orgasm. Even better, finish carpentry has multiple climaxes. Attaching the kitchen cabinetry hardware literally transforms the space. We affix wall sconces, hang the wedding-gift chandelier, nail shoe molding into place, and cope crown molding. We stand back, exhausted, and survey the completed kitchen.

"Do you like it?" I ask.

She purrs, "Yes."

The Addition

"It's been two hellish years of marriage," Susan exhales.

I cut her a look. Even acknowledging what we've been through, I'm surprised by her candor at this moment. "Hellish?"

"Not the marriage," she backpedals, "but the *years* have been hellish. It's been a lot."

"Yeah, that sounds a whole lot better," I say, not letting her entirely off the hook, yet agreeing wholeheartedly. It feels good to acknowledge it, as if recognition helps to secure it in the past. Now, finally, we are living an existence that is decidedly not hellish. We sit. We watch TV. We nap when we can. Most important, we jump up and down responding to the demands—only and always food—of our newborn son, Jackson.

He was born in New York City on January 3. After twenty-four hours of labor. Ready in the delivery room to hold onto the helpful hubby token ankle and coo "Good job honey," I was alarmed to find myself at seven A.M. grasping both my wife's knees and barking "six, seven, eight" like a drill sergeant. Teams of nurses and a trio of doctors filed in and out of the delivery room in a choreography that was confounding. I should have been over-taken by the momentousness of the occasion, I suppose, but I was really wondering, *Who the hell thought husbands should be in the delivery room?* It felt like hospital cost-cutting, passing off some of the work to unpaid labor. More to the point, it was humbling to be so helpless to assuage the pain of someone I love.

Days later we drove out to Sag Harbor and met up with the furniture and belongings we had just had delivered by a pair of grumpy Ukrainian movers. For the first time in two years, Susan and I—and our belongings—would be under the same roof. A roof that we wanted to be under. A roof that we built. Under simpler circumstances, it would have been a romantic time, but with our firstborn with us to share the experience it was a miraculous event.

Our punch list was still a mile long, but now we didn't give a damn. Hand towels were stuffed in door cutouts where knobs should be, club chairs propped against doors kept them closed during heavy winter winds. Coats hung in closets without doors. The back deck was not even started. The tasks that hovered over us like unwelcome relatives with unspeakable pressure—exploding into our marriage with unnecessary arguments—had been divested of their forcefulness.

After we exhaust the offerings at the local video store, and after we are bestowed with a solid three hours sleep, we are ready to spend some time working on the house. Susan initiates another round of paint considerations, and I begin to work on the ground floor addition in earnest. The routine is becoming familiar: framing, wiring, Sheetrocking, spackling, sanding, and painting. It's becoming second nature. Almost. The floors, however, are another matter. Since the concrete slab of the floor is too uneven and cold for flooring to be placed directly on top of it, I nail down ACQ (the new environmentally friendly treated lumber) sleepers and a plywood subfloor. The flooring on top of that should meet up, roughly, with the brick patio we will eventually build out the back doors. Since it will be highly trafficked from the backyard, we want something tougher than the wide-plank pine we've installed upstairs.

We decide on bamboo, which has the added benefit of coming prefinished. Once cut and nailed into place, it won't have to be sanded and polyurethaned. This is attractive, not only in terms of time savings, but also to avoid the issues of fugitive dust and deadly fumes hanging out in the house during the unventilated months of February and March.

As conscientious as we are about what Jackson might inhale from any continued renovation, we are also surprised to find that he doesn't respond badly to the racket going on downstairs. Muffled but by no means quiet, nail guns, power planers, and a chop saw squeal from time to time during the days and weeks. Jackson is unflappable. Or deaf. Then we conclude: What else does he know but construction noise? From his earliest moments in his uterine condominium, his unruly neighbors have been creating a noisy din. It is well documented that babies respond at a very early age to noise outside of the womb. They even have a memory of those sounds. In a study that tested this phenomenon, one group of pregnant mothers was asked to watch the same soap opera every day; another group was asked to watch TV randomly or not at all. After the children were born, the second group of babies cried and were calmed with expected effort; but with the first group, crying babies were calmed and quieted almost immediately when they heard the theme song from the soap opera. It was familiar and comforting to them. We joke that Jackson's fetal soundtrack is an avant-garde cacophony of hammers, abraded materials, and power tools. Perhaps it is oddly comforting to him, this familiar din. In truth, as long as I am downstairs cutting something up or nailing something down, he is preternaturally content. Maybe he gets that from his mother. Of course, we do eventually learn what sets him off. Sitting in his baby-sized Barcalounger, he suddenly shrieks. I rub his head, trying to comfort him, but he is inconsolable. Terrified.

"Susan," I say, waving my hand, "you'd better turn off the vacuum."

Now that we are home, finally *home*, we are able to enjoy not only our son, but each other. And the unalterable and crushing fatigue also teaches us something we hadn't previously divined during the years of agonizing renovation: a division of labor. We long held on to the romantic notion that we could choose everything together, that our dream home would be the manifestation of all of our shared decisions. But there is no surer way to drive each other loony. Assuming it would bring us together, it did just the opposite. We started earnestly, engaged in an overly deferential matrimonial consensus building. Then we turned sarcastic and strategic, making outlandish suggestions to exhaust the other's veto power. Finally, with too many decisions and too little expertise, we became argumentative and brittle. Progress slowed. Eventually, necessity jump-started the process: There was no time, and less money, for philosophical considerations of grout color and electrical outlet placement. One choice was pretty much like another, and our lives weren't going to be improved or diminished remarkably by one shade's difference. At last, we learned to work in tandem, rather than like two corporate vice presidents wary that their company influence might erode if they weren't in on every decision, every action. We were ready to let go.

"All yours," I say munificently.

"I was last time, really," Susan says, batting her eyelashes, coaxing me to act.

I recite the only guiding principle I've been able to come up with in situations like this: "You're holding him, you get to change him."

"That's so unfair," she protests insincerely, laughing.

"Hey, it's not my area."

"Oh yes it is," Susan lights up. "You can say that the flooring or cabinets are 'not my area,' but this kid's butt, definitely your area."

"I make breakfast, build walls, I cook lunch; my work is never done!" I complain disingenuously. In truth, whatever I do, I've come to feel, pales in comparison to what Susan has been through for our nascent family. I pick Jackson up to be changed and hold him momentarily next to Susan. I'm proud that we've made it. Created this amazing being. Built our house. Stared divorce in the eye and took the hard road, stayed together. I couldn't be happier, and occasionally marvel at the twist of fate that brought us together. Our complementary strengths, enthusiasms, and psychopathologies got us through some tough years.

As I soothe Jackson, Susan grabs a magazine that was resting next to the sofa. I notice that some of the pages are dog-eared.

"What's that?" I ask, warily.

"*The East Ender.*" A real estate circular. "Here, I want you to look at something."

I sit back down, cradling Jackson.

"There," she says, folding back a page and pointing to a forlorn federal somewhere in Sag Harbor. Overgrown shrubs hide much of the house, but the sky blue paint is visibly cracking from the upper rows of clapboard. Badly. Windows are missing, and a column has fallen from under the front entryway, letting the small roof sag in place.

"Yeah?" I say.

"It looks like an interesting project," she says brightly.

I look at her, at the circular, then back at her. Speechless.

"Well," she presses, "what do you think?"

"That old fucking house?"

Epilogue

I was recently unpacking some cardboard boxes that have been in storage since we began our home renovation. On top of the second box was a book about Matteo Ricci, the Jesuit missionary. Ricci (1552–1610), an Italian, was the first westerner since Marco Polo to be in China. He assimilated into a population suspicious of outsiders by dressing as a Buddhist and, later, as a Confucian scholar. To make contact with others and to spread his faith, he taught Confucian students tricks to improve their memories. These skills, he thought, would communicate the intellectual strength of western civilization and thereby the validity of mono-theistic Christianity. Ricci told his pupils that memory palaces could be wholly fictive or drawn from reality, whichever was most helpful, and these palaces would provide ample storage spaces for the knowledge one wanted to store and recall when required. Additional rooms could even be added on—without going through a zoning board, presumably—when more space was needed to house additional knowledge. To Ricci's credit, his efforts had a good deal of success as he converted many Chinese to Christianity.

What intrigues me most about his story is that in teaching people how to improve their memories Ricci was able to coax them to forget who they previously were. To put down one faith and pick up another. Whether they were "better off" as Bud-dhists or Christians is a meaningless discussion to me; what *is* interesting is that they chose to make a change. They opted to embrace a different way of looking at the world, and their place in it. Similarly, I've come to realize, my little palace, my little shit hole of a house now gloriously refurbished, is the transformative event that taught me how to be married. Each room, each wall, each floor in our house has memories attached to it. The front bedroom is the repository for bouts of anger, told and untold, where Susan and I had our worst days, worst arguments, and came closest to calling it quits several times; thankfully, those events have been painted over in that room, several times. The front porch speaks frustration to me, using a power nailer for the first time and nailing the fir strips in the groove rather than through the tongue. I think that was the day I threw the phone, feeling impotent in my fledgling carpentry career, after Susan suggested I "just call Dexter" for advice. It would have saved me hours with a nail sink had I swallowed my pride and done so, for days after the porch was done I saw Doug flooring a Corinthian job floor and realized my mistake. The first floor is doubtless the heart of our renovation and indeed our marriage, for never did we work as well or quickly as those days spent putting in the pine floors, our crew of two, experiencing and enjoying the transformation fully. As well, the kitchen—though it will no doubt be repainted—holds our best memories of cooperation and accomplishment. An ingenious cabinet solution finished with a granite countertop neither one of us had even thought of, resulted in a kitchen even better than we dared to hope for, despite some vocal friends' doubts along the way. "Celadon cabinets and black granite countertops?" Gavin chided sarcastically. "Oh, everybody's doing it." Today the kitchen is being photographed for a magazine layout.

The realization came in the basement—while cutting through concrete with a diamond blade, trying to contain the dust storm by holding the saw under a cardboard box—that it was not solely our house but our lives that had been renovated. Not built new, as if we had been married as twenty-year-olds, but opened up, gutted, and painstakingly put back together with hard work and too much Sherwin-Williams. The process revealed very quickly, perhaps too quickly for a new marriage, our old assumptions about sex roles, money, convictions about money, tolerance for debt, and the near-debilitating realization that marriage means *two* sets of opinions.

Much is made of marital "compromise," and I think this house has taught us that valuable skill, though not as an act of concession or of finding the middle ground, but of finding a better ground. Which is to say that now I leave all the paint decisions to Susan. When I married her all she wanted was white. Now that she is a latex-crazed repainter—indulging whims of mango, Cherokee, and Milwaukee sunset at thirty dollars a gallon—I have no one to blame but myself.

It is January now, and no less than three gallons of differently colored paint sit in a box by the coat closet. The red might be for the kitchen. "If not, we'll use it in another room," Susan faux reassures me. In any event, it won't be used today, for the kitchen is crowded with our family and our extended family—friends and subcontractors. We are celebrating the completion of the house—save phase three, perpetual redecoration—and Jackson's first birthday. Yesterday I thought he was getting big, but today, held in the crook of our plumber Paul's tattooed arm, he looks smaller than the day we brought him home. Our parents are here, appropriately, for we wouldn't be here without them. Ray is mixing Bloody Marys; Monica is passing out food. My mother checks, surreptitiously, on the header she said we could cut into. Maybe she's afraid she'll get a call back. Cliff sits on the kitchen sofa, his ankle propped on the ottoman, playing with Dan and

Cyndy's year-old son, David Dean. Jackson's fifth grandparent is here, too; Susan's long-lost mother from Michigan reconnected when Jackson was born and has been a loving presence, unintentionally proving some good things do come out of Detroit. Also in attendance are our neighbors Veronique, Mark One and Gary, Mark Two, Ted and Steve, and Norm and Ellen. Dexter cracks jokes that he can't believe the place is still standing.

Dan brings me a drink. "Did Cyndy tell you?"

"Tell me what?" I ask.

"She solved it," he says, grinning. He calls Cyndy over to tell the story herself.

I bite. "So what did you solve, CSI Cyndy?"

"The riddle," she beams with accomplishment. "The Witchie Poo question." For months Dan and I have been threatening to follow the Wicked Witch of the West on one of her bereted missions, variously speculating that she was a call girl for the elder hostel, or running hoagies to Al Qaeda hideouts.

"No *way*," I say theatrically. Dan and I have been on the case for how long, and this rookie cracks the case?

"I was getting my hair cut . . ."

"Homicide Harriet?"

"Of course. And when I went out the back way, toward Yo Yard Sale! . . ."

"Uh-huh."

"There she was, straddling her bike behind the movie theater talking to . . . someone . . . in . . . a . . . Town Car."

"Get out!"

Dan starts to laugh. "It gets better."

"So," Cyndy says, "she's talking to Hannibal, right? And the curious thing is that cardboard box on her bike rack?"

"Yeah?"

"Nowhere to be seen."

I lower my tone, "What do you make of that, Inspector?"

"Clearly, she's working for the man," Cyndy says.

"Body parts, I think," Dan interjects. We crack up at the thought of Witchie Poo biking around Sag Harbor delivering kidneys to Hannibal Lecter for an evening repast.

"Or," I say, raising my index finger skyward, "there's manuscript pages in that box."

"I like it," Dan barks.

"So," Cyndy says, "you're suggesting . . ."

"That some of the masterpieces of psychological fiction are written *not* by Thomas Harris, but by a bereted bicycle freak."

"Obviously," Dan concludes.

"Susan," I call out, "Cyndy solved it." Susan looks up from her conversation with Deepak the Mason. "You gotta hear this."

I walk away to answer the door—while Dan wonders aloud, "Is Harris even out here in January?"—and greet the newest arrivals, my friend James and his new girlfriend, Sophie. After the hellos and introductions, James excuses himself to get their drinks. Sophie, who obviously heard some of our house story on the drive over, compliments the work we did and asks for a tour. I comply. And then some. As we stroll from bedroom to bedroom, to bathroom to downstairs office, I quickly lay it all out in Technicolor. The early planning, the Architectural Review Board, the idiotic draftsman, the terrifying confrontations Susan and I had. Sophie looks fearful, and I wonder if I've gone over the line, scaring this poor woman in the throes of a new courtship, with nightmares of renovation and fraying marriage. Moreover, I surprise myself that these emotions are so accessible, so close to the surface. Part of me is joking, but another part of me is willing to spare her nothing: not the cost overruns, not the credit card debt, not the disappearing sex life, not the (ominous and metaphorical) hairline cracks that appear in newly spackled walls even before the house is finished. When we finally make it back upstairs, I gently tell her that it's the end of the tour, worried that I might be cited for emotional abuse.

But I couldn't have read her more wrongly. After my entire harangue, she is buoyant. Intrigued. She doesn't utter the code word, she doesn't offer the secret handshake, but I wonder if she is a fellow masochist, a no-pain-no-gain loony ready to embrace the sweat lodge metaphysics of home renovation. Maybe she's just humoring me. "It really *does* look fantastic."

"Thank you, Sophie, that's very nice of you to say."

"And, despite the rough patches, I mean, well, it's all been worth it now, hasn't it?"

The question catches me off guard. She couldn't have heard me arguing with Susan so many months ago.

"Is it worth . . ."

"I mean, would you do it again?"

I consider it for a moment, then formulate the scariest thing I can say:

"In a heartbeat."

Later, after Jackson is abused with a Lamontagne–LaRose rendition of "Happy Birthday" and the cake has been passed around, we get down to the serious business of unwrapping gifts. Jackson is awed by a rocking horse, a toy gas station, and a police car, but Susan and I unwittingly gravitate to the new Lego set. It's a good one, with a green dimpled sheet that acts as a foundation, and interesting windows and doors. We haphazardly construct a preposterous tower, with skywalks and spires. The clicking of the blocks attracts Jackson's attention and he is upon us in second, quickly knocking over the tower, dismantling its component parts gleefully.

Truly, the demo never ends.

Acknowledgments

I am grateful to many people without whom this book would not have been completed.

For early advice, encouragement, cat-calling, and inadvertently inspiring "You're fucking crazy" salutes, I'd like to thank Peter Gethers who first (yes, of course, except for you Susan) damnably said "that's a book," as well as A. J. Jacobs, Ira Silverberg, Nan Shipley, Binky Urban, Peter Jennings, Rick Marin, Tad "Let's do some heavy lifting" Floridis, and that guy at Starbucks who was reading over my shoulder, tittering.

Thanks to my agent, David McCormick, for the superlative effort and skillful navigation.

At Bloomsbury I am indebted to my publisher, Karen Rinaldi, whose enthusiasm and support were so limitless I was convinced she had me confused with someone else. (But, given the circumstances, was I so wrong to ask her to paint my house?) As well, her fantastic team of Amanda Katz, Greg Villepique, Marian Brown, Yelena Gitlin, Stephen Morrison, Alona Fryman, Sabrina Farber, the inspired Alison Lazarus, Roger Haskins, and Andrew "Mad Sexy" Hetherington. Countless thanks (and double combat pay) are due Panio "the Alchemist" Gianopoulos, who refused sleep until his edit was complete, his newborn daughter diapered.

Home renovation contractors bear a stigma as schemers, flim-flam artists, and cheats. I was lucky to avoid most of them. Greatest thanks and highest respect for Bill Dexter, Bill Alves,

Kevin Mance, Tom "seriously, I'm swamped but you're on my priority list" Gardella, and Mark Danowksi. As well, the men and women at Riverhead Building Supply—when they weren't affecting the rebarbative hauteur of Parisian bistro garçons—were a great source of information and guidance when I wasn't too embarrassed to ask for it.

Our parents—Barbara and Cliff, Ray and Monica—paid a hefty price to insure that we would not land back on their doorsteps, and we are grateful. They were not only generous, but wise. Had they invested that money in the market at the time they would have lost it all; loaning it to us they can count on at least half of it back.

The house would have been put together with glue—and at odd angles—were it not for David Berridge, who magnificently loaned his chop box and table saw even before he knew my last name. Other tools were loaned by, or pilfered from, Jeff Steele, Dan Bragg, and James "Where the hell's my Sawzall?" DeMartis.

As well, in one way or another, the house and the book would not be the same if not for Alexandra Leigh-Hunt, Jeffrey Wolf, Robert LaRose, Julia Tardio, Mel Jarvis, Darlene Haut, Esteban Ledezma, David Lamontagne, Frances Trunzo, Cyndy Cecil, and everyone at the Double 'D' Writer's Ranch. Über thanks.

For her daring, determination, and sharing the dedication I owe Susan—the chop saw jockey I'll always love—everything.

A NOTE ON THE AUTHOR

Lawrence LaRose is a seasoned editor and writer, an amateur home builder, and a freelance smart-ass. He coauthored the internationally bestselling *The Code: Time-Tested Secrets for Getting What You Want from Women—Without Marrying Them!* and then promptly forgot his own best advice. He lives with his wife and son in the paint section at Kmart.

A NOTE ON THE TYPE

The text of this book is set in Berling roman, a modern face designed by K. E. Forsberg between 1951–58. In spite of its youth it does carry the characteristics of an old face. The serifs are inclined and blunt, and the g has a straight ear.